# The Ha

*An Anthology of Australian*
*and New Zealand Military Poems*

Selected and Compiled by
Paul Barrett, Warrant Officer Class 2
and Kerry B. Collison

Published by: Sid Harta Publishers

P.O. Box 1042
Hartwell Victoria   Australia 3124
email: author@sidharta.com.au

Internet sites:
http://www.sidharta.com.au
http://www.publisher-guidelines.com
http://www.temple-house.com

for "The Happy Warrior Trust"

45 Strickland Drive
Wheelers Hill, Vic  3150

Australian Internet site:
http://www.anzac.sidharta.com

First Published:  April 2001
Copyright:  Kerry B. Collison and Paul Barrett
Cover Design:  Mario Cicivelli
Design, Typesetting, Graphics:  Alias Design
Photographs courtesy of the Australian War Memorial

Collison, Kerry B. and Paul Barrett

ISBN: 0 9577824 7 0 (cased edition)
ISBN: 0 9577824 6 2 (trade paperback)

Printed by:
Australian Print Group,
Maryborough, Victoria Australia

## Copyright

# Contents

## In Flanders Fields

In Flanders fields the poppies grow
Between the crosses, row on row,
That mark our place; and in the sky
The larks, still bravely singing fly
Scarce heard amid the guns below.

We are the dead. Short days ago
We lived, felt dawn, saw sunset glow,
Loved and were loved, and now we lie
In Flanders fields.

Take up our quarrel with the foe;
To you from failing hands we throw
The torch; be yours to hold it high.
If ye break faith with us who die
We shall not sleep, though poppies grow
In Flanders fields.

*The red poppy, the Flanders poppy, was first described as the 'flower of remembrance' by Colonel John McCrae, who was Professor of Medicine at McGill University of Canada before World War I. Colonel McCrae had served as a gunner in the Boer War, and went to France in World War I as a medical officer with the first Canadian contingent.*

*At the second battle of Ypres in 1915, when in charge of a small first aid post, he wrote the poem above in pencil on a page torn from his dispatch book.*

*The verses were apparently sent anonymously to the English magazine, 'Punch', which published them under the title 'In Flanders Fields'.*

*Colonel McCrae was wounded in May 1918 and died three days later in a military hospital on the French coast. On the eve of his death he allegedly said to his doctor: "Tell them this, If ye break faith with us who die we shall not sleep."*

## For the Fallen

With proud thanksgiving, a mother for her children,
England mourns for her dead across the sea.
Flesh of her flesh they were, spirit of her spirit,
Fallen in the cause of the free.

Solemn in drums thrill: Death august and royal
Signs sorrow up into immortal spheres.
There is music in the midst of desolation
And a glory that shines upon our tears.

They went with songs to the battle, they were young,
Straight of limb, true of eye, steady and aglow.
They were staunch to the end against odds uncounted,
They fell with their faces to the foe.

They shall grow not old, as we that are left grow old;
Age shall not weary them, nor the years condemn.
At the going down of the sun and in the morning
We will remember them.

They mingle not with their laughing comrades again:
They sit no more at familiar tables at home;
They have no lot in our labour of the daytime;
They sleep beyond England's foam.

But where our desires are and our hopes profound,
Felt as a wellspring that is hidden from sight,
To the innermost heart of their own land they are known
As the stars that are known to the night.

As the stars that shall be bright when we are dust,
Moving in marches upon the heavenly plain,
As the stars that are starry in the time of our darkness,
To the end, to the end, they remain.

*Laurence Binyon*
*(1869 – 1943)*

*This RSL Ode is taken from the elegy 'For The Fallen', by English poet and writer Laurence Binyon, and was published in London in 'The Winnowing Fan; Poems of the Great War' in 1914. The verse, which became the Returned Servicemen's League Ode, was already used in association with commemoration services in Australia in 1921 and not only adorns war memorials throughout the British Commonwealth but is also at the heart of all rites of the RSL.*

# Foreword

From: Lieutenant General P.J. Cosgrove, AC, MC
Chief of Army

Army Headquarters
R1-4-B003
Russell Offices
CANBERRA ACT 2600

Telephone:   (02) 6265 4311
Facsimile:   (02) 6265 5446

// October 2000

This anthology of poetry is rich with emotion, vibrant with diversity and strong with sentiment.  The poems tell stories everyone should read, to gain insights into the minds, hearts and souls of our warriors who have defended our great country, Australia.

The editors, Warrant Officer Paul Barrett and Kerry B. Collison have been most successful in setting out these captivating tales in a well-blended mix of irony, humour and the horrors of war, allowing the reader to empathise and identify with the authors.

This collection is an important anthology.  It captures the essence of human spirit and the warriors behind the poems themselves.

I commend this work for you to read.

*Peter Cosgrove*

# Acknowledgements

The Happy Warrior Trustees wish to thank the following donors for their financial support in the production of 'The Happy Warrior'.

**Mitsubishi Motors Australia Limited**

**Mincom Limited**

**Independent Building Products Limited**

**Rio Tinto**

**Adacel Technologies Limited**

**Safe Air Limited**

**Total Logistics Management Pty Ltd**

**Bill Sutton**

# Compilers' Note
## *Paul Barrett, Warrant Officer Class 2 and Kerry B. Collison*

This anthology of poems about the military is by members and ex-members of the Australian Defence Force and others, including some by our Kiwi cousins. They span the whole of the twentieth century, from the Boer War to peacekeeping in East Timor. The title 'The Happy Warrior' is taken from 'Character of the Happy Warrior', by William Wordsworth. Although this poem was written about 200 years ago, its uplifting message is just as appropriate today, with Australians adding their own unique 'character'.

In making our selection, we searched far and wide for words from 'unsung heroes' who had responded to the touch of the Bard. Many of the poems are courtesy the Australian War Memorial, Canberra. Others came to us by word of mouth as news of our project spread. In some cases we had to choose from several versions of a poem. Many were not signed or dated.

The writers of these verses are not professional or established poets. They are straight from the war zones, the training grounds, the home front or somewhere in between. Some went to 'the front' in their tender years, or for other reasons had little education. So much the richer, then, are these verses, which show so many skills of the seasoned poet: rhyme and rhythm or free verse in robust narrative or quiet reflection; imagery and 'Aussie talk' galore; pathos and hyperbole, heroic and mock heroic styles. At times imperfect, of course (beware the purist!), but all with undeniable soul, spirit and 'character'.

The people within these pages represent the thousands who have given of themselves so generously towards Australia's heritage, our traditions and our hope for the future. So this anthology is of a special kind, with a special purpose. It is partly to entertain. It is also partly to provide insight into the minds and hearts of soldiers, sailors and airmen and women who have served or are still serving their country, thus to reach those little aware of their effort and sacrifice.

Editing has been minimal, retaining the original 'text' (at times no more than a scribble) and adding an extra word only where it appears to have been missed by mistake. Remember while reading that most of these poems were written at a time when there was no such thing as 'political correctness'! Punctuation, where non-existent, has been inserted; where confusing, amended as far as possible to honour the intention of the individual poet. Verse and line structure have been arranged for visual variation according to the era and style of poem. Ranks are given as written at the time.

If you buy this book: Thank you! The poems for the anthology have been given free of charge and proceeds from its sale will help ex-service personnel. Or you might pick the book up in a library, or see it on the desk or bookshelf of a friend. If so, and if you feel moved, you can make a donation to the Returned and Services League or Legacy office, or the Regular Defence Force Academy in Canberra. To reassure you, there are no administration costs: all moneys will go straight to the point of need.

By the way, if you recognise a poem by 'Anon', and know its author or anything about it, we would be grateful if you would contact us with the information. Enjoy (and weep over) this book — we did!

## *Character of the Happy Warrior*

Who is the happy Warrior? Who is he
That every man in arms should wish to be?
– It is the generous Spirit, who, when brought
Among the tasks of real life, hath wrought
Upon the plan that pleased his boyish thought:
Whose high endeavours are an inward light
That makes the path before him always bright:
Who, with a natural instinct to discern
What knowledge can perform, is diligent to learn;
Abides by this resolve, and stops not there,
But makes his moral being his prime care;
Who, doomed to go in company with Pain,
And Fear, and Bloodshed, miserable train!
Turns his necessity to glorious gain;
In face of these doth exercise a power
Which is our human nature's highest dower;
Controls them and subdues, transmutes, bereaves
Of their bad influence, and their good receives:
By objects, which might force the soul to abate
Her feeling, rendered more compassionate;
Is placable – because occasions rise
So often that demand such sacrifice;
More skilful in self-knowledge, even more pure,
As tempted more; more able to endure,
As more exposed to suffering and distress;
Thence, also, more alive to tenderness.
'Tis he whose law is reason; who depends
Upon that law as on the best of friends;
Whence, in a state where men are tempted still
To evil for a guard against worse ill,
And what in quality or act is best
Doth seldom on a right foundation rest,
He labours good on good to fix, and owes
To virtue every triumph that he knows:

Who, if he rise to station of command,
Rises by open means; and there will stand
On honourable terms, or else retire,
And in himself possess his own desire;
Who comprehends his trust, and to the same
Keeps faithful with a singleness of aim;
And therefore does not stoop or lie in wait
For wealth, or honours, or for worldly state;
Whom they must follow; on whose head must fall,
Like showers of manna, if they come at all:
Whose powers shed round him in the common strife,
Or mild concerns of ordinary life,
A constant influence, a peculiar grace;
But who, if he be called upon to face
Some awful moment to which Heaven has joined
Great issues, good or bad for human kind,
Is happy as a Lover; and attired
With sudden brightness, like a Man inspired;
And, through the heat of conflict, keeps the law
In calmness made, and sees what he foresaw;
Or if an unexpected call succeed,
Come when it will, is equal to the need:
He who, though thus endued as with a sense
And faculty for storm and turbulence,
Is yet a Soul whose master-bias leans
To homefelt pleasures and to gentle scenes;
Sweet images! which, wheresoe'er he be
Are at his heart; and such fidelity
It is his darling passion to approve;
More brave for this that he hath much to love: –
'Tis, finally, the Man, Who, lifted high,
Conspicuous object in a Nation's eye,
Or left unthought-of in obscurity, –
Who, with a toward or untoward lot,
Prosperous or adverse, to his wish or not–
Plays, in the many games of life, that one
Where what he most doth value must be won:

Whom neither shape of danger can dismay,
Nor thought of tender happiness betray;
Who, not content that former worth stand fast,
Looks forward, persevering to the last,
From well to better, daily self-surpast:
Who, whether praise of him must walk the earth
For ever, and to noble deeds give birth,
Or he must fall, to sleep without his fame,
And leave a dead unprofitable name –
Finds comfort in himself and in his cause;
And, while the mortal mist is gathering, draws
His breath in confidence of Heaven's applause:
This is the happy Warrior; this is He
That every Man in arms should wish to be.

*William Wordsworth*
*(1770 – 1850)*

# Chapter One
# The Boer War

## En Avant
## ("Let us be going")

There's a voice from 'way down under,
Ringing 'round the circling foam,
And it says, in tones of thunder –
"Send, at once, my Bushmen home!"
'Tis Australia that's calling,
And we echo, everyone,
Sick of this ignoble brawling –
"Send us home; our work is done!"

In the hour of Britain's trial,
When successful foes assailed,
And the noblest self-denial
And heroic courage failed,
Never one did flinch or falter,
But we bared our bosoms leal
On the sacrificial altar
Of our nation's common weal.

Through the marches, fever haunted,
Whence pale Death chill arrows drew,
And his ghostly banner flaunted
Ever on our straining view;
Onward, where the straight neck rested
Far below each frowning height,
We have hewn a path and wrested
Vict'ry in our foes' despite.

And the brown veld knows us, passing,
And our foeman know us too,
On their rocky kopjes massing,
For our bullets travel true.
So they greet us when they meet us,
Along the distant way,
[*Missing Line*]
Is that they've found that it will pay.

On our native hills and sandy plains,
In peaceful lands afar,
We learned things that come in handy
In the deadly game of war.
For in tracking, dodging, feinting –
Tricks which every huntsman knows –
Lies the art of circumventing
Still more cunning human foes.

Well enough for child or zeny
To be dumbly, blindly, led,
Governed like a tossed-up penny –
Tail, defeat; a victory, head.
Independent thought and action,
Trending to a given goal,
Bind together sum and fraction
In a strong, cohesive whole.

Strange that, for these vital factors,
In our measure of success,
Academical detractors
Condemnation strong express.
True, we don't go 'Nap' on polish-,
Soldiers' business is to kill,
And we'd cheerfully abolish
Half the service form and drill.

Though the vile 'by numbers' racket
I may aptly use in rhyme,
Plain horse-sense, with pluck to back it,
Suits the Bushmen every time.
Of mere regimental antics
We are wearied, and would fain
Quit these senseless corybantics
And take to the bush again.

Pleased for once, we'll do a double
To the stations in the west,
Where the non-coms cease to trouble
And a fellow gets a rest
Bosses there don't care a (blessing)
Whether Smith keep step with Jones,
And there's no 'eyes right' and dressing
Heelpegs, nosebags, saddles, stones.

We can sit the war-horse fairly
When we're out 'upon our own',
And a 'want of training' rarely
Proves the 'power behind the thrown';
But we're bound to take a tumble
When red tape replaces brains
And some military bumble
Comes and takes away the reins.

Not so much we blame the person
When official acts annoy;
What we stop to heave a curse on
Is the system they employ,
With its hidebound regulations,
And its blind obedience rules –
Well designed abominations
For the stock-in-trade of fools.

True, the starred, an ill-starred Johnny,
Dollars many, gumption 'nix',
Though in drill book lore a Don,
He caps the blessed bag of tricks.
For these embryo tacticians
Humbug hath attractions rare
And the 'Army's best traditions'
Find their best exponents there.

Such may form a theme for joking,
But the humour's not so gay
When we find John Bull revoking
As to our Rhodesian pay.
Things are crooked with an Empire
Upon which the sun never sets
When the military vampire
Cannot pay its lawful debts.

I've no wish to pose as mentor
In respect to shady modes
Shown by that financial centaur
Johnny Ball and Cecil Rhodes,
But his paper credit's riddled
Since he broke his bond to pay,
And we're dished and jerry diddled
Out of sixty pence a day.

Thus, we're 'fed up'. Others phrase it
In a manner less polite,
Which, being the sad case, it
Wouldn't do for me to write.
So I'll wind up with a chorus,
And all hands will join the strain –
We have other work before us:
Kindly send us home again!

### Epilogue

Away, my bush-bred Pegasus! My nimble brumby go!
Let's spread aboard the joyful news all Bushmen long to know:
For fourteen months we've battled with the drill book and the Boer,
And which has been our direst foe I cannot tell, I'm sure;
At all event we've knocked both out and now, our troubles past,
Fling up your hat and kick it, boys –
WE'RE GOING HOME AT LAST!

*Trooper Fred H. Wyse*
*1st Australian Bushmen*
*(AWM 3 DRL 6070A)*

## *When Other Lips and Other Hearts*

When other lips and other hearts their tales of love shall tell
In language whose excess imparts the power they feel so well,
There maybe perhaps in such a scene
Some recollection of days that have happy been;
And you'll remember me, and you'll remember me.

When coldness of deceit shall slight the beauty now they prize
And deem it but a faded light which beams within your eyes,
Then you will remember me.

When hollow hearts shall wear a mask
T'will break your own to see in such a moment –
I but ask, that you'll remember me.

*C. T. Mealing*
*14 August 1900*
*(AWM PR 00752)*

## *Oh, Give Me Back the Days...*

Oh, give me back the days of long ago,
When life was one long glad and everlasting dream
When things that were less than things that seem
No thought of sorrow then no thought of woe;
Oh give me back, give me back the days of long ago!

Oh give me back the days of long ago
When first fresh breezes breathed from far away,
When morning's splendour lingered through the day,
No thought of sorrow then no thought of woe;
Oh give me back, give me back the days of long ago!

Oh give me back the days of long ago,
When life with flashing power was all agleam
And love took up and changed it to a dream
No whisper then of heartbreak nor of pain;
Oh give me back the good old days of long ago!

*C. T. Mealing*
*14 August 1900*
*(AWM PR 00752)*

## *Ah, He Kissed Me When He Left Me*

Ah, he kissed me when he left me
And he told me to be brave,
"For I go," he whispered, "Darling
All that's dear to me on earth to save."
So I stifled down my sobbing
And I listened with a smile
For I knew his country called him
Though my heart should break the while

Chorus: Ah he kissed me when he left me,
His parting words remain
Deep within my bosom, "Dearest
We shall meet again."

Oh, the sun shines just as brightly
And the world looks just as gay
As on that fatal morning
Which bore my love away
Now, alas, the dust is resting
On that bold and manly brow,
And the heart that beat so proudly
Lieth still and quiet now.

Yes, he fell, his clear voice ringing
Loud to cheer his comrades on,
But now much of you and gladness
Is with him forever gone.
Where now the pine tree rustles
And the southern branches wave,
There my own true love is lying
Low within a soldier's grave.

*C. T. Mealing*
*18 August 1900*
*(AWM PR 00752)*

## *Untitled*

Oh, are she dead and be her gone
And is I left here all alone?
Oh cruel fate you is unkind
To take the fort and leave I behind;
Her never will come home to we
But we will surely go to she!

*C. T. Mealing*
*10 August 1900*
*(AWM PR 00752)*

## *A Love Poem*

'Tis you I love and shall forever
You may change but I shall never
Let separation be our lot,
Dearest Ethel forget me not.

Take this little bunch of flowers
And the ribbon that is around them,
Take them to cheer your lonely heart
And take the boy that bound them.

When rocks and hills divide us
And you no more I see,
Remember dearest Ethyl
'Twas Christy that sent this to thee.

*C. T. Mealin*
*19 December 1900*
*(AWM PR 00752)*

## *A Love Poem*

My dearest Dear my heart's delight,
Don't fret because I am out of sight,
But bear me in your mind for what I write I am sincere
I am still in love [with] you my dear
And as the sand lies on the shore
It's you I love and no one more.

Written by a loving hand and sealed with a kiss
Think of me, Darling, when you are reading this;
Think of me [as] the miles between us lay,
Think of me when far away;
Think of me and love me true
When I am far away from you.

When distance rolls between us shall I forgotten be
Or will you, when far away, fondly remember me?

*C. T. Mealing*
*19 December1900*
*(AWM PR 00752)*

## In the Starlight

In the starlight, in the starlight, I am dreaming of the past,
While the soft breezes fan me gently and the time is speeding fast;
I am dreaming of my darling and all thou art to me,
I am longing, I am dreaming, in the starlight by the sea.
In the starlight, in the starlight, once you promised to be true
And my heart is broken for all its faith was placed in you;
Oh, thou false forgetting cruel maiden! Dost thou think of me,
And all the vows we uttered in the starlight by the sea?

*C. T. Mealing*
*27 September 1900*
*(AWM PR 00752)*

# Chapter Two
# World War I

## *Untitled*

*This poem was annotated with the following: – "This poem was put together by a mate of mine and not long after he finished it - he got killed. (signed) Bob"*

The Turks thought the Australians
Did not know how to fight
But we soon taught them a lesson
On that awful Sunday night.

We drove them from the ridges
Midst shrapnel, shot and shell,
Our officers were falling
And for us they made it hell;

And on that Monday morning
The sun shone on our heads,
Saw the stretcher-bearers busy
With the wounded and the dead.

They were as thick as rabbits
And so we took a deadly aim,
For the men there in our trenches
Will keep Australia's name.

They fought and fell like heroes
And our rifles getting hot,
For they plainly burnt our fingers
As we fired every shot.

They were using their artillery
But we never had a gun
And the odds they were against us
Yes, they numbered us four to one;

From hill to hill we bounded
And before us they were driven;
There was not a bugle sounded
And not an order given.

Our officers – there's very few
Left in the first, our Brigade –
They fought and fell with hearts so true,
'Twas a gallant charge we made

It's the old British saying
What we've got we'll hold,
And the Turks we still keep slaying
For this country dearly sold.

And when the battle ended
And a roll-call has begun,
And a lot of our young comrades
Lie bleaching in the sun,

There will be some anxious faces
Waiting on Australia's shore,
Watching as the troops come home
For a face they'll see no more.

When they turn away sad-hearted
They all will think the same,
That men that died in Turkey
Helped to make Australia's name.

*Pte R. Thompson 1191*
*D Company 2nd Batt*
*(AWM PR 85 273)*

## *At Sea*

'Tis night.
Across the sea the silver crescent moon
Is slowly sinking, following to rest
Her sister orb. The high-arch'd dome above
Glows with a myriad lesser lights that shine
Upon the track we follow. All is peace
In this our little world, while far away
On Europe's bloody shores Australia's sons
Are giving of their best amid the lust
and tragedy of war. How strange it is
That very soon we too perhaps may be
Enveloped in this dreadful sickening strife!

God knows what's held in store for us, and yet
On such a night as this the joy of life
And love of home and friends, enwrap the heart
In such tranquillity that only those
Who know the Saviour Christ can hope to keep
Throughout these troubled, storm-tossed years of woe.

The agony will pass, thank God, and then
Humanity will rise from out the mire
To better, finer things and thus will come
The glorious kingdom of the Lord, our God.

So we have offered all we have and are
That by our sacrifice mankind shall learn
To live for others is the highest life,
And truest peace is born of truest love.

*Sgt Alan J. Kerr*
*24th Battalion AIF*
SS Euripides *May 1915*
*(AWM 1 DRL 397)*

## *Adieu!*

O ye who live
Beneath the splendour of the Southern Cross
In peace we mourn with you the awful loss
Of thousands of our brothers who have shed
Their lifeblood in the world war's stream of red,
A humbler cross its vigil sad now keeps
O'er many a spot where some brave hero sleeps

O ye who love
The beautiful, the true, the pure and sweet
Let not a madman crush beneath his feet
All you hold dear, the music and the art
Of centuries. Be strong and play your part
And show the world that he who will not give
A helping hand has lost the right to live.

O ye who see
Beyond this turmoil and chaotic strife
Beyond this sinful waste of human life
An age of gold wherein mankind shall dwell
In highest heaven instead of deepest hell,
Be not afraid to spread your faith abroad,
But trust to God for strength – He is the Lord.

*Sgt Alan J. Kerr*
*Gallipoli, 16 December 1915*
*(AWM 1 DRL 397)*

### *Christmas, 1915*

'Tis Christmas Eve. In all the camps
There gleam a host of tiny lamps
That make the hill on which I stand
A veritable fairyland.
For friends at home and far away
Have helped us celebrate the day
By sending each and every man
A present of a billycan
Crammed full of wondrous things inside,
You couldn't guess them if you tried.
Tobacco, socks and butterscotch,
And for some lucky chap, a watch;
Tinned cheese, and ham, and bloater-paste,
Sweet biscuits (which we will not waste)
Toothbrushes, chocolate, lanoline,
Bootlaces, cocoa, vaseline,
Stewed fruit, cigars, a Christmas cake,
And writing pad all helped to make
A gift as pleasant to receive
On service as it was to give.
Now the first excitement o'er
And as I listen from the shore,
A wave of song towards me floats
From fairy choirs in fairy boats
Bearing the message of love and praise
And a prayer for purer, better days.
The Spirit of God is hovering there
In the wondrous calm of the still night air,
For the roughest heart has seen again
A vision of peace and goodwill to men.
So here's to you, good friends and true,
And 'hands across the oceans blue';
We wish you all both far and near:
A happy Christmas, a prosperous New Year!

*Sgt Alan J. Kerr*
*(AWM 1 DRL 397)*

## *The Dardanelles*

*A Tribute to Our Boys at the Front*

Who said our boys were laggards?
Who called Australia black,
The home of sports and spielers,
From Sydney and way back?

    Who taunted us with wanting
    Discipline, courage, go?
    Who said we were not soldiers,
    But just an idle show?

Not Kitchener or Joffre,
Not Hamilton or French;
Not Uncle Sam or Poincaire –
But critics at the bench.

    They judged us as rough bushmen,
    Who gape like gawking fools
    At every bloomin' hustler,
    Too raw for rods or schools.

They passed us by as stockmen,
Forgot we learnt to ride
The toughest mounts with hoofs on
When school boys, with a pride

That equalled any leader
Of dauntless cavalry;
Forgot, too, that our shots were
More than ABC

We never missed a target,
Nor failed a pal when down;
For hearts are warm in our land –
What matters to a crown?

Our fathers' blood is in us
The British pioneer!
And those who scorn Australians;
Old Britain's sons must sneer.

Let ev'ry tongue defame us,
Let braggarts scoff and scorn,
We've made a page for history
That never dare be torn.

We've shown our pluck and courage,
We've rung the grim death knells,
At Turkey's gates we thundered
In the famous Dardanelles.

At school we learnt that Turkey
Had built her forts supreme,
And nations looked upon her strength
More than an idle dream.

The Dardanelles was hell's gate,
The world's great monster fort,
Too powerful to be charged at
Or ever to be caught.

Yet our boys braved the monster,
Charged up the flaming mounts,
Unheeding tongues of flame and shell
From iron jaws and founts.

The shells were screaming 'round them,
The flames of hell burst forth ;
But their blood was up and boiling
With a fiery 'vengeful wrath.

They took no thought of danger,
They only saw the heights,
And knew the Turks were hiding
Behind those bursting lights.

"Now for it, boys!" they shouted,
"We'll break their jaws asunder;
Don't have them say Australia let
The British flag go under!"

Nor did they make an idle boast –
They stormed, and charged, and thundered!
Right down the ages will be read
How every nation wondered.

Australia's men had courage,
They were a priceless white men.
Don't mourn their dead – the honoured dead –
Thank God they were the right men.

Who says our boys are laggards now,
Who calls our country black?
Where is the laggard that would dare
To blaze that Turkish track?

Come, give your countrymen three cheers-
Three good Australian yells –
You cannot shout too loudly for
The Dardanelles! The Dardanelles! The Dardanelles!

*E. Power-Pinn*

## *ANZAC!*

Would but some wingéd angel, ere too late,
Arrest the yet unfolded Roll of Fate,
And make the stern Recorder, otherwise
Enregister; or quite obliterate !
*Omar Khayyam*
*(d 1123)*

On Turkish coast it woke to life
The symbol of a budding fame!
And 'ere the annals made it rife
The world had breathed the wondrous name.

Like letters writ in human fire
And burning through the Nation's brain
The mystic word seemed to inspire
The Empire's courage yet again.

Australian and New Zealand men
Had fathered it on foreign soil,
And what they made it stand for then
No human pow'r on earth can spoil.

While History remains to tell
The thrilling story to the world;
Australia and New Zealand will
Be famous as the flag unfurled.

At Gaba Tepe they won their fame,
At Suvla and Gallipoli;
And 'ANZAC' was the wondrous name
They gave it with their victory!

Illustr'ous spot, illustr'ous name,
That holds the mem'ry of their deeds!
No finger points to coward's shame,
But bravery where courage speeds.

On to the end of Life's decree,
On to that eternal close;
When ev'ry light has ceased to be,
And ev'ry nation's lifeblood flows.

Out through the channel into space,
From whence we never can come back;
The world will want to keep in pace
With army lads we call'd: ANZAC!

*E. Power-Pinn*

## *Our Heroes*

### *A Tribute to Our Wounded Soldiers*

We sent you out with heartbreaks
    Tho' we smiled as we said good-bye,
For we knew you were brave lads,
    You would conquer or you would die.

What tho' there was danger before you!
    What tho' it was hell's own gate!
You would face the danger as bravely
    As any who shared your fate.

What tho' there were loves behind you,
    And mothers, and children, and wives!
The Empire needed your arm, lads,
    To help her to save those lives.

Are you sorry you fought that battle,
    And sorry you faced those shells;
Sorry you helped to storm those great heights
Back there in the Dardanelles?

What was the pain to the glory, lads,
    What was the price to the gain?
Your country is proud to claim you hers,
    To immortalise your name.

Heroes for ever, thro' all time
    On hist'ry's pages to shine
What are the marks of the campaign
    To the names on ev'ry line?

You can stand before the coward,
    A man amongst men today;
Tho' the marks of the battle remain,
    'Twas a noble price to pay.

In the years that face you, soldiers,
    There may be some who will scorn,
Because you are not as robust
    As you were on the battle morn.

But you need not fear those jibes, lads,
    You have earned a crown more fair
Than all the beauty they can claim,
    In the battle scars you bear.

*E. Power-Pinn*

## *Heliopolis : Egypt : Land of Sand*

Oh! Egypt, land of dreams and visions
Of dirty towns and street collisions,
Where Arabs sell their greasy wares
And cabbies charge you double fares,
Where sin and wickedness, dirt and smells
Makes this a disease-stricken hell,
A land of sand and desert plain
Where no such thing is known as rain,
A drink of water is a treasure
And tucker's issued in half measure,
Where donks and camels bear huge loads
Across loose sand in place of roads,
Where donkeys, goats, fowls, dogs and natives
All live together, like relatives:
Such sights are common over here
Where Soldiers drink cheap doped-up beer
Then fall, drunk, helpless in the sand;
It makes your hair on end to stand
Two drinks will make a man dead tight
And make him argue all the night
Until his sleepy mates rebel
And wish him and his beer in hell;
'Tis here, midst sweltering sun and skies,
Tormented by insects and flies
The soldier trudges, sick and sore,
Cursing the Kaiser, and the war,
Which brought him from his home to dwell
In this dreary dried up land of hell.

*Tpr W. H. Johnstone (?)*
*8th ALH, AIF*
*(AWM PR 84/049)*

## Over There

Over there, it's in the air,
The smell of death is everywhere,
Unburied bodies lying 'round,
Bits of flesh upon the ground.

Grotesque shapes of shattered bone
Stand like sentinels alone;
Where once were living breathing men,
Now hidden, now turned up again.

Tiny flags of flapping rags
Flutter in the air,
Or stiff with mud and dried in blood,
Mutely cry, "Beware!"

Beware of man for he has been,
And look what he has done.

Before another moon does rise,
Once more man will come,
Leaving death and darkness
Ever in his wake.

*Greg Brooks*

## Night Attack

Do you see the cannon flashing?
Do you hear their fire crashing
On the enemy emplacements far away?
With the infantry advancing,
In expectation prancing,
Eager to move up and join the fray.

Our eyes are blinded by the flash,
Our ears are deafened by the crash
Of rapid firing high explosive rounds,
While the cordite smoke surrounds us
Spreads an eerie haze around us,
And the cartridge cases gleam upon the ground.

The artillery is booming,
Their muzzle flash illuming
Shedding temporary daylight all around,
While the enemy is quaking,
In trenches they are shaking,
Trying to dig deeper in the ground.

But they really needn't bother,
The artillery will smother them,
And bury them in craters deep and wide;
Then any who are left to fight,
By bayonet will be put to flight,
As the infantrymen sweep them all aside.

*Greg Brooks*

### The Show Went on Forever

They came in the summer of 'fourteen.
Like daytrippers from Dover they crossed,
With expectations of glory, swaggering proud.
Whilst the lie that war is noble dripped
Like poison from insipid lips
Of politician and statesman,
And urging angry crowd.

They thought it would be a short war:
"Give the Hun a bloody nose,
By Christmas it will all be over –
Come early, don't miss the show!"

They faced off in their tunnelled rows,
Lines of green on grey;
A whistle blew the grave command,
Then all was disarray.

Metal streamers filled the air
In intersecting lanes.
Deadly ribbons tore their flesh
And hammered through their veins.

They died in droves amongst the groves
And in the fields of France,
Pirouetting line on line,
Danced their deathly dance.

The neverending rending
Of the earth and of the air
Saw fragments once were living men
Now scattered everywhere.

They hung upon the sagging wire
Like clothing spread to dry,
Khaki flags of flapping rags,
Stark against the sky.

The living mud entrapped them,
Drew them down in watery holes,
Tightly clung, enwrapped them,
Filled their eyes, took their souls.

The beast of carnage sucked the flesh
And marrow from their bones;
Belched the stark white excrement
Back to the killing zones.

Where is war's nobility?
What price war's romance?
Their blood as tears the angels shed,
The agony of France.

A generation bled to death,
Sacrificed in Christian war,
Fodder to the holy beast
To sate its hungry maw.

They waited for the final curtain,
But the curtain never came.
And the show went on forever
To popular acclaim.

*Greg Brooks*

## *Camp Topics*

I wonder what they're doing now
   In France and Germany;
I wonder why our Government
   Sent us across the sea?
Wonder where the others are,
   That left soon after we;
I wonder what we're going to have
   Next Sunday night for tea?

I wonder why we've got to lead
   Our horses thro' the sand,
While officers and NCOs
   Can canter round the land,
I wonder why our boys go out,
   And act so very queer
I wonder is it natural,
   Or is it only beer.

I wonder if the 3rd Brigade
   Are going to start the band;
I wonder will they practice in
   Some distant foreign land,
Or if they wake the Colonel up,
   And all his staff as well,
I wonder will he tear his hair
   And order them to ____?

I wonder when the heads will wake
   And issue us our pay;
I wonder do they understand
   We're all stone broke today:
And if this state of things goes on
   I wonder what they'll say,
When half the men clear out and get
   A ship to old SA?

I wonder when our government
    Will start a decent store;
We're paying more for foodstuffs now
    Than e'er we have before.
I wonder when the trumpeters
    That practice on the plain
Will be shot as peace disturbers
    Or be sent back home again?

I wonder why we march to church,
    And stand well in the rear;
I wonder why the clergy preach
    Too soft for us to hear;
I wonder did the angels blush
    When at this said parade,
A gambler netted thirty bob ,
    Without the clergy's aid?

I wonder, yes, I wonder,
    What the _____ is in the wind;
I wonder, yes I wonder,
    How on earth this show will end.
I wonder, yes I wonder.
    How my dear ones are tonight.
That settles all my wondering, so –
    I'll bid you all goodnight.

*BAC*
*(AWM 1 DRL 572)*

## *When Your Number's Up*

You may dodge fatigues and duty if the Sergeant's on your side
You may shirk a kit inspection and some have even tried
To avoid (and quite successfully) an airman flying low
But you cannot dodge your bullet when your number's up to go

For this is a law of warfare not every man must die
Since some must live to tell the tale and no-one shall say why;
Bill Jones is killed while Tom is spared but so the gods decree
And it's no use trying to dodge it for the likes of you and me.

There was Jimmy Green of the Durhams; he'd done his buckshee year,
Waiting to go with the transport, busy packing his gear,
"One more shot at the blighters! Lend us a Bondook!" he cried,
Popped his head over the parapet, stopped an explosive and died.

And I shan't forget that afternoon when Ginger Cook came down
The muddy ditch we called a trench to speak to Topper Brown.
He lit a fag, said "So long, Boys," turned back and gave a shout –
A German sniper had him set and laid poor Ginger out.

Perhaps you've left the trenches which are commonly called hell
You think you've clicked and found a job away from shot and shell,
But high explosives travel far and aeroplanes range wide
And behind the lines they oft cop out worse than they do inside.

The moral then is surely writ quite plain for all to see:
You chance your arm a thousand times wherever you may be,
The gods on high they play this game, we are the pawns below
And when they put your number up, it's up you've got to go.

*Sgt A.M. Dick (?)*
*(AWM PR 00187)*

## *Australians*

We stand on the shore of Durban
And watch the transports go
To England from Australia
Hurrying to and fro,
Bearing the men of a Nation
Who are heroes to the core
To stand or fall by the motherland;
And they're sending thousands more

We've watched the ships returning
With the crippled and the maimed,
With limbs that trail and falter
Theirs an immortal name!
The deathless name of "Anzac"
That thrills from pole to pole,
The remnants of the heroes
On the long and glorious roll.

And now in their tens of hundreds
Come the men to fill their ranks,
And what can we do to show them
Our love, our pride, our thanks?
We can't do much (I own it)
But give them a passing cheer,
While the real elite beat a shocked retreat –
Why, they saw one drinking a beer!

*Sgt AM Dick (?)*
*(AWM PR 00187)*

### *Assignment*

Laughingly he told us before he went away
To look inside his wallet, we'd find his last weeks pay,
And should he not return we were to spend the bloomin lot
On a stimulating beverage at the first inviting spot.

We said "Good luck!" and watched their shapes fade dimly in the west
And I thought how many a truthful word is often said in jest;
So we went about our work until the boys returned at three
Then we heard that one missing and I knew at once 'twas he.

And now that we are back a bit we all agree it's best
That we go on leave together and fulfil his small request;
And we'll spend his well-earned money and we'll drink to one who knew
That we'd be with him in spirit just the way he asked us to.

*Pte A. Morrison*
*QX4534*
*(AWM PR 00392)*

## Rhyme of War Gasses

If you get a choking feeling
And the smell of musty hay
You can bet your bottom dollar
That there's phosgene on the way,

But the smell of bleaching powder
Will inevitably mean
That the enemy we are meeting
Is the gas we call chlorine.

When your eyes begin a-twitching
And for tears you cannot see
It's not mother peeling onions
But a dose of C.A.P.

Should the smell resemble pear-drops
You had better not delay;
It's not your mate that's sucking toffee
It's the awful K.S.K.

If you catch a pungent odor
As you're going home for tea
You may safely take for granted
That they're using B.B.C.

If for garlic or onions
You have cultivated a taste
When in war you meet these orders
Leave the area in haste:

It's mustard gas, that hellish stuff,
That leaves you one big blister
And in hospital you will need
The attention of a Sister.

White geranium looks quite pleasant
In a jar beside the bed
You must learn that smell in wartime –
If it's Lewisite, you're dead.

*Cpl M. M. Carroll*
*2/4 Aust. Field Bakery*
*(AWM PR 00544)*

## *"Stand To"*

Between the night and the morning,
When the vigilant sentry's wet through,
Comes an hour by all soldiers detested,
Which begins with the order "Stand To".

Then the tired soldier puts on his sheepskin,
And his words turn the atmosphere blue,
For he knows that he'll freeze for an hour,
Then the OC's voice rings out "Stand To".

How his anger will rise 'gainst the Kaiser
And he'll curse all that Sauerkraut crew,
And it's God help the Hun that he catches,
When the Sergeant repeats the "Stand To".

Is your magazine loaded and ready,
Is your bayonet fixed on firm and true?
'Tis the questioning voice of the Sergeant,
When the word's passed along to "Stand To".

And then when his vigil is over
In his heart blossoms forth hope anew,
And once more he feels life is worth living,
When he's finished the daily "Stand To".

But we're working and hoping for victory
And when we have smashed our way through,
Every day for the twenty-four hours
We'll see that the Germans "Stand To".

*Pte Charles H. Breckell*
*19th Batt. AIF*
*(AWM 1 DRL 148)*

## Boxing On

There's a heavy, distant rumble
As the lingering sun sinks low,
And there's flashing of artillery
In the battle's ebb and flow;
And the searchlight ever flickers
Seeking, seeking for a sign
Of the enemy in motion
Down the line.

Now the din creeps ever nearer
Till the air is rocked with sound,
And the rifles and machine guns
Get to business, all around;
And there sounds the devil's chorus,
The discordant notes of hell,
When the guns boom forth their greetings
In unceasing bursts of shell.

But at last the gunfire slackens
And reluctantly draws to a close,
As the sound-stunned weary gunners
Seek a short, hard-earned repose;
And only the sentry's rifle
And machine gun's deadly breath,
Remain to remind the wakeful
Of nations in grips to the death.

*Pte Charles H. Breckell*
*19th Batt. AIF*
*(AWM 1 DRL 148)*

## *Thoughts on a Cottage Wrecked by Gun Fire*

Ere yet the contending hosts in battle wrought,
It stood, a humble wayside home;
The labourer after toil its sanctuary sought,
Not ever far from its old roof would roam;
Content to spend the autumn of his life
Amid the circle of his bairns and wife.
But now, alas, his Joys and Hopes are dead,
Scarce stone on stone of that fair cottage stands;
The labourer and his family far have fled,
The striving armies desecrate his lands.
The gunner who, in thoughtless pride of aim
With cold precision, wrecked that cottage so,
Gave not a thought to humble folk bowed low,
Eating the bread of charity in shame.

But such is the reckoning mankind must pay,
When monarchs' wild ambitions are given play.

*Pte Charles H. Breckell*
*19th Batt. AIF*
*Killed in Action, Flers, 14 November 1916,*
*Aged 23 years*
*(AWM 1 DRL 148)*

## *How Rifleman Brown Came to Valhalla*

To the lower Hall of Vallalla, to the heroes of no renown,
Relieved from his spell at the listening-post, came Rifleman Joseph Brown
With never a rent in his khaki nor a smear of blood on his face
He flung his pack from his shoulders and made for an empty place.

The killer-men of Valhalla looked up from the banquet board
At the unfouled breach of his rifle, at the unfleshed point of his sword;
And the unsung dead of the trenches, the kings who have never a crown,
Demanded his pass to Valhalla from Rifleman Joseph Brown.

"Who comes unhit to the party ?" A one-legged Corporal spoke,
And the gashed heads nodded approval through the rings of endless smoke.
"Who comes for the beer and woodbines of the never-closed canteen,
With the barrack-shine on his bayonet and a full-charged magazine?"

Then Rifleman Brown looked 'round him at the nameless men of the Line,
At the wounds of the shell and the bullet, at the burns of the bomb and the mine;
At the tunics virgin of medals but crimson-clotted with blood,
At the ankle boots and the puttees caked stiff with the Flanders mud;

At the myriad short Lee-Enfields that crowded the rifle-rack,
Each with its blade to the sword-boss brown and its muzzle powder-black:
And Rifleman Brown said never a word; yet he felt in the soul of his soul
His right to the beer of the lower Hall, though he came to drink of it whole;

His right to the fags of the free canteen, to a seat at the banquet board
Though he came to the men who had killed their man with never a man to his sword.
"Who speaks for the stranger Rifleman, O boys of the free canteen?
Who passes the chap with the unmaimed limbs and the kit that is far too clean?"

The gashed heads eyed him above their beers, the gashed lips sucked at their smoke:
There were three at the board of his own platoon, but not a man of them spoke.
His mouth was mad for the tankard froth and the biting whiff of a fag
But he knew he might not speak for himself to the dead men who do not brag.

A gun-butt crashed on the gate-way, a man came staggering in;
His head was cleft with a great red wound from the templebone to the chin,
His blade was dyed to the bayonet-boss with the clots that were scarcely dry,
And he cried to the men who had killed their man: "Who passes the Rifleman? I!"

By the four I slew, by the shell I stopped, if my feet be not too late,
I speak the word for Rifleman Brown, that a chap may speak for a mate."
The dead of lower Valhalla, the heroes of dumb renown,
They pricked their ears to the tale of the earth as they set their tankards down.

"My mate was on sentry this evening when the General happened along,
And asked what he would do in a gas attack. Joe told him, "Beat on the gong."
"What else?" "Open fire, Sir," Joe answered. "Good God, man," our General said,
"By the time you'd beaten that bloodstained gong the chances are you'd be dead.

Just think lad!" "Gas helmet of course, Sir!" "Yes damn it, and gas-helmet first!"
So Joe stood dumb to attention and wondered why he'd been cursed.
The gashed heads turned to the Rifleman and now it seemed that they knew
Why the face that had never a smear of blood was stained to the jawbone blue.

"He was posted again at midnight." The scarred heads craned to the voice,
As the man with the blood-red bayonet spoke up for the mate of his choice.
"You know what it's like at a listening post, the Verey candles aflare,
Their bullets smacking the sand-bags, our Vickers combing your hair,

How your ears and your eyes get jumpy till each known tuft that you scan
Moves and crawls in the shadows till you'd almost swear it was a man;
You know how you peer and snuff at the night when the north east gas-wind blows."
"By the One who made us and maimed us," quoth lower Valhalla, "we know."

Sudden, out of the blackness, sudden as hell there came
Roar and rattle of rifles, spurts of machine-gun flame;
And Joe stood up in the forward sap to try and fathom the game.

Sudden, their shells came screaming; sudden, his nostrils sniff
The sickening reek of the rotten pears the death that kills with a whiff.
Death! And he knows it certain, as he bangs on his cartridge-case,
While the gas-cloud claws at his windpipe and the gas-cloud wings on his face.

We heard his gong in our dugout, he only whacked on it twice,
We whipped our gas-bags over our heads, and manned the steps in thrice
For the cloud would have caught us as sure as Fate if he'd taken the Staff's advice.

His head was cleft with a great red wound from the chin to the templebone
But his voice was as clear as a sounding gong, "I'll be damned if I'll drink alone!
Not even in lower Valhalla! Is he free of your free canteen,
My mate who comes with the unfleshed point and the full-charged magazine?"

The gashed heads rose at the Rifleman o'er the rings of the Endless Smoke,
And as the roar of a thousand guns, Valhalla's answer broke,
And loud as the crash of a thousand shells their tankards clashed on the board:
"He is free of the mess of the Killer-men, your mate of the unfleshed sword;

"For we know the worth of his deed on earth; as we know the speed of the death
Which catches its man by the back of the throat and gives him water for breath;
As we know how the hand at the helmet-cloth may tarry seconds too long,
When the very life of the front-line trench is staked on the beat of a gong;

By the four you slew, by the case he smote, by the grey gas-cloud and the green,
We pass your mate of the Endless Smoke and the beer of the free canteen."
In the lower hall of Valhalla, with the heroes of no renown,
With our nameless dead of the Marne and the Aisne, of Mons and Wipers town,
With the men who killed 'ere they died for us, sits Rifleman Joseph Brown.

*Gilbert Frankau*
*39th Batt. AMF*
*(AWM PR 83/34)*

# CHAPTER THREE
# WORLD WAR II

## *After the First Battle of Alamein*

Shaded by desert sand dunes,
Lulled by the murmur of waves;
Quickly we went back to nature,
Forgetting Syria and old Tobruk's caves.

The roar of the guns at Tel Eisa
Brought war and reality near;
We soon had a big job before us,
No time for reflection or fear.

Then came the war-wounded weary,
Shell-torn wounds covered in flies;
Sick of the war and the desert,
The reflection of hell in their eyes.

There on the dunes of the desert,
For many the war had its end;
All they had they had given:
Their life, Freedom's cause to defend.

Some the Grim Reaper defeated,
Back from the shadow they came;
Saved by the skill of a surgeon,
Once again they've a number and name.

Back they can go the furnace
That is fed by man's malice and hate;
Given lease to a life full of sorrow,
Mayhap Death were a kindlier fate.

Some paid a price that was lighter,
An arm, or a leg, or a hand.
Back on the trail they were started
That ends in dear Aussie land.

We are leaving old 'Figtree Alley'
We are going up further they say;
Does it mean that the blood wasn't wasted?
Does it mean we are nearer the Day?

## Epilogue
Let us hope that the crosses which we leave behind,
Let us hope that the blood and the tears of our kind,
Will be 'membered when we reach our own sunny land,
May they serve to remind us: War isn't grand!

*NX.8448*
*2/11 Aust. Field Ambulance, MDS*
*(AWM MSS 1221)*

## *An Airforce Guard, New Guinea 1942*

It's dark like inky blackness,
    Your eyes just pierce the gloom,
The palms like ghostly figures
    From out the jungle loom.

Like weird and dancing phantoms
    They stand out in the night,
The jungle all around you
    A dank and dismal sight.

The rain drops pitter-patter,
    A tattoo on the kite,
Like some prehistoric monster
    It stands there in the night.

The muzzle of your rifle
    Is shining with storm,
Beneath that dripping rain cape
    You feel your body warm.

The wing gives slight protection
    From the beating jungle rain,
Like a million phantom drummers
    It plays a haunting strain.

Your mind is just attracted,
    It seems to catch the eye,
A twinkling, hovering spectral,
    A drifting firefly.

That tiny little creature
    With its body all alight
Gives a fraction's comfort
    In the long and dreary night.

The breeze like devils' voices
    Whispering out of space,
Whistles round the main plane
    And fans your shining face.

A light shines in the distance,
    Like some orb'd evil eye;
It stabs the dark around you
    Casting shadows to the sky.

Then as the light approaches
    It fades towards the hill,
The darkness round you gathers
    The night is once more still.

The rain has stopped its beating,
    Just a drizzle trickles down;
You think of home and people
    In some far and distant town.

Then as the night grows older,
    Comes the silver creeping dawn,
The scene that stands around you
    Seems strange and much folorn.

The birds around awaken;
    Their song is soft and sweet
To the ears of a standing figure –
    A sentry on his beat.

*W. A. Dutton*
*(AWM MSS 1481)*

## *His Dream Girl*

Jungle, jungle, jungle,
Humid, wet and green.
Entangled vines and creepers,
Like some horrid, awful dream.

The order it is given,
The advance stops for a spell;
You fall fatigued and tired,
In this jaded jungle hell.

As you sit there in the jungle,
Your mind drifts into space;
In a mud-hole filled with water,
You see a charming face

Of a pretty dark haired lady.
Her smile is soft and sweet.
Her eyes are gay, alluring,
Her face is small and neat.

Her face it seems to sparkle
Like an elegant morn in June;
It lingers in your memory
Like the strain of a haunting tune.

You bend down to her closer,
To kiss those ruby lips;
Instead of scented lipstick.
Just muddy water sips.

Your dream girl, she has vanished
The pool is stirred and black;
You wish that pretty lady
To that mud pool would come back.

*W. A. Dutton*
*(AWM MSS 1481)*

## An Airman at Milne Bay

Beneath the spreading palm trees,
Flat in the bloody mud,
The Zeros scream above you,
And down the bombs they thud.

    Up go six P40s
    The War – it's on at last!
    You listen to the chatter
    As the Brownings start to blast.

The Japs they are not frightened,
As they streak across the sky,
Our boys are right behind them –
They're out to do or die.

    You shiver in the trenches,
    As one comes rather low,
    Then down swoops one P40
    And lets her six guns go.

A Zero does a sort of bank,
With flames from nose to tail,
And disappears behind the palms
In a fiery, smoky trail.

    Then one of our lads gets the works,
    The Jap caught him a beaut;
    But from that flaming kitty,
    He bails out in his 'chute.

The dog fight's nearly over,
Our losses: two to five;
Although we've lost one pilot,
The other's still alive.

    The sky is cleared of Zeros,
    The Kitties just remain
    And hope to fight those yellow swines,
    If they come back again.

*W. A. Dutton*
*(AWM MSS 1481)*

## *Remembrance*

*In remembrance of the Officers, NCOs and men of the AIF and AMF who fell at Milne Bay, 1942*

When shadows fall and night has come
    At the close of a glorious day,
The birds have all flown home to rest
    And silent lies the bay.

It brings back tender memories
    Of the eve before the dawn,
When everything was peace and still,
    The evening breeze was warm.

But on that bloody morning
    War's dread drums did beat,
The battle raged with fury
    With powder smoke and heat.

And now the battle's over,
    And peace reigns on the bay
We hear it at the sunset
    And at the close of day.

Sounding across the still night air,
    Reminiscently soft and sweet,
A voice of a distant bugle
    As it plays the last retreat.

Its notes are soft and soothing,
    Like a voice they seem to say,
"Sleep on ye valiant heroes,
    Who fell beside the bay."

A symbol of Remembrance
    Is that starry cross on high,
Like God's own guiding angels,
    It stands there in the sky.

Throughout the long and dreary night,
    God's guiding angels keep
A watch on graves beneath the palms
    Where gallant heroes sleep.

*W. A. Dutton*
*(AWM MSS 1481)*

## *The Men in Green*

These jaded sons of Anzacs,
Valiant in every deed,
Their daring and their courage,
An example we might lead.

From Milne Bay and Buna,
Of Lae and Kokoda fame,
Their blood on the beaten jungle
Has written their glorious name.

Through rivers, creeks and jungle
And land that no one knew,
They overcame the setbacks,
These men in Nature's hue.

 A cross stands in the jungle,
A  tin hat on its frame,
It bears the scribbled letters
Of a fallen hero's name.

Perhaps a kiddy's daddy,
Perhaps a mother's son,
Lies down beneath that heap of earth,
His life and duty done.

Nippon's scattered remnants,
Retreat before their might.
Broken in disorder,
They leave the bloody fight.

Onwards, ever onwards,
Their work and fight unseen,
These gallant sons of Anzacs,
Who wear the jungle green.

*W. A. Dutton*
*(AWM MSS 1481)*

## *The Road to Kokoda*

*Dedicated to the Gallant Australians who battled through the Owen Stanley Ranges*
*New Guinea, 1942*

The road to Kokoda;
Through the pages of history we'll look back
Of the hardships and the suffering
On that jungle beaten track.

Their goal was always onwards,
Up high and perilous slopes;
In spite of the setbacks
Their hearts were full of hopes.

The weary, worn and wounded
Who had stopped a knife or shell,
Were carried back to safety
From this unforgotten hell.

Their bearers they were gallant,
Their skin was shiny black;
Through unseen work and glory
They brought the wounded back.

These Fuzzy Wuzzy Angels
Their childlike actions odd,
Had surely come from heaven
And were sent to us by God.

Every inch a hardship,
Every mile a woe,
Carried our boys nearer
Toward a cunning foe.

So on this road of glory
With many a turn and bend,
Towards a well earned victory
When they reach their journey's end.

*W. A. Dutton*
*(AWM MSS 1481)*

## *Bomb Happy*

We are the bomb happy children
We play around the drome every day
We just love to build a dispersal
Or help at constructing a bay.

As we dive in and out of slit-trenches
Our officers say it's a shame
But they don't understand that it's only
Just part of our bomb happy game.

*Lt Alfred William Salmon*
*(AWM PR 00297)*

## *I Joined Up in the AIF*

I joined up in the AIF,
Just eighteen months ago,
To get a blinking uniform
And see the ruddy show.

My mother waved goodbye to me,
Her eyes were pools of pain
As she said, "God bless you, laddie,
And bring you home again."

My brother laughed and jeered at me
And said, "It's ballyhoo!
You're one of Menzies' tourists
Of the war you'll have no view."

So he's still home in civvies
With my sheila and my job,
While I'm stuck in the Army
Scared to open up my gob.

A billiard cue's his rifle,
A racecourse 'No-man's Land',
While I'm stuck in the desert,
With plurry flies and sand.

Or away up in the trenches,
Too afraid to lift my head,
For fear a blasted sniper
Will plug it full of lead.

Sometimes I'd sell my rifle
And chuck away my gear,
For a night out with a sheila
And a belly full of beer.

But when I think of Aussie
And my brother loafing there,
I pull a hitch upon my belt
And strive to do my share.

I've made a lot of cobbers
Of men and just mere kids,
And wouldn't lose a one of them
For all of Nuffield's quids.

So when I'm feeling kind of blue
Or rotten for a while,
I shove a round up in the spout,
Then face old Fritz, and smile.

*L/Cpl A. W. Clark*
*QX5546*
*(AWM PR 83 151)*

## *Ass*

In a certain women's paper
That is published once a week
There are many lying statements
About which I must speak.

They use a national crisis
As a purpose for this end,
Then send a woman writer
And say that we're her friends.

She said: "We like the country,
The climate suits us swell."
She forgot it's only training,
For when we go to hell.

Long after our arrival
The mail plane brought her in,
If only she'd stayed longer
Her waist would soon get thin.

She mentioned leave in Singapore,
Although she failed to say
That once a year we get this leave,
We have to train each day.

She may have liked the country;
Perhaps we would like it too,
If we travelled round in cars
With nothing else to do.

Because of women waiting
For news of men abroad,
They paint a perfect picture,
The truth, it is ignored.

They create a wrong impression,
It's sure to boost their sales;
Though truth may be stranger
Lies make the better tales.

Our unit never saw her,
Our camp was far from town;
Think of the discomfort
In a weary travel down.

Now she's back in Aussie,
We'd like to be there, too.
She goes on writing falsehoods –
There's nothing we can do.

*Raymond John Colenso*
*(AWM PR 00689)*

## *Leave in Malaya*

You've heard of scrumptious parties
And tiffin feasts galore
That the AIF are having
At Kuala Lumpa and Singapore,

And tales of taxi dancers
So soothing on the eyes;
I'll stage for you the dinkum facts
Without such varnished lies.

To make it more authentic
I'll tell you what I've seen;
Perhaps your views will alter
When you find out what I mean.

The first Australian convoy
To land troops in the East
Had no honoured welcome party
Or celebration feast.

They whipped us straight up country
Two hundred miles or more,
I cannot quote the figures,
The censor would be sore.

We landed in the jungle,
And settled down to work;
We never had the chance to rest,
Let alone to shirk.

It appears some high official
Thought it would be good
To make us work four times as hard
As any white man should.

They had to prove our toughness;
To them it seemed great fun,
To show the seasoned Tommies
Just how the job is done.

No man can beat the tropics
Be he white or brown,
Yet we worked for nine long weeks
And never saw a town.

If you stop and think a moment
You'll know what happened next,
I'm afraid I cannot tell you;
Our friend the censor would be vexed.

And then without a warning
They shocked us to the core
With a very generous offer
Of leave in Singapore.

Like everything that's pleasant,
This scheme had a catch –
Twice a week leave parties left
With fifteen in each batch;

So even if the planters,
All the Englishmen from here,
Escorted us to parties
And filled us up with beer,

We wouldn't be on velvet
As many seem to think;
Every man would wait a year
Before he got free drink.

Like the easier glamour
These parties are a myth,
So also was the woman
Whose husband's name was Smith.

She wrote about our parties
And how we liked the clime
Although she never saw us –
She didn't have the time.

I visited the island
On my three days' leave,
The way I found the English
It really makes me grieve.

Perhaps they'll love their prestige
And say, "How do you do!"
If the Japs move southward
And we stop them getting through.

The way they act at present
If they owned a jeweler's shop
And an Aussie was to ask the time
They wouldn't even stop.

I am not vindictive,
They don't have to talk;
I'd forgive most anything
But at rudeness I will baulk.

We may be only privates
On a lousy army pay,
But even if they're millionaires
We're better men than they.

This poem is not libel;
There's truth in all I say.
I hope I'll never have to work
If this is a holiday.

*Raymond John Colenso*
*(AWM PR 00689)*

## *This Place They Call ...?*

There's places that I've been in
    I didn't like too well,
Scotland's far too blooming cold
    And Cairo's hot as hell.
(The Pilsner beer is always warm…)
    In each there's something crook
But each and all are perfect [compared] to
    This place they call ...

We reckoned El Agheila
    Was none too flash a place
El Abiar and Beda Fomm
    Weren't in the bloody race
At the towns this side of Benghasi
    We hadn't time to look –
But I'll take my oath they're better than
    This place they call …?

I've seen some dust storms back at home
    That made the housewives work;
Here there's enough inside our shirts
    To smother all of Bourke.
Two diggers cleaned their dugout
    And their blankets out they shook
Two Colonels perished in the dust in
    This place they call …?

There's militant teetotallers
    Who abhor all kinds of drink;
There's wives break good bottles
    And pour them down the sink.
This place would suit them to the ground;
    We've searched in every nook
But booze is rare as hens' teeth in
    This place they call …?

There's centipedes like pythons
    And there's countless hordes of fleas
As big as poodle dogs they come
    A' snapping 'round your knees
And scorpions large as AFVs
    Come out to have a look;
There's surely lots of livestock in
    This place they call ...?

The shelling's nice and frequent
    And they whistle overhead;
You go into your dugout
    And find shrapnel in your bed.
And when the stukas dive on us
    We never pause to look;
We're down our holes like rabbits in
    This place they call ...?

Sometimes we go in swimming
    And float about at ease
In water clear as crystal
    And nice clean salty breeze.
When down comes blasted Hermann
    And we've to sling our hook,
We dive clean to the bottom in
    This place they call ...?

I really do not think this place
    Was meant for me and you;
Let's return it to the Arab
    And he knows what he can do.
We'll leave this God-forsaken place
    Without one backward look
We've called it lots of other names
    This place they call ...?

*A. W. Curran (?)*
*Tobruk 15 September 1941*
*(AWM 3 DRL 3527)*

## *Greece*

We left the Dago on the run
And moved to Greece to fight the Hun,
Outnumbered there we gave them hell
Not stopping for a breathing spell.

We held the pass at Vi Vi ridge
This line of hills we could not bridge,
Machine gunned, shelled and bombed as well
The Germans could not make us quell.

Our first positions were withdrawn;
The boys were feeling tired and worn
While Jerries lying dead – three deep,
Gave others time to catch some sleep.

Grecian soldiers – not alone –
Fighting for their wives and home,
But treacherous power holding sway
Just waiting for the final day.

A high official, quite well known,
Would like to see us overthrown;
Underestimating British fervour
His hand was called in this last hour.

But now the damage has been done
And once again we had to run;
An organised retreat was planned
Though every man would rather stand.

No threat of Germans in the rear
Only bombers should we fear;
Villages and roads complain,
Machine-gunned by the diving planes.

Caught like rats on a mountain pass –
How long will this nightmare last?

*A.W. Curran (?)*
*(AWM 3 DRL 3527)*

## *Somewhere in Malaya*

We are somewhere in Malaya, where they very seldom pay yer,
And conjecture and opinion now runs free,
For the troops grow daily thinner on what they'd like for dinner,
But we're soldiers in Malaya, by the sea.

After working hard for hours we come home to find no showers,
And no matter how the troops protest or plea,
We are told we should know better, just to go and don a sweater
Cause we're living in Malaya, by the sea.

Drains and ditches breed mosquitoes which are big enough to eat us
And with scorpions like monsters from the sea,
Add to these the snakes and lizards and the lot get in our gizzards –
Wish we'd never seen Malaya, by the sea.

Now according to the papers we are cutting fancy capers
And our life is just eternally a spree,
But to us it's quite apparent that our bright reporters haven't
Ever seen Malaya, by the sea.

When we're done with camps and bivvies and we all go back to civvies
Swapping lies and pitching yarns and feeling free,
Not one second would we wonder, if for all the blood and thunder
We'd go back to Malaya, by the sea.

So in passing, let's remember, when life's just a glowing ember,
And our name perhaps a hallowed memory,
Just despite this old 'hard-bitten', we will find his deeds are written
In the history of Malaya, by the sea.

*Cpl. C. W. Lewis*
*(AWM PR 00074)*

## *Full Moon*

Robed in a garment of silver splendour,
    Fair and clear she walks the sky
And the troubled earth is a world beyond her
    Where men may live, may love, may die...

Tonight the gods of love will waken
    In a thousand hearts in her silver glow
Heart to heart the world forsaken
    They walk the roads that dreamers know.

But death will ride the skies tonight
    And race the wind on silver wings,
And laugh aloud in mad delight
    At all the terror that he brings.

The rain of bombs on men below
    The lurid fires beneath the moon
That does not care that may not know
    How much she helped to cause that ruin.

Tonight along our eastern shore
    Our soldiers wait and watch the sky,
And all the people tense with war
    Look up and curse the moon on high.

She rides serene as the night grows late
    As the planes return –
And the soldiers wait...

*Ft Lt Thomas L Stewart*
*(AWM MSS 1250)*

## Faded Suits of Green

I am standing at my window, I can hear the tramp of feet,
I can hear the soldiers marching down the bush road and the street,
They are coming into vision, now they can be plainly seen,
That swinging line of figures in their faded suits of Green.

Suits that went into the dye pots – in a hurry as you know,
For the Jap was at our door step, a crafty cruel foe –
No time for fuss or finish, very little lay between
Those screaming hordes of Nippon, and those faded suits of Green.

The dye came out in patches of pale yellow, green and brown,
They were fashioned for the jungle, not for touring round the town
They were not meant for dancing, to strut in or to preen,
They were made for men of action, streaky faded suits of Green.

There were men who went to outposts, to the flies and dust and heat,
To monotony and boredom, no offensive, no retreat;
And they missed the path of glory with their mates at Alamein
They were left to guard Australia in their faded suits of Green.

On the battle fields of Papua, on the shores of Milne Bay
On the road to far Kokoda, and down Gona-Bura way,
Through the fever stricken jungles where the Nippon lurked unseen,
Into slime and slush and slaughter, went those faded suits of Green

Pressing onward, ever onward, rivers crossed and pathways strange,
Facing death, defying danger, on the Owen Stanley Range,
Up the cliffs and down the valleys, through the deep and dark ravine,
Torn and tattered, splashed with crimson, glorious faded suits of Green.

Standing, watching at my window, my thoughts wing as before
To the ricefields of Malaya, to the docks of Singapore,
To the prison camps of Nippon where our loved ones, gaunt and lean,
Weary, wait there to be rescued, by those faded suits of Green.

They are coming, captive soldiers, tho' the way be grim and hard
They will fight on to a finish, inch by inch and yard by yard,
For no suits of shining armour, worn by knights before a Queen,
Ever held such pride and honour as those faded suits of Green.

When the bells of peace are ringing as they did in days of yore,
When the hated sound of war drums shall have ceased for evermore,
When we live in love and laughter and happiness serene,
OH, AUSTRALIA! PLEASE REMEMBER – THOSE FADED SUITS OF GREEN!

*Rebecca Morton*
*(AWM PR 87 062)*

## Moratai

I've left the Sunny Southern land
And sailed across the sea,
I've left behind me all the ones I love;
I've landed on a coral isle
Beneath a foreign flag,
But yet the Southern Cross still shines above,

And when the daily job is done
I lay upon my bed,
And gazing upward to the heavens bright,
I think of how those very stars
Shine on my loved one too,
And wonder if she thinks of me tonight.

*Pte Jim Baker NX 139320*
*Moratai NEI, 1944*

## *The Unwrapped Chocolate Soldier*

You saw him in your town a-strolling down the street,
You saw him in his uniform that always looked so neat,
You heard him in the dance hall, with your hand upon his shoulder
Cursing fate and his bad luck – the Unwrapped Chocolate Soldier.

    You labelled him a coward, because he did not fight,
    You thought he didn't have the guts to stick up for the right,
    You heard him in the bar, and if you felt a little bolder,
    You didn't hesitate to say – another Chocolate Soldier

But how your song is different when war is at your door.
You rarely hear the saying 'Chocolate Soldier' any more,
By heaven you'll thank your Maker, before you are much older,
For the man who kept the Japs away – the Unwrapped Chocolate Soldier.

    You don't know how he cursed the flies, and swore at dirt and heat,
    He put away the uniform that always looked so neat,
    He wears a pair of ragged shorts, a shirt when it is cooler,
    He puts up with pests and flies – the Unwrapped Chocolate Soldier.

He is living in a reeking tent, his rations often short,
He thinks of all the steak and eggs and the beer that once he bought,
But when the bombers fill the skies his rage begins to smoulder,
When he sees his cobbers fall and die – the Unwrapped Chocolate Soldier.

    His ack-ack guns and small arms too were shields to your defence,
    His body first to take the blow and if you are not too dense;
    You'll take your hat off to the man, before you are much older,
    The man you used to spurn and rail – another Chocolate Soldier.

*Anon*
*AAMWS, AIF*
*(AWM PR 88 019)*

## *Doing Our Best*

There's talk just now of leaving here,
    And going to pastures new,
Of leaving all the work we've done
    Behind, it just won't do.

This place is like a home to us,
    We're happy and content,
We've built it up to what it is,
    The time has been well spent.

We do our work, of course we do,
    Yet busy tho' we be,
We, most of us, have done our bit
    Working unitedly.

Of course there are some careless chaps
    Who do not care a jot,
Smashing trucks and shunning work –
    Efficient they are not.

It may be only want of thought,
    Not realising the fact,
That all these bad marks mounting up
    Can put us on the track.

Meaning to say, that those in charge
    Cannot put up a fight
To keep us here, if we do not
    Assist them as we might.

We all must strive to do our job
    And give no chance at all
To those who'd try to put us out
    And cash in on our job.

We have a very decent lot
Of officers – They're men,
Who one and all will stand by us,
If we will stand by them.

So let us do our very best
That we may still enjoy
The comfort of this best of camps,
With nothing to annoy.

*Pte Jim Baker*
*NX139320*
*116 Aust.Gen Trans. Coy*
*Marrickville, NSW, 1947*

## Army Days (Daze)

I said I'd join the Army
But they said, "Don't do it lad,
You'll find conditions dreadful
And I hear the food is bad."

But being kind of willful said,
"I'll just give it a fling",
To me the Army life appeared
To be the very thing.

But when into the showground
We were herded like the sheep,
And marched around Centennial Park
And Showground roads three deep.

I thought I'd made a big mistake,
The Army life was not
Just what it was cracked up to be,
Not by a jolly lot.

But then they sent me out at last,
To GT 116
And if I had my way at all,
It would be there I'd stick.

The only thing I did not like,
Was getting out of bed
And falling down the stairs the night
The Japs came through the Heads.

The workshop boys are all OK,
They like their fun of course,
But still they work and really are
A credit to the Force.

The drivers – well, we mend their truck
And really ought to know...
But p'raps I'd better not throw muck –
Still, we wish they'd drive more slow!

*Pte Jim Baker*
*NX139320*
*116 Aust.Gen.Trans.Coy*
*Marrickville, NSW. 9 September,1942*

## *"Fight 'em Back!"*

When you read in daily papers of another air attack,
Do you think of all the gunners standing by
Pushing mighty stacks of ammo through the bores of every gun,
Giving hell to Tojo's bombers in the sky

When you hear of Zeros strafing, you can picture gunners laughing
As the Aussies and the Yanks hop to attack?
You can bet your bottom dollar that the yellow rat will holler,
For the ack-ack gunner's creed is "Fight 'em back!"

Who wants to be a gunner, and live beside the drome?
It's the target for tonight you cop the lot
And you haven't time to wonder as the guns are crashing thunder,
What it is that makes a shell case so darned hot!

They're the 'Heavies' and the Bofors and the deadly point-fives too
And they're manned by Yanks and Aussies who won't crack;
So at a hundred shells a minute, sure the Japs just won't be in it,
For the ack-ack gunner's creed is, "Fight em back!"

*Gunner*

## *Without Glory*

Not for us the raging combat when the blind instinctive urge
    To kill and kill and kill is ever near,
When the thought of hardships suffered, in a wild ensweeping surge,
    Obliterates all normal sense of fear.

Not for us the tense excitement of the coming zero-hour,
    The weary thrill of savage victory gained,
The grim glad satisfaction, to have smashed the other's power,
    A milestone to the final win attained.

Not for us the ringing tumult of the people's wild acclaim
    As home-come heroes march through city streets,
Never decorations, medals, battle honours to our name,
    No tales of epic awe-inspiring feats.

We are not the stalwart heroes of the hard held battlefront
    We are not the lads with iron-seeming spines
We're an overseas WORKS company up here to bear the brunt
    Of humdrum jobs a mile behind the lines.

If it's ship with ammunition or with food for forward troops,
    We are there to swiftly get it safe ashore,
While the bombers speed our tempo with their hell-for-leather sweeps
    We are merry little wharfies playing war.

If the bridges need repairing or the roads are shelled to bits,
    We fix them so the guns won't be delayed
Or we lump the ammo forward while the gunner starts his blitz
    And try to kid ourselves we're not afraid.

We're the Army's jack-of-all-trades, and its rouseabout to boot,
    There is not a job of war we haven't done;
Though we seldom see real action, and we very seldom shoot –
    Just men behind the men behind the guns.

For our labour is our weapon and our symbol is our sweat,
    We're average and unfit might-have-beens;
We're packhorse, navvy, wharfie, we're a motley crowd and yet
    We are blokes on whom the Army gladly leans.

Without Glory, Praise or Glamour, we plug silently away,
   We're humble men who fill a humble role:
We're the troops you never think of till one sudden, startled day
   You send for us because you're in a hole.

*"Black Bob"*
*(Lt A. L. O'Neill?)*
*Solomon Islands, November 1944*
*(AWM MSS 1328)*

## *Tribute*

Roar of Stuka, whine of shell,
Blast of bomb and mine as well,
Crack of rifle, whine of Spandau,
Opening up the door of hell.

This and more did not deter you
From the path you had to blaze,
Though you saw your comrades falling
Only dimly through the haze.

On you went and ever onward
Through the field of steel and gore,
Right into the new made trenches,
Diggers always to the fore.

Once again in this long struggle,
Amply backed by plane and gun,
You have proved that you are better
Than the frenzied, ruthless Hun.

Now my comrades, I salute you,
For that hard and bitter fight,
For the hardships you have suffered,
For our freedom and our right.

They shall never be forgotten,
They who sleep 'neath desert sand,
Ever may their name be sacred
In our own Australian land.

*Anon*

## Remember - Centaur *14 May 1943*

This is a memorial to those who sleep
Before their time on unknown golden sands,
Locked with the secrets of the eternal deep,
Remote in their last rest from restless hands.
To those who, 'mid the clamours of the battlefield
    Brought soothing art which many a wound has gently healed.

This is an act of thanks – to those who saved
The lives of brave men, bravely, under fire,
Who selflessly and sleeplessly have slaved
In night and day. Courage was never higher
Than in these hearts whose very veins ran living love,
    Whose minds thought only duty as bombs burst above.

This is an act of thanks – for those who smiled
Where pain had creased the brow, and thinned the lips,
Whose mien was tranquil when the world was wild,
Who cheered the dullness of the Red Cross ships.
To those whose word or laugh made searing pain seem light,
    Whose presence made the suffering days seem sunny bright.

A memorial to those who loved not life
E'en unto death, to those who might have stayed
To lead their gallant brethren out of strife,
But that some cruel and treacherous hand betrayed
A memorial which keeps their memory evergreen
    And shouts for vengeance of the harsh inhuman scene.

The pale and anguished bosom of the deep
Sighs out its foamy sorrow on the shore,
Is restless for the souls new-laid to sleep,
Nurses whose healing hands will heal no more.
The *Centaur's* wood flows broken, useless on the wave,
    Cries payment for those lives who nought but mercy gave.

*Frank S. Greenop*

## Centaur

Skulk to your hole, you yellow-bellied cur,
Apeing the boldness of the lion without the lion's heart!
No sea seclusion will protect your hide,
No sea can be too wide or yet too deep
But that the vengeance of this outraged land
Can root you out.

Well you may rise to watch the crippled ship
That trusted to your honour – you have none.
Well you may surface and through insolent eyes
Observe the work your perfidy had wrought.
Think you so vile an act will profit you
Or rouse a flame of terror in our souls?

Reprisal! Already I can hear it on your lips.
Already I can hear you tell the world
'Twas done for some fictitious vengeance,
Some deed for which it is not possible
For us to stoop unless we hacked away all decencies.
Skulk to your hole, for your success was failure!

A few there may have been who gave to you
The benefit of doubt at recent times,
Countenancing your treacheries because
There was a possibility of doubt.

Even in the face of such atrocity,
While yet the sea was boiling where the ship
Had drawn her splendid cross beneath the calm,
A woman in a lifeboat sang.

*Russell J. Oakes*

## New Guinea Exile

This is a land where men have fought and died.
Here in these mountains they have toiled and known
Day after day in mud, on steep cliffside,
Tangled with vines, together or alone,
Such fear as none can know who have not been
In this wild land, this hell of jungle green.

Here is a world apart from that of man;
A world in which the savage even seems
Civil and tame compared with that wild clan,
Whose savage lust, whose mad ferocious dreams
Have driven them and us to its strange shore
To fight — some to remain for evermore.

Will there, in some dim future, dawn a day
When we who led this crazy, unreal life
Waken again to see, in trim array,
The radiant form of a beloved wife,
Our children without fear, the little lawn,
And flowers in the quiet, warless dawn?

*Cpl. J.J. McAuliffe*

## We'll Capture Tarakan

( To the tune of Lili Marlene)

Here comes the Aussies to capture Tarakan,
It is just the kick-off, we're heading for Japan.
It you could see these grim-faced men
With their mates, the RAN,
And backed up by the Air Force – We'll capture Tarakan.

Kenny has promised the Air Force a Douglas full of beer,
While the boys who do the landing can't crack it for a cheer.
All they will cop from this lousy joint
Is one long look at the water point.
But they don't buck, you know it, they'll capture Tarakan.

Resting on Manoora is Fraser and his crew,
Messing around as usual, he doesn't know what to do;
But you can bet that he enjoys
The rousing cheers from all the boys
When he sends up the munga, we'll need in Tarakan.

Where is Colonel Ainslie? About eight minutes late.
We can't stop to worry, 'cause soldiers do not wait;
We've got to climb the razor-back,
The oil fields there are on our track,
And straight from there we're heading – to capture Tarakan.

The barrage is lifting, we're just about to land,
There's fire from Nippy's pill-box, he's trying to starve our hand.
Company in position, we're all in line,
The first wave's off, we start to shine,
Then push up, from the beach-head – to capture Tarakan.

'Oboe one' is over, we're ready for Number Two.
Throwback on your gear, Rats, we're in 'another blue';
Though some of us may go down,
The rest will carry on without a frown.
We're sure to have the memory – of the capture of Tarakan.

*Colby Corrigan.*
*2/48 Aust. Inf. Batt.*

## *Dawn Patrol*

The day was breaking, heralding the light of dawn,
    Seeping through the foliage a new day is born;
And with creeping fingers showed up where one boy lay
    Silent in Death, never again to laugh or play;
The pride of Australia, the pride of us all,
    This boy had answered willingly his Country's call.

All day yesterday they had fought from dawn to dark,
    Not without loss, for it had surely left its mark;
No sleep, no rest, they had been on picquet all night
    But with day breaking, they still held onto this height;
Then the word came that a patrol would have to go
    To find out his strength, the positions of the foe.

These men, gaunt, unshaven, with a glint in their eyes,
    Nothing but their senses could they use for their guides;
Their automatics slung, their senses all alert,
    Thought first of their loved ones, their loss they knew would hurt;
And with hearts that throbbed madly, with pulses that raced,
    Only they knew the perils they would have to face.

Wiping out their thoughts of home and all they love,
    They mingled with the shadows, trusting that God above
Watched their every movement; their lives they left to Him.
    It was a path of Life and Death, a path so dim,
Shrouded by the tree tops, and undergrowth so thick,
    To make no false step needed every jungle trick.

With stealth, and with silence, using every jungle law,
    Stalking and creeping, they knew that every yard more
Brought them close to Death. But did anyone stop?
    Not they – only the Japs' bullets could make them drop.
Then with suddenness the silence was broken,
    A Jap machine gun to their right had spoken.

Down to ground! Their thoughts were in a chaotic mess.
    Had they been seen? No, it was impossible – but yes;
For still the machine gun bullets were passing by
    Just three feet over their heads, they were whining high.
Where was the danger that now impeded their way?
    They puzzled this out as in the bracken they lay.

Someone then remembered, higher up, to the right,
    A woodpecker had been seen in the waning light,
And the Jap from his greater height could easily see
    Any movement that could be caused by brushing a tree;
For the foliage above would then shiver and shake;
    The command went back, "Be careful, for goodness sake!"

So with head bent low, dodging trees, protruding vines,
    They passed a dead Jap, and on the right were sure signs
Of tracks and Jap doovers, with the nauseous stench
    That pollutes the air in the region of their trench;
A muttered curse, with those softly whispered words;
    "Death is too good for you, you mongrel yellow curs!"

Cautiously forward, yard by yard, with bated breath
    Past those doovers they crept in defiance of death;
Then the sound of a bolt with that metallic click
    Swung them 'round with a speed undeniably quick,
Searching for the danger that made its presence felt –
    But on they must go, so in the shadows they melt.

Looking forwards and sideways they managed to go,
    Keeping to shadows, till within nearly a stone's throw
Of Japs digging doovers and jabbering aloud,
    (There's one thing about them. they make plenty of sound),
Their job is now completed, they silently withdraw
    To report their success and all the things they saw.

So with joy and light hearts they wended their way back
    Past those concealed doovers by the side of the track,
Side-stepping the Jap corpse that was gruesome and stark,
    For this was the last phase, the last reminding mark
Of the fingers of Death, and the fingers of Fate,
    That had waited to grasp them with relentless hate.

Love, Life and Joy once more seemed to seep through their veins,
    These feelings they had curbed while the danger had reigned;
But now they were themselves, laughing again once more,
    Throwing off this cloak, this terrible cloak of war.
They lay back and reclined, resting their weary minds,
    Looking upward to where their future path would wind.

*G Bowles*

## *The Night Patrol*

It's zero hour, there's a hushed command
As out of the shadows move a band,
Each man knows of the task ahead
As he moves to the wire with a stealthy tread.

There isn't a sound or glimmer of light,
Only the stars to guide them right;
A thousand yards to reach their goal,
A race ere the rising moon unfolds.

To hesitate would be too late,
For the moon-lit rays seal their fate;
So on through booby traps and mines
On 'til they reach the enemy's lines.

A clattering stone someone spoke,
A burst of fire from the stillness broke
As the shadowy forms of a dozen men
Sprayed hot lead from rifle and Bren.

Forward they rush, like men insane,
To take and hold all they can gain.
They won't face steel is the Aussies' boast
And they find it so when they reach that post.

There's a quick check up, a note or two,
Then back to their lines for some warmed up stew,
A dixie of tea or a noggin of rum,
A smile from their mates for a job well done.

Then down in the dust of their holes they creep
Like desert rats, they are soon asleep
And dream of parties and folks at home,
Of the girls they have loved – or a mutton bone.

The sun is up, there's a harsh command,
It's five hundred hours don't be alarmed!
Yesterday's gone. Now call the roll.
I want twelve men for tonight's patrol.

*Anon*

## Isle of Tarakan

From afar I saw this lovely isle,
It looked a romantic, exotic pile,
And I thought I'd like to stay awhile,
On lovely Tarakan.

But the longer I live upon its shore,
My interest decreases more and more
And I long for the good old days of yore –
To hell with Tarakan!

As the rain pours down, my temper sours,
It's the dinkum stuff, not April showers,
And I'm up to my ruddy neck for hours,
In mud on Tarakan.

When the clouds roll on and the day is fine,
With an azure sky and bright sunshine,
The sweat will cascade from my spine,
On humid Tarakan.

But when I walk it makes me boil,
I'm up to my blinking knees in oil,
And I can't thrive on the oily soil,
On greasy Tarakan.

I even tried to learn Malay,
But I find my efforts do not pay,
The dumb cows dunno what I say,
On ignorant Tarakan.

I've stood the sight of hill and glade,
And I've heard the sound of the war's tirade,
But when the Japs start crashing a mess parade,
I give you away, Tarakan.

If I had five hooks on my sleeve,
I tell you straight, and you must believe,
That I would neither howl nor grieve,
On leaving Tarakan.

*Anon*

## *Souvenir Poem*

We are nearing the end of our journey,
A trip we were eager to take,
For a chance of a joust in the journey,
For our own and the Motherland's sake.

We know nought of what may be lurking
Ahead and we care not a damn –
We'll just take the chance without shirking
Any job we're assigned in the jam.

So here's to what may be before us,
Whatever the cost we will gain,
The deeds of our Dads will immure us
To hardship and physical pain.

And our wives and sweethearts and Mothers,
In their worry and sorrow and pride,
Will reverence the memory of 'others',
Who are left on the other side.

*Anon*

## "Sayeeda"

When first we landed on these shores
To do our bit and help the cause,
In busy street and passing throng
We heard one word, most all day long,
"Sayeeda"

It followed us where'er we went,
And seemed for every purpose meant,
"Good day!!", "Good night!" and "How are you?"
Upon our tongues it almost grew:
"Sayeeda"

Through dust and heat and burning sun,
Through pelting rains and work and fun,
At every hour of day and night,
It came to haunt us like a blight –
"Sayeeda"

And when we leave this foreign land,
With parting shout on every hand,
This word I'm sure above the noise,
Will still be heard by all the boys:
"Sayeeda"

*Anon*

## *To a Wooden Cross*

No thought to win a medal, no chance to gain real fame,
But just to save your comrades – that's why we sing your name.

Your riddled coat stands witness, four buried Huns lie near,
And here's to you in Glory, for death you had no fear.

You stormed alone this gun-pit and alone you fell,
You taught them all a lesson their nearby graves now tell.

Your Dear Ones must have knowledge, that you did not die in vain,
For by such deeds of valour, our troops have won this plain.

*Anon*

## A Tribute

*Dedicated to those who fell whilst holding the "Hill of Jesus" on 22nd July 1942*

To desert desolation has been given
A sacred symbol, where brave men have striven,
In sight of Tel el Eisa stand the crosses
That speak of greater gains that come through losses.
And He, whose name on yon hill is inscribed,
He spake of love, greater than which is none,
Where man forfeited his life in death lay down.

By those immutable and universal laws
That bind humanity as one, and thereby cause
The clash and strife, when greed and selfishness
Exclude from view the vaster world, where stress
On things that make us petty and secluded,
(By little dreams of paltry gains deluded)
Is but a relic of a passing phase
That leads onward to more glorious days.

By those same universal laws, perchance
We faced a foe, so eager to enhance
Advantages won in recent rapid rush
Eastward, and thereby his opponent crush,
That dreams of domination of the world
Might to fulfilment be brought nearer, and unfurled
O'er Egypt and the East the banner borne
By host whose loyalty to Fatherland was sworn.

The sudden bursting forth of morning violence
That July day in nineteen forty two,
That twenty-second day! Now pride in silence
Honors. Sorrows doth our pride subdue
The boom of gun, the whine and crash of shell.
The crush of mortars, rifles spitting hell,
Machine guns pouring death on every crest
Did brave men face, and facing them could jest.

Though willing be the flesh of gallant men,
The strongest, bravest spirit is subdued,
And overwhelming weight of force and fire
Batters and blasts, as wounded rise again
To reach a comrade's side to render aid
Or to press on in desert's heat, where shade
And water are but things to torment those
Who think and suffer lying near their foes.

Oft victory comes to us in some disguise
That mocked faint hearts, perceived but by the wise
Who perseveres with courage to endure
And make the fruits of victory secure.
Awhile the outcome of the awful night
Seems doubtful, but with break of morning light
The verdict o'er the conduct could be given –
Our enemy once more was backward driven.

The price? Men in the pride and strength of youth
Preferring death, with loyalty to truth,
Is that the price must be, which faint heart chills,
Accept the hazards of their own free wills;
No cheap bravadoes but a deep sincerity
Called them from distant shores and homes and love,
And Tel el Eisa's crosses of eternity,
And forgotten as our deed shall prove.

*Chaplain B. C. Archbold*
*2/48th Aust. Inf. Batt.*

## *The Rats of Tobruk*

"Good morning Rats!" The donkey brayed,
"Rats at the end of your tether,
I heard your nerves are somewhat frayed,
Shall I snap them altogether?"

And he called to his birds of prey:
"Swoop low on the British Rats,
They're afraid of the light of day,
They live in caves like bats."

So the vultures flocked to the kill
And they dived on the hospital ships
And the hospital high on the hill
And they blew all the wards to bits.

Full gorged with easy game,
The vultures flocked once more,
A hundred plus they came,
And dived on the shattered shore.

"Crash!" went the big Ack-Ack.
"Bang!" went the Bofors guns –
And the Rats stood back
And shot lead at the hated Huns.

*Anon*

## *The Wounded from Tobruk*

You come limping down the gangplank,
Or you're carried down instead,
Carried in a blanket with a boot beneath your head,
And you look all lean and hungry
Beneath your good old Aussie grin,
Sick of bully beef and biscuits
But the sort that won't give in.

You're smiled at by a bearer,
Who's muscular and big
Fishing fags out from his pocket
With a "Better have one, Dig!"
And you take it as he lights it,
And return a wiry grin,
Making little of your trouble,
Though there's no one taken in.

For they know that you've been through it,
And there's nothing much to say,
You're a base-job or a blighty,
And they'll help you on your way,
For the skies were full of zoomers,
And the sand bags fairly shook,
Like the good old Bondi boomers
When you stopped one at Tobruk.

And I'm proud that I'm Australian,
When I look at men like these;
They're the men who marched beside me,
Back in Woodside Camp in threes.
In the days when life was rosy,
Full of laughter, love and beer,
And I never thought I'd see them
Carried down a gangplank here.

Well they've done their best for England,
And they've done their best for home,
For the girls they left behind them
And the pals across the foam;
And may Australia not forget them
When they are invalided back,
Nor leave them, poor and jobless,
For the dole queue or the track.

*Anon*

## The Emperor: 1945

Oh, fearful he who plays the game
  Of treachery and strife,
With free men's license now to count
  The cost of human life!

'Tis not the Khan's armada
  That presses to the shore,
But vengeance, dark, within these ships
  That stand outside the door.

Oh wasted Kamikaze!
  Divine warriors from the sky!
You fell like cherry blossoms
  And like cherry blossoms ... died.

Now a sun god shrinks from black defeat,
  And an Emperor quakes as his empire shrinks;
No majesty, no honour, no mystery now,
  Just the muffled drum of a lone heartbeat.

*Grahame Fooks*
*PM7560*

*Grahame Fooks served on HMAS Quickmatch from 1944 - 1946 and, as part of Task Force 57 on 'Operation Iceberg,' had first hand experience of Kamikaze attacks on the fleet.*

## Quickmatch

The oily water laps her sides
In the blackness of the night;
Asleep, her breathing can be felt
And she's restless for the light

"Let go forward! Let go aft!"
She shudders at the cry,
Slips out to sea with an eager look,
For it's where her pleasures lie.

She dips her bow in salute to the waves
And they become as one,
While the bos'n's pipe is lost in the wind
And her shrouds sing a song to the sun.

*Grahame Fooks*
*PM 7560*

## *The Tale of Tobruk*

We got in a ship and sailed out to the sea
And each of us then were in spirits of glee,
For 'twas farewell to Egypt and old King Farouk;
We were bound for the beautiful town of Tobruk.

A night and a day we sailed over the waves
Then arrived in Tobruk with its harbour of graves.
There were ships all around us, but sad to relate
They were all under water – a terrible state.

We gazed and we thought as our eyes met that sight
Of all the good ships in that terrible plight.
There were British and Jerries and Ities galore;
Oh! the price that we pay when we're going to war!

Now we sighted this town which before us did lie
And most of us then heaved a mighty big sigh,
For this was our home right down to the sea
And none of us knew for how long it would be.

We walked through the streets 'twas a pitiful sight,
Each shop in a turmoil, just a ragman's delight;
Devastation lay around us where the bombs had come down –
Man's folly had wrecked this once beautiful town.

As the weeks passed to months and the weather grew hot,
Each mother's son groused at his terrible lot,
With fags unobtainable and no hope of beer
We all cursed the man who had sent us out here.

We worked with a will and enjoyed all the fun,
For the Ities turned tail and started to run,
But we worked just as hard, we couldn't relax,
For our troops reached Bengazi and stopped in their tracks.

They had fought along way their strength was depleted,
When they met Jerry's army our boys soon retreated
For Jerry was strong and fresh in the fray,
We were vastly outnumbered that tragical day.

You've all heard the story of the thin long red line –
Our boy's rearguard action was equally fine;
But the tenth day of April, the bugle was sounded,
Alas and alack – Tobruk was surrounded!

We couldn't surrender, our morale was still high
When suddenly there came a roar in the sky;
They machine gunned us and bombed us and shelled us as well,
To be in Tobruk was like living in hell.

We all now look forward to that glorious day
When once more on a ship we shall sail out the bay,
And as we glide out we shall take a last look
At the wreck that was once the proud town of Tobruk.

*Sgt John Patrick Hampton*
*9th Aust. Div. Salvage Section*
*(AWM PR 00759)*

## The Raid Song

Here they come, their bombs to rain
Lurid lingo's merely vain
So we'll sing this old refrain:
"The rotten bastard's here again."
When the sirens weirdly wail
Even heroes, they turn pale,
Phar Lap who we never fail
Funk homeward setting sail
In the drowsy heat of noon
Or beneath the silver moon,
When we hear the dreaded tune
It's under cover bloody soon;
In the night we rise from bed
When we hear them overhead
If no pants on, let it be said
We've each a tin hat on our head;
Loafers drop their tired roles
It's a tune when no one 'poles'
Rabbits, rats or bloody moles –
We can beat them to their holes
When ack-ack starts to roar
Downwards bombs they start to pour
Deeper still we try to bore
No one ever shouts "Encore!"
Hear the flaming crash of guns,
Bombs are dropping by the tons,
Duck your head, now here she comes –
'Blast', the Dagoes or the Huns
But they fall like April rain
Soon the 'All Clear', sounds again
So once again the old refrain:
"The rotten bastard's gone again!"

*Sgt LK Bailey*
*4 M Batt.*
*(AWM PR 00526)*

## *Action*

The twenty five pounders flash & roar,
Their defiance they tell to the Hun,
The mortar bombs whistle, as upwards they roar
And the fun has only begun.

Yes, the fun has only begun lads,
Just wait till the break of day
For then we shall see at the end of the spree,
The enemy running away.

The 'Vickers' guns chatter in bursts loud & long
And the gunners chuckle with glee,
While the Brens & Tommy guns sing their songs
Where the bullets are flying free.

The shrapnel is bursting right overhead
With a rush of flying steel
And the air is filled with the droning lead,
Its breath on your cheeks you feel.

The Lee-Enfield rifles flare & crash
And the line is a line of fire
While the enemy sends his bullets bash
As our men advance to the wire.

Our boys go up to his wire by loads
That fence so cruel & strong
But the boys are bright this deathly night,
On each one's lips is a song.

And now its the Engineers turn to shine;
They crawl forward with bated breath
While away on the right explodes a mine
And someone meets his death.

Now the 'Bangalores' blow with a deafening crash
And the wire goes sky high,
And the charge is reckless & sometimes rash
As the boys from the South go by.

The Bayonets flash in the moonlight clear
As they storm the sangars built
By the Dago & Fritz in the months they've been here,
And the steel goes home to the hilt.

Yes, the steel goes home to the hilt my lads,
And many close their eyes
In death in the field where they would not yield,
They will never see sunrise.

The fighting is fierce & deadly & hot
The bayonets are dripping red,
And the air is heavy with shell & shot
While the ground is strewn with dead

But the battle is over the victory ours
The enemy is in full flight
And we look back with pride & the last few hours
As the eastern sky turns bright.

Though many a comrade has fallen tonight
And our hearts for their loved ones bleed,
We know that they fell in a glorious fight
In the hour of their country's need.

In the hour of their country's need, my lads,
No braver you'll find here;
Through the world will run those deeds they done,
Those comrades tried & dear.

As the rising sun mounts into the blue
And the shadows swiftly fly,
The stretcher bearers come two by two
As they bring the wounded by.

While the men go back to their well earned rest
Proud of the victory won,
And the land for which they gave of their best
Will bless each Mother's son.

*N. C. Lord*
*NA.25906*
*(AWM PR 00526)*

## The 'Isle of Doom'

Here I sit on the Isle of Crete
Bludging on my blistered feet,
Little wonder I've got the blues
With my feet encased in big canoes

In khaki shorts instead of slacks
Living like a tribe of blacks
Except that blacks don't sit & brood
And wait throughout the day for food.

'Twas just a month ago – not more –
We sailed to Greece to win the war
We marched and groaned beneath our load
While bombers bombed us off the road.

They chased us here, they chased us there,
The bastards chased us everywhere
And while they dropped their loads of death
We cursed the bloody RAF.

The RAF was there in force
– They left a few at home of course –
We saw the entire force one day
When a Spitfire spat the other way.

Then we heard the wireless news
When portly Winston, gave his views
He said the RAF's in Greece
Fighting hard to give us peace.

And then we scratched our heads & thought
This sounds distinctly like a "rort",
For if in Greece the Air Force be
Where the bloody hell are we?

And then at last we met the Hun
At odds of thirty-three to one
And though he made it bloody hot
We gave the bastard all we got.

The bullets whizzed, the big guns roared
We howled for ships, to get aboard,
At last they came and on we got
And hurried from that cursed spot.

Then they landed us in Crete
And marched us off our bloody feet;
The food was light the water crook,
I got fed up and slung my hook.

Returned that night full of wine
And next day copped a fiver fine
My paybook was behind to hell
So when pay was called I said, "Oh hell!'
They wont pay me I'm sure of that!"
But when they did, I smelt a rat.

But when next day the rations came
I realized their wily game,
For sooner than sit down and die
We spent our 'dough' on food supply

So now it looks like even betting
A man will soon become a Cretan,
And spend his days in black & gloom
On Adolf Hitler's 'Isle of Doom'.

*Anon*
*(AWM PR 00526)*

## AIF Brigade

Cherished sons and bloody crooks,
Oxford Dons with learned looks,
Farmer boys and city rooks,
Clever clerks and greasy cooks,

> Boundary riders, station owners,
> Out of work and fate bemoaners,
> Pianists and poor tromboners,
> Butchers, bakers, float-a-loaners,

Bagmen, bludgers and school teachers,
Civil servants, sons of preachers,
Navvies, touts and social leaches,
Everything from bush to beaches,

> Con-men, cabbies, counter jumpers,
> Men who used to pick up dumpers,
> Paper peddlers, petrol pumpers,
> Policemen, painters, wild wharf lumpers,

Pugilists and poker players,
Pensive poets, pious prayers,
Boarders who were not good stayers,
Bookies who were not good payers:

> We joined the bloody AIF,
> To every warning we were deaf;
> We started off a motley crew
> Like ingredients of Irish stew.

We consisted of the best and worst,
Sometimes prayed, mostly cursed,
From every walk of life became
Soldiers, treated all the same.

> In training learned to give and take
> For every bloody body's sake,
> Shared our joys and shared our fears,
> Shared our girls and shared our beers.

We staggered down the city street,
We fought and spewed and lost our feet,
Taunted 'Chocos', wrecked cafes,
Made a name that stank always.

> We trained and learned the art of war,
> Often weary and footsore,
> Our former lives began to fade
> As into soldiers we were made.

Soon we came to embarkation,
'Soldiers' in our estimation,
A title that is only earned
By lessons but in action learned.

> We crammed aboard the sweaty ship
> And sweated right throughout the trip,
> Soldiers crammed from stem to stern,
> Hardly room to twist or turn.

We misbehaved ourselves in Perth,
Most hospitable city on earth,
Played merry hell in Old Capetown,
Likewise Durban, also Freetown.

> We kissed the girls in Blighty,
> And mixed with high society,
> Got gloriously drunk without much dough,
> They insisted on paying – we let them go.

Egypt heard our hearty voice,
And didn't seem to quite rejoice;
A land of dirty wogs and stinks
Of pyramids and sour sphinx,

> In cabarets we drank and danced,
> In Sister Street sometimes romanced;
> Read their books of foul perversion,
> Saw the can-can with aversion

In Libya we met the Wop,
Quickly got him on the hop,
Soon we took complete control,
Had the "Itie" up the pole.

> We captured lorries, stores and guns,
> Of all equipment there was tons;
> Guzzled wine, ate vermicelli,
> Regardless of the poor old belly.

But German leaders took the reins
Reorganised the wop remains,
With new equipment, guns and tanks,
Threatened to engage our flanks.

> As most had gone to Greece or Crete,
> We had make a quick retreat,
> And barely kept ahead a lap,
> In the great Benghazi Handicap.

We made our stand in old Tobruk,
To stop the Hun by hook or crook,
For months we fought with visage grim –
Chances then looked pretty slim,

> We lived with fleas in filthy holes;
> The sand entered our very souls
> Shelled and shot at, daily stukered,
> No wonder we were nearly euchred.

Rumour said we'd be relieved,
But most of us just disbelieved;
We thought that by the world forgot,
Our bones would in the desert rot.

> How it happened no one knew,
> But at last our dreams came true;
> We limped out of our lousy holes,
> Relieved by several thousand Poles.

Long hours by the sea we waited,
Anxiously with breathing bated,
Expectant ears alert to hear,
The drone of Herman coming near.

Our ships stole in across the bay
Where battered hulks in dozens lay;
We jumped aboard, were on our way –
No place for shipping to delay.

Back to Egypt – Amariya,
And buckshee bottles of Aussie beer,
So sudden breaking of the drought
Nearly made us all pass out.

In Palestine we met the wogs,
Dressed in their expectant togs;
Allah will be born in pants
And every Arab has a chance,

Flies fed round their filthy eyes,
Most of them were German spies;
They'd steal the milk from out your tea,
Then coolly bite for buckshee.

The dusky little Arab bints,
With their seductive autumn tints,
Were devilish hard to quite convince
And very seldom took our hints.

Their beer was barely drinkable,
Their spirits quite unthinkable,
But some who wouldn't knock it back
Went crazy drinking cognac.

We roamed around Jerusalem,
The begging wogs abusin' 'em,
Spent money on pretty Jewesses,
Barely bought a few caresses

We went to all the holy places,
Bitten by a dozen races,
Learned the way to go to heaven,
Then went down to Kilo Seven.

    To Syria we soldiered on,
    Like lorries in a marathon;
    Women waved from every town,
    One even pulled a garment down.

While we lingered at El Aine
Many beakers did we drain,
Of queer concoctions labeled 'wine'
From grapes but recent off the vine.

    At last we landed at Alep,
    The girls were gay and full of pep;
    We trod the streets with airy step,
    Established our distinctive rep.

In cafes sat and sipped vin blanc,
And to the music added song;
A wild and woolly khaki throng,
We often drank the whole night long.

    All over town you'd hear our call,
    The parody of "Bless 'em all!"
    We lived on chicken, steak and eggs –
    They must have thought we'd hollow legs.

We mounted any passing gharry,
Took the reins and didn't tarry;
Despite the drivers sad demurs
Drove around like mad Ben Hurs.

    For miles we wandered underground,
    A great bazaar was all around,
    Even may have gone – who knows?
    To the street of a thousand so-and-sos.

Our Christmas spirit of good cheer,
Was arak, rum and Aussie beer,
Champagne, gin, Vat 69,
And rare Italian altar wine.

> Dear old ladies played hostess,
> Entertained with great success,
> The best of all was, on the whole,
> Madame Lola – dear old soul!

They welcomed us to Pension Blighty
Even though we acted flighty;
The good clean fun at Pension Badre
Might well be fit for any padre.

> Such happy homes were very handy,
> They frequently had cherry brandy,
> When other ranks had gone away,
> The officers came in to play.

When we had nowhere else to go
We saw a sensuous Wog Show;
Dancing girls with swaying hips,
Attentive wogs with parted lips,

> At seventeen degrees below
> The place lay under feet of snow,
> Snowballs whizzed in all directions,
> Made some pretty good connections.

We saw the ancient citadel,
Learnt its history and its smell,
Constructed good defensive works,
Fraternised with cautious Turks.

> Now the Japs were in the war,
> Would soon be knocking at our door,
> We said goodbye to Madamoiselle;
> Soldiered on to – who could tell?

Down to Suez, onto the sea,
Oh, Middle East, farewell to thee,
You gave us hell sometimes, it's true,
But often gave us good times too.

"Whither?" was the general query,
Everyone produced a theory:
Even money Malaya, Burma,
The odds on home were even firmer.

Bombay was a port of call,
A heavy time was had by all,
But those who visited Grant Road
Later carried all the load.

Singapore fell to the Japs,
Then the Indies quick collapse,
Java held out for a while,
But soon succumbed to yellow guile.

Thus ended weeks of speculation
On what would be our destination;
We slowly slipped across the foam
And knew we headed right for home.

At thought of home our spirits rose,
We washed and pressed our service clothes,
Let ourselves fondly believe,
We'd soon be going home on leave.

They sneaked us out to Sandy Creek
And granted us a lousy week;
Whose home were in another state,
Had many, many weeks to wait,

We traveled on to Tenterfield,
Our vicious natures quite concealed;
The people all showed naïve amaze,
That we behaved in decent ways.

Another move to Kilcoy,
Where people really did enjoy
Seeing that everything was done
To make our stay a pleasant one.

    The training here was pretty tough,
    In country pretty close and rough;
    Were quite content to go to beddie
    After going out on a 'Don Freddie'.

Then we grizzled and grumbled and swore,
Knew we were on our way once more
Over the sea to a foreign shore,
'Twas harder this time than it was before,

    En route they told us to beware,
    Many evils await to ensnare,
    Told us how we'd get our share,
    Of tropic disease and disaster to spare.

Then we landed at Papua,
Our moods got rapidly bluer,
Each sharpened up his trusty bayonet,
So the Japs could with ease contain it.

    Presently we fought the Jap
    And showed him how to fight a sarap,
    A fast and furious affray,
    Known as the Battle of Milne Bay

'Twas his first defeat in any land,
We dished it out with lavish hand,
Hardly any got away,
The rest of them are here to stay.

    (So our story waits in Milne Bay,
    How much more, no one can say;
    The final verse will mark the day
    When worldwide peace is here to stay.)

*B. T. Woods*
*(AWM PR 00359)*

## *Our First Stunt*

It was Saturday night in the boozer,
When the word was passed around
That our convoy would leave next morning
When we heard the bugle sound.

At four ack emma we were out of bed
Before the sun arose,
The breakfast was stew and not so hot
And the work was on the nose.

We travelled through the desert
Known to us now as Sinai,
And hour after hour
Saw nothing but sand and sky.

At last we reached our barracks
A place called Mersa Matruh,
Where Cleo and Anthony used to make love
And the Duke and Duchess too.

We had a lot of Ities there
And didn't like the hicks,
So we stood around and smoked and yarned
While those bastards swung the picks.

*Stan Pinson*
*(AWM PR00526)*

## Spring Offensive

In where the smoke runs black against the snow
And bullets drum against the rocks he went
And saw men die with childish wonderment
Where bayonets glitter in the sudden glow;
And sleek shells scream and mortars cough below
There tanks lurch up and shudder to a halt
Before the superb anger of the guns
Then flares go up – the rattle of a bolt.
Rifles stutter and voices curse the Huns
And then he jerked and toppled to the ground,
His ears too full of noise, his eyes of light,
His scattered cartridge clips glint brassy bright
A Vickers cackles madly from the mound.
Oh, where the red anemone brims over
To swarm in brambled riot down a rise,
There we will lay him, lay your widow'd lover,
And wipe the poor burnt face and gently cover
The look of startled wonder in his eyes.
Let beauty come, let her alone
Bemoan those broken lips with kisses of her own.

*Sig M. Biggs*
*(AWM PR 00526)*

## *Libya*

Oh, Libya! thou land of pests,
With Nature's wiles one never rests
And Jerry shows his nasty ways
By shelling us for days and days.

The CQ sends the rations short
And drinks the rum, we've always thought;
Of our CO I cannot speak –
We have a new one every week.

The morn it shines so awfully bright
The bastard snipes with ease at night
And makes us jump and swear with fright
And cry: You bastard, come and fight!

We live in holes dug in the ground
Where moles and rats and fleas abound;
There's flies and ants and nasty chats
And bloody beetles as big as bats.

There's Messerschmitts and good old Foux
(We always have a shot at you)
And Whispering Willie winds his way
And where he'll land no one can say;

And Verey lights go up at night –
They are a most delightful sight
And raiding bombers come and go
To be chased by onions, to and fro.

There's booby traps and tangled wire
To be erected under fire;
So Libya now rest content
You're all the evils ever sent.

*Anon*
*(AWM PR 00526)*

## *The Pillbox on the Rise*

Now this land is hot and dusty
Not worth a bloody hoot,
It would take a million acres
To support a bandicoot

Out towards where the escarpment
Rears beneath the lower skies
My mates and I are living
In a pillbox on the rise.

Well, it wasn't built for comfort
But we stand some heavy knocks
The ventilation's not hygienic
And it smells of sweaty sox.

At night the sand fleas eat us
And by day we have the flies,
A delightful little mansion
Is this pillbox on the rise.

We live on army rations –
Bully beef or beans or stew,
Some Mungaree and margarine
And Nelsons' evil brew.

To stretch and sleep in comfort
We would need one twice the size,
But we've got to be contented
In this pillbox on the rise.

Oft the Sigs drop in upon us
When they're running out their lines,
They've got them stretched about the place
Like bloody pumpkin vines.

They sit and smoke and yarn awhile
And tell the latest lies;
We have our little gatherings
At the pillbox on the rise.

It's not a fast existence
But we've heard a bomber or so
And when the ack-ack opens up,
Come out and see the show.

Now Smithy's quite disheartened
But he'd better dry his eyes –
He won't be always waiting
In a pillbox on a rise.

But someone's got to man it
And I guess we are the mugs
While we dream of leave in Alex
And of beer in foaming mugs;

And if the worst should happen
We've a job quite man size,
Defending Aussie and Egypt
In the pillbox on the rise.

*Anon*
*(AWM PR 00526)*

## *To the A.A.S.C.*

They have toiled their loads o'er the far flung roads
And the labour has been their pride
They have hauled the clip to the waiting ship
Through the streets to the waterside.

They have brought the grain from the stubbled plains
Till the silo siding was full
Through the days that were long they have loved their song
Of the engines thrust & pull.

When the gales wild lash made the branches crash
Spite of perils old & new,
Down the winding grade not a whit dismayed
Came the transport roaring through.

Through the coastal rains, over black soil plains
Through flood & dust & flame,
No matter what the odds, by all the gods,
They'd get there just the same.

Now they've left the roads, they have no loads
To the wharf or the outback store
For the Empire's call has brought them all
To the days & the ways of war.

Now the engine's song sounds stern & strong
And its theme is the common will,
For the foe of old grows overbold
And we love our freedom still.

Yet the part they played in the nation's trade
Their motto now shall be,
Equal to the task to all that's asked
Of the men of our ASC.

In the peaceful years they got no cheers
And they seek none now, it's true
But this we know, where wheels can go,
They'll get their war freights through.

They'll haul each shell to the gates of hell
To the maw of each hungry gun,
O'er countless roads they'll bring their loads
And the job will be well done.

Let the spotlight shine on the firing line
On the guns & the infantry
But save a cheer for the trusty Rear,
The men of our AASC.

*Anon*
*(AWM PR 00526)*

## *1941*

That year it rained death like apples
It did not matter at all about the dead
For what better than death in battle,
(The sick voice said in the belly
What death better than death in battle?)
That year the wicked were strong but remember
That the time comes when the thing that you strike
Rouses itself suddenly, very terribly,
And stands staring with a terribly angry look
And says, "Why do you strike me brother? I am a man."
One man is like another,
One strength like another strength
And the wicked shall not prosper for ever,
When the turns of history
Bring the innocent –
To Victory!

*G. W. F.*
*(AWM PR 00526)*

## The Australian Volunteers

This war is just beginning,
By a man who has no love
For the lives of human beings
And the God we know above.

So to victory we're marching,
The possessors of no fear
And throughout the world we're known as:
The Australian volunteers.

When we left our wives and mothers
It was sorrowful, I'll say,
And for the pain they supplied
Someone will have to pay.

That someone's Adolf Hitler
For he's caused them many tears,
And revenge will be the bayonets
Of the Australian Volunteers.

Our fathers fought in 'fourteen
When they made their big advance,
And they wrote their names in history
As the bravest men in France.

We'll follow in their footsteps
Tho' it's after twenty years
To keep the old tradition
Of the Australian volunteers.

When we return to Australia,
Victorious from the strife,
There's many a man we left behind
Who gave his gallant life

So freedom may continue
As it has in former years,
With the Empire's gains assisted
By the Aussie Volunteers

*Anon*
*(AWM PR 00526)*

## Bound'ry Riders of Tobruk

We're riding Shank's pony,
    Round the boundry of Tobruk
And looking to the traps at night as well;
    We're rounding up all the boobies
And we have our share of luck
    And now and then we yard a straying shell.

We're used to yarding cattle
    On a brumby mountain bred,
We can use the whips and spurs in proper style,
    But the boundaries here are different
And the whips are Brens instead
    And our spurs are made of barbed wire by the mile.

We see the Jerry rustler
    As he sneaks about at night,
No doubt he is a trier, is old Fritz,
    But he's found the Boundary Rider
Ever ready for a fight
    If he decides to start on a blitz.

We are gathered from the outposts
    Of Australia over here
And if we chance to leave slip and rail down,
    It's just a trap for Jerry,
So you needn't have a fear,
    All you blokes that work back near the town.

Just send us up our rations,
    Keep the ammo well supplied
And see we get our mail and parcels too;
    We'll route the Jerry rustler out
And tan his bloody hide
    Ere we round him up and send him back again.

*Anon*
*(AWM PR 00526)*

## Headlines

A mighty island fortress,
The guardian of the east,
An up-to-date Gibraltar,
A thousand planes at least.
"It simply cannot be taken,
'Twill stand a siege for years
We'll hold the place for ever,
'Twill bring our foe to tears.
Our men are there in thousands,
Defences are unique."

The Japs did not believe it –
So they took it in a week.

*Anon*

## *The Battle of Jahore*

There's a strip of rubber country
North of Singapore;
To the Diggers it was a death trap,
On the map it's called Jahore.

'Twas against tremendous odds
The boys put on a show
That was the equal of the Anzacs
At Gallipoli long ago.

But men on the ground can never fight
The terrors of the sky;
Without air support they just lie still
To wait on death and die.

Face to face odds matter not
For the Digger loves a scrap,
But when the sky is full of planes
And every one a Jap,

It's then you wonder, was it a dream,
For in the paper that you read,
Air support will soon arrive
As production goes ahead.

There's a strip of rubber country
Which some day we will take,
For that is all he asked of us
The chap who was our mate.

Then we'll hand Malaya over
And with it goes Jahore,
And we'll pray to God we're never called
To defend it any more.

*Anon*

## *At Anchor in Aden*

There's a cobalt blue that's brilliant
As I gaze into the sky,
There's a sheen of blue-green waters
And a dhow is sailing by.

　The fleecy clouds are fading
　As the sun climbs further still,
　The sullen sea reflects its glare,
　Its heat frowns on the hill.

There's a range of rocks so rugged,
Some million years gone by,
May have held a valley verdant
Beneath a kindlier sky.

　They rise up stark and sombre
　From out the Gulf's green wave;
　They are barren as the desert,
　As forbidding as the grave.

Gaunt hills that girt the harbour
And guard the dead Red Sea,
To ships that sail the ocean
A sign of sanctuary.

　It's one more Empire outpost,
　A bulwark of the Nation,
　That earns an exile's edict,
　A place of desolation.

Where strategy commands the sea,
Where ships across it sail,
Where wealth is won from toil and trade
A port must mark the trail.

　And thus it is that Aden,
　Sheer rock and desert dust,
　Was found and won by Britain
　And hold to it we must.

For all of us the fight is fought
And play our parts we will,
And though our thoughts stray far away,
Our eyes are on the Hill.

The day will dawn, the tide will turn,
Our term in exile ended;
We'll greet again our hearth and homes
And reap the vision splendid.

*John L. Wylie*
*(AWM MSS 1375)*

# Tulagi

*In commemoration of the sinking of HMAS* Canberra *in Tulagi Bay, Solomon Islands, 9 August 1942*

We sailed north, invasion our aim,
Not for honour or fame,
Just to teach the Japs to play the game.
When we reached Tulagi,
The invasion barges were in the Bay,
How many soldiers was hard to say,
But when they landed there was hell to pay
on that island of Tulagi.

The sailors were quiet, the atmosphere tense,
The Admiral kept them in suspense,
And nobody knew the Japs defence
When we sailed into Tulagi.
The Japanese bombers left Rabaul
To answer the island's desperate call
And some of them were seen to fall
into the Bay of Tulagi.

The torpedo bombers came to attack,
All we heard was the sharp ack-ack
As our ack-ack guns drove them back
Away from Tulagi.
Then late at night action sounded,
And to their guns the sailors bounded,
As into the *Canberra* many shells pounded
just off Tulagi.

The sailors were almost in their stride
When a Japanese torpedo hit our side,
And many a brave sailor reeled and died
Near the Island of Tulagi.
Although we could not help the fleet,
Our wounded Captain kept his feet,
He was one who didn't admit defeat
when we sank in Tulagi.

*Able Seaman 'Happy' Fellows*

## *A Survivor*

### *A Tribute to Greece*

I ask no nobler task than to portray,
As one fate spared to flee your fire-raked shore,
The glorious martyred courage that today
Flames fiercer than the brilliant meteor.
I'd write Your valiant fight two years ago
That stained the scales of Liberty with blood!
What more vivid memory could I know
Than Athens, warm and gay, steeped in the flood
Of Grecian sunlight, like a vibrant maid,
Splendid with life and love, with head held high?
Though ruthless rape still holds its ghastly fate,
You'll not cringe and cry the plea that Byron made;
For there will come a new Thermopolae,
To give rebirth, to purge the German hate.

*Tpr W. L. Johnson*
*VX8303*
*(AWM PR 87/062)*

## Gundeck Reverie

### (RAN Reverie)

Where the deep blue of the ocean meets the brighter blue of sky,
Where white capped waves and wind swept clouds are scudding gaily by,
From east to west, from north to south, as far as eye can see,
That ever distant circle, the horizon, calls to me.

It calls me with a yearning only sailors can define,
Ports and harbors, sailing ships, the tang of ocean brine;
There's magic in the surging sea, the trackless ocean way,
There's music in the lullaby of wind and flying spray.

When golden sun gives way to night, with myriad stars a throng
The moonlit sea, the rhythmic throb of engines is my song.
Yet the call of hearth and homeland intrudes my reverie,
For there's sadness in a woman's heart, who lonely waits for me.

On duty on the gundeck as we plough across the sea,
All the action and adventure, all the splendor fades from me –
Far beyond the distant skyline, beyond the boundless foam,
There's a wistful woman praying that his ship comes safely home.

There's a cosy little cottage and each night a vacant chair,
And a loving heart is heavy, for a loved one isn't there.
The children, as they go to bed, kneel down at night to pray:
"Dear God, Will you bring Daddy back? Please bring him home some day."

*L/Sig John L. Wylie W 769*
*Aden, Arabia, December 1940*
*(AWM MSS 1375)*

## On the Sanananda Beach

The palm trees sway at the close of day
On Sananand Beach,
A cloud-filled sky bids the sun goodbye
Beyond the jungle's reach.

Each swirling wave seems to engrave
A pattern on the sands:
A silent word, unseen, unheard,
Cut out by nature's hands.

A shadow falls and a wild bird coils
To the sinking sun and the sea;
The fast fading light, and the still of the night
Bring a breath of a mystery.

The bird's call stops and the night breeze drops,
And an awful stillness reigns;
A soothing calm like a healing balm,
But the sound of the sea remains.

As if in a dream, there comes a wild scream,
As aeroplanes roar overhead;
With bombs and with fire, they leave a huge pyre,
Of wounded bodies and dead.

The jungle recesses and lost wildernesses
Resound to the battle's affray;
The earth splits asunder, and echoes like thunder
Roll onward and echo away.

Far into the night continues the fight,
And the noise of the struggle is heard,
Where silence was breathless and stillness once deathless
Excepting the call of the bird.

After ages, at last, the battle is past,
The noise and the action no more,
The trees maimed and broken, a grim tragic token
Of the terrible havoc of war.

A soft quietness steals and the moonlight reveals
The result of this death-dealing game;
The sky rains its dew, as if all nature too
Were weeping with pity and shame.

An unseen hand has sketched on the sand
A pattern just out of reach,
Of many a wave that flows o'er a grave
On the Sanananda Beach.

*Pte C. R. Shaw*
*Q126475*
*(AWM PR 87/062)*

## The Ringers from the North

They have finished with the riding, down the lonely cattle trails,
They are through with swapping stories, watching riders from the rails,
And the moleskins and the leggings that are sweaty, old and torn
Are discarded for the glory of a Khaki Uniform.

They won't be drafting bullocks for many days to come
And the noise of rushing cattle will yield to roaring guns,
And those nights spent by the campfire in the stock camps near the yard
Will just be pleasant memories to a ringer doing guard.

They are using, now, a field gun where they once just used the reins,
And they're marching and they're drilling getting cusses for their pains,
But they know the job's worth doing, as they know a good man's worth,
They are number one good fellows are the ringers from the north.

And when they're cold and hungry, sitting shivering like lost souls
There will come some fragrant memories of grilling rib-bones on the coals
With a damper in the ashes and a quart pot full of tea
And the black boys hobbling horses singing native songs of glee.

And when the war is over and the bugle calls no more,
Then the ringers will be moving to a southern tropic shore
And as the sky grows crimson beneath the setting sun
You will see each ringer heading for a distant cattle run.

*Lance Bombardier Sydney Kelly*
*(AWM PR 87/062)*

## Bomber

As darkness covers the tarmac,
The bombers grasp the sky;
Their crews are cold with sweat,
For fear that they might die.

    A pilot sits transfixed
    Before his knobs and dials and switches;
    His navigator sits and stares,
    Not a muscle twitches.

The engines drone regardless,
The gunner tests his guns,
Assures himself that they will work
When he must down the Huns.

    The planes roar out across the sea,
    The target drawing near,
    Until the sounds of those before them
    On the wind the crews could hear.

Burst of flack and wicked tracer
Lacerate the night;
Bomb run commenced,
The pilot must not deviate in flight.

    Ahead there is a blinding flash,
    A bomber bursts in flames –
    All the men aboard are dead,
    Glorious are their names.

Planes are falling from the sky,
Torn blazing from the night,
Balls of fire with smoking trails,
They plummet out of sight.

    The cry of "Bombs away!" at last,
    Time again to breathe,
    Power on to climb and turn,
    A lifetime to achieve.

The 109s are all around;
Cannon and machine gun fire.
Silhouetted against the flames,
The bombers' funeral pyre.

    The survivors claw their way
    Towards the coast and homeward bound,
    Trailing smoke and glycol –
    Still the fighters hound.

A badly damaged straggler
Limps across the sky;
The surviving crew are cold with sweat,
For fear that they might die.

    The navigator's lifeless form
    Lies twisted on his sight,
    Near stalling speed the plane
    Prepares to slip beneath the night.

The gunner stares through sightless eyes,
At nothing to be seen,
Reflecting tiny images
Where once such life had been.

    The pilot, numbed by pain and shock,
    Sits rigid all alone;
    He tries to keep his plane aloft
    To reach the aerodrome.

The altimeter is winding down,
Airspeed reaching critical,
Heartbeats measure lifetime,
Survival hypothetical.

    Shattered screen and instruments,
    The air an icy flow,
    The engines cough and splutter,
    Oh, how the wind does blow!

*Greg Brooks*

## Egypt? For Australia We Fight

*We're here because we're here* is a song we used to sing
  Before we left Australia for the fray
Well, we're here now, with a vengeance and here we've got to stop
  For there's not the slightest chance to get away.

We said farewell to loved ones e're we left Port Melbourne Pier
  To fight against big odds on land and sea,
But the freedom of Australia must be guarded at all costs
  And we'll fight like hell to keep our country free.

We long to leave these lands of strife, of misery and pain,
  We long to see our homes and loved ones too,
But until our foe is conquered and the Kaiser sheaths his sword
  We'll clench our teeth and see this matter through.

*Tpr W. H. Johnstone (?)*
*8th ALH, AIF*
*(AWM PR 84/049)*

## *Of Courage and Fear*

What thoughts through [a] warrior's mind might pass,
What scattered gems are there?
Memories fond, of times long past,
Tomorrow's dreams to share.

That darkest time, await the dawn,
The chill of night a cloak,
Lonely, midst the milling crowd
Where seldom a word is spoke.

Embraced in silent solitude
Yet part of a common bond,
For here all souls react as one,
Ponder fate, which waits beyond.

To live, to die, what fortune hides
In heavy thoughts aquired?
Yet too soon, to feel the rush
When first the shots are fired.

What feeling stirs this pounding heart
Dark thoughts, yet far from clear,
Perhaps a threatening warrior bold
Or a lonely soul with fear.

Confronting soon, as warriors must
When decision time draws near,
The conflict of courage and duty
Against his basic, mortal fear.

For without fear, there is no courage,
Gone all values held so dear;
A warrior, who would be a hero
Needs the emotional catalyst, fear.

*James D. Young*

# Chapter Four
# Other Conflicts

## *I'd Like to be There*

I would like to be there in November
To talk with you, just like old times;
I'd like to see who will remember,
And walk for a while in the lines.

    Hear the noise of the cooks in the morning,
    Steal a smoke on picquet at night,
    Dodge the RSM as he wanders,
    Ready to give me a fright.

And I'd like to play football on sports day
And shoot on the old rifle range,
Catch a tram to the B.E. on weekends,
Or Grand Central just for a change.

    I wonder who you all married?
    And how many children you had?
    Where you worked, and if you succeeded?
    See – proves you weren't all that bad.

And I'd like to visit the chapel,
Maybe see all the trees in the rain,
Polish my boots on a Sunday
And stand on parade once again.

    But I can't be there in November.
    I lie here in Korea's cold clime.
    But thankyou for planting the trees
    And thankyou for taking the time.

To Remember a Mate.

*Margaret Gibbons*

## *I've Had Me Share of Rubber Trees*

I've had me share of rubber trees and screamin' Sergeant-Majors
And livin' like a mongrel dog in those stuffed-out canvas cages;

'Ad me share of screamin' jets and whoopin' bloody rockets,
Beetles in me under dacks, bull ants in me pockets.

Had me share of mud 'n slush and raining like a bastard,
And when it rains, it rains here mate – a fortnight once it lasted.

'Ad me share of crawling things and human ones is with 'em
Bitin' round your tender spots and at the bosses bum they're sniffin',

I've had me share of sweaty gear and rashes on me belly
And watchin' Yankee football on the stuffed out canteen telly;

'Ad me share of dipping out on sex and lovin' and boozin',
Yeah I'm in this bloody place, but it sure wasn't my choosin.'

Had this bloody Vietnam and a war that ain't fair dinkum,
Had the swamps and chook-house towns and everythin' is stinkin',

Had me share of countin' days and boots with ten foot laces,
I've had me share, I've 'ad it mate – 'up' all them foreign places!

*Anon*
*(AWM MSS 0870)*

## 105's 105s

*A tribute to the Officers and Men of 105 Field Battery Royal Australian Artillery, the Battle for Long Tan and the 105mm Pack Howitzer and its role during that battle. This poem is dedicated to all of the Veterans who took part in this battle and kept alive the spirit of the Anzacs.*

"Take Post! Take Post!" They'd heard it before,
They were quick to their guns, a few even swore,
But this was a fire mission like none in the past
And so it had started the battle at Long Tan.

The boys from D Company were in a fix,
Not far from the Dat, about two clicks,
The call came in for support to survive
And to the fore were 105's 105s.

In the rubber plantation the boys on the ground,
Facing enemy fire from all around,
Conditions appalling the mud and fierce rain,
Visibility a problem but confusion restrained;

The position more clearly with bright blue flashes,
From the guns in support landing rounds in the ashes;
The gunfire was loud, bright and blaring,
Placed a look on the diggers surprised and glaring.

They knew there was hope with accurate fire
To help them survive the mud and the mire,
The guns so constant with dangerous close fire.

Back at the Dat the actions were true,
The boys on the guns they knew what to do;
The weather so bad the rain teeming down,
Strong cordite mist was hugging the ground,
Empty cart cases were forming a mound,
But the guns would not cease until the very last round,
From 105's 105s.

The battle raged on through that terrible night,
Uncertain the thoughts of the men in the fight,
But the soldiers had been trained for a job to be done
And all fought and battled until it was won.

At the end of it all they all looked around,
They were tired, drenched and spent,
And looked at each other in wonderment.
Through the days that had passed battle honours had been won,
You could not but admire the Australian Son,
But then a glance at that little gun, 105's 105s.

*WO2 Bill Pritchard*

## Body Bags

Body bags slick, shining green,
    white nylon zips unable to stem
    the knowing of limp slack lines
    and men who once were friends.

Floppy hands and heavy carry
    to waiting helicopter doors,
    and mates who once smiled
    now stacked on aluminium floors.

Congealed blood and torn boots
    by the bamboo groves,
    and thumping rotor blades
    taking away the stiffened hands.

Stacked, flopped, almost liquid
    in the obscene formlessness of plastic,
    hiding the end product of insanity
    and the awful work of jumping mines.

Taking from your pocket a letter
    still unread, but opened by shrapnel,
    and here an arm, and there a leg,
    neatly body-bagged, and bloody well dead.

The ashes of unshown grief choking us
    along with the red dust as you go away,
    now a mere dot in the vault of the sky,
    wrapped with your memories in a bag.

*Lt John A. Moller*
*RNZIR Whiskey Two*
*Vietnam*

## The Last Step

Had enough time to cry
"My God!"
As the innocent track
Leapt up in a moment
Of sound and fury
And the jumping mine
Cut him in two
At his pubic hair line.

And in the dark shadows
On the sides of the track
His friends all retched
And gently reached back,
Pulling their bayonets
To prod the bloody track.

Fighting down their fear
And wanting to run,
But knowing if they did
They'd be dead, every one;
Feeling for the trip-wires
And the shining prongs,
Inch by inch all prodding
The leaf mould and the slime.

*John A. Moller*

## *A Salute to the Men of Long Tan*

Kiss your wives and farewell your friends,
  it's time my lads to stand with the men;
Bloodied red bayonets and mouths painful dry,
  bandage your brothers, and try not to cry.

The Vietcong are coming all black down the road
  so take up your rifles and aim well and load;
Forget all your dreams and remember your past,
  I fear that this battle may well be your last.

Stay firm in the trenches, shoot slightly low,
  ignore dying friends as the cannon mouths glow,
The enemy are evil and slavery their name,
  so fix tight your bayonets and mark well the aim.

So kiss all your wives and hug tight your child,
  for today is the day when death will run wild;
The tracer bright ribbons will cut them down clean
  in the eddies of battle by dirty brown streams.

So hold tight your brothers and farewell your babes,
  today is the day you'll be in your graves;
Falling and calling in cordite's white cloud
  the jungle forever your lonely brave shroud.

So remember my friends those D Company men
  who laid down their lives in Long Tan's green glens,
Salute all your sons and the seventeen lost
  who paid for our freedom – the ultimate cost.

*John A. Moller*

## *Forgotten Heroes*

We marched for seven days and nights,
We marched with heavy feet and hearts,
We marched along the dusty roads,
We marched with weathered heavy souls.

We saw the children and the farms,
We saw the choppers and napalm,
We saw the smoke and then the flames
And deceived ourselves to hide the shame.

We closed our eyes to restless sleep,
We prayed the Lord our souls to keep,
We counted days until we went home,
To the country we loved, to the country we'd outgrown.

We hid in the jungle from our foe,
We played our parts in this terror filled role,
We sighted guns and dug our pits,
And in between we took the hits.

We numbed our minds to the pain we felt,
And drank to forget the death we dealt,
We showed no fear except to ourselves,
And tried to protect our mental health.

Our lives were changed in those fateful years,
Scars were forged with blood and tears,
We did our time and paid our dues,
We returned home spat on and ridiculed.

We served our country,
For the good of democracy,
We returned home like criminals,
Chained to hypocrisy.

*Pte J. Harris*
*17 March 1998*

## Just Us

I've never done this thing before
"Pick 'em up and take 'em to war."
What could be so hard in that?
We load them on, and it's off to Nui Dat.

> I watch these blokes real close,
> They're tough, keen and different to most;
> They train and train and some more –
> This must be some hell of a war

We're getting close, I can see a change,
Gun crews ready, check the range,
All the lights are turned down low,
Black curtains are now the go.

> Whispers from the mess decks low,
> No one sleeps and cigarettes glow;
> Tracer fire fills the night,
> A young sailor hugs his lifejacket real tight.

The morning light it comes at last,
Let's get these blokes off real fast;
The sound of choppers fills the air;
There are bloody things going on everywhere

> Look them in the eye before they go:
> What will Fate on them bestow?
> Their faces you'll remember for all time –
> Farewell, fall in line, great Aussie, shine!

*Barry Buttle*

## CHAPTER FIVE
# PRISONERS OF WAR

## Escape

If you can quit the compound undetected
And clear your tracks nor leave the smallest trace,
And follow out the program you've selected
Nor lose your grasp of distance, time and place,

If you can walk at night by compass bearing
Or ride the railways in the light of day
And temper your elusiveness with daring,
Trusting that sometimes bluff will find a way,

If you can follow sour frustration
And gaze unmoved at failure's ugly shape
Remembering, as further inspiration,
It was and is your duty to escape,

If you can keep the great Gestapo guessing,
With explanations only partly true
And leave them in their heart of hearts confessing
They didn't get the whole truth out of you,

If you can use your 'cooler' fortnight clearly
For planning methods wiser than before
And treat your first miscalculations merely
As hints let fall by fate to teach you more,

If you scheme on with patience and precision
(It wasn't in a day they builded Rome)
And make escape your single sole ambition –
The next time you attempt it you'll get home.

*F/Lt G. Bretel*
*(AWM PR 88 160)*

## Stalag Luft III

Here we are at Stalag Three,
Drinking beer at the bar
With lovely girls to serve the beer...
  like bloody hell we are.

We traveled here in luxury
The whole trip for a quid,
A sleeping berth for each of us...
  like bloody hell we did

Our feather beds are two feet deep
The carpet's almost new,
In easy chairs we sit all day...
  like bloody hell we do.

The goons are bloody wizard chaps,
Their hopes of victory good,
We'd change them places any day...
  like bloody hell we would.

When winter comes and snow's around,
The temperature at nil,
We'll find hot bottles in our beds...
  like bloody hell we will.

It's heaven on earth at Stalag Three,
A life we'd hate to miss,
It's everything we've always wished...
  like bloody hell it is.

*F. O. J McCleery (?)*
*(AWM PR 88 160)*

## *There's Always Bloody Something*

Bloody times is bloody hard
Bloody wire for bloody guard
Bloody dogs in bloody yard,
Bloody, Bloody, Bloody.

Bloody tea is bloody vile
Bloody cocoa makes you smile
Cocoa made in bloody style,
Bloody, Bloody, Bloody.

Bloody ice rink, bloody mud
Bloody skates no bloody good
Sat where once I bloody stood
Bloody, Bloody, Bloody.

Bloody salmon's bloody queer
Looks at you with bloody leer
Is it good? no bloody fear!
Bloody, Bloody, Bloody.

Bloody bridge all bloody day
Learning how to bloody play
Bloody Blackwoods bloody way,
Bloody, Bloody, Bloody.

Now and then tho' bloody stale
Censor hands out bloody mail
Better draw the bloody veil,
Bloody, Bloody, Bloody.

Bloody girlfriend drops me flat
Like a dog on bloody mat
Gets a Yank like bloody that,
Bloody, Bloody, Bloody.

Bloody sawdust in the bread
Must have come from bloody bed
Better all be bloody dead,
Bloody, Bloody, Bloody.

Don't it get your bloody goat;
Was it Shaw who bloody wrote
"Where the hell's that bloody boat?"
Bloody, Bloody, Bloody.

Now I've reached the bloody end
Nearly round the bloody bend
That's the general bloody trend,
Bloody, Bloody, Bloody.

*F. O. J McCleery (?)*
*(AWM PR 88 160)*

## *This War*

It started back in '14
    And it's just kicked off again,
Another war to end all wars
    In the good Lord's sacred name.

The British blame the Germans,
    The Jerry blame the Poles,
But it's poor silly B___!
    Who lie fighting in the holes

They decked us out in khaki
    With buttons shining bright,
With a rifle and a bayonet
    They taught us how to fight.

They taught us the art of battle
    In a most efficient way
With church blessings every Sunday:
    God speed you on your way!

But the day is shortly coming
    When we will all be free
To board the good old steamer
    That sails Pacific seas.

With sweethearts there to meet us,
    And friends and pals galore,
They'll line that golden waterfront
    Along old Aussie's shore.

And when the boat is anchored
    And the birds are at the nest
We'll think of our fallen comrades
    Who have done their very best.

*POW unknown*
*(AWM 3 DRL 3527)*

## *Mail*

Nothing is so cheering
To a POW in camp
As a letter, good news bearing,
With a good old Aussie stamp.

Everyone in camp is waiting
Everybody without fail,
Be it officer or rating,
For the coming of the mail.

"Anything for me?" asks Larry
When the postman comes around,
"Sorry old boy; one for Harry,
But nothing from your home town."

Many men feel heavy-hearted
When they hear old Larry say:
"Not a letter since we parted,
But one may come some day."

When this b___ war is over
And at last are homeward bound,
Sailing up the straits, in clover
No need to wait the postman's round.

*Anon*
*(AWM 3 DRL 3527)*

## *Half Way There*

Despite all the carnage around us
We always believed we could cope,
For through all the darkness of evil
There was always the Lantern of Hope.

So slowly the days dragged onward,
Each getting worse than before,
Each morning a maximum effort
Each Prayer "Please God, only once more!"

The column climbed over the saddle
And stopped in the snow on its crest
As we saw for the first time before us
The plains stretch away to the West.

Below, The Bohemian Basin
As far as the eye could behold,
White with the mantle of winter
The streams frozen solid with cold.

Slowly we marched through the snow drifts,
Where Wenceslas' footstep once trod,
Past quaint little roadside chapels,
Reminders of man's faith in God.

The pain that accompanies starvation
Increased to the nth degree;
The Grim Reaper sat on our shoulders
Like Sinbad's *Old Man of the Sea.*

The limit of living had reached us,
I sat with Patrick my friend;
We could march no more with the column
This day would be Journey's End.

But 'ere the Grim Reaper could claim us
A Swedish white wagon arrived,
Handing out Red Cross foodstuffs
So thus once again we survived.

The Lantern of Hope, rekindled,
Burned bright when the wagon had gone;
We picked up our miserable bundles
And those who could stand carried on.

O'er the Elbe to the Erzgebirge Ranges
Plodding the sodden tracks,
With the Lantern of Hope growing dim now
And the Reaper again on our backs

Whilst struggling along the by-roads
Something affected my soul
There was a gap in the pain that enclosed me
And my spirit slipped out of the hole

Up, up and away I went floating
Away from the noises of war
Away from the horror of living
And all that had happened before.

Contented and painless I floated
In wonderous peace of mind,
Not dreaming, but thinking and seeing,
Though my body was left far behind.

Below me the column, still marching
I could see front to the rear,
All in the sharpest of detail
Each man showing separate and clear.

On the head of a man in the centre
The Russian-made headgear of Pat,
On the left flank beside him a figure
Wearing my battered slouch hat.

I studied that pitiful creature
That I knew was the body of me
And wondered what kept it going
When the part that mattered was free.

At last when the daylight was dying
I came back to the world of pain,
Dragged through the gap that was closing –
I was back in the column again.

I believe that there is an Almighty,
I believe in the power of prayer,
I believe there is life after dying.
I know. I have been Half Way There.

*Pte J. Wright*
*(AWM MSS 1586)*

## POW Day

No doubt that we were bunnies
To swallow all their talk
Of Yankees at Port Dickson
And Pommies' air support

    They marched us out to Changi
    Ten thousand men or more;
    The fallen by the roadside
    Made us yearn no more for war.

We're planting beans by numbers
We're sloping arms no more,
We're through with bloody fighting
For Tojo topped the score.

    We live in shell-torn barracks
    Minus water, roof and tile,
    The NCOs and Pippers
    Eat with rank and file

Our clothes they are most scanty,
Our trousers ripped and torn,
We're bloody near as naked
As the day that we were born

    Our charpoys they have taken,
    We sleep on them no more;
    There's naught for us to do
    But doss upon the floor.

We rise around eight hundred
And creep down to the tong
And think of old Rexona
And hope it won't be long.

    We fall in on the A Parade
    And answer to our names
    It's "Stand at ease!" "stand easy!"
    Then the OC cries again:

"You're still in the AIF lads,
And no matter where you go
The Government of Australia
Expects you to earn your dough."

Next up we have breakfast
Our appetites to sate,
In single file we get it –
It's rice upon our plate

The greasy babblers moaning,
The backups standing by
And Corporal Death a leading
With hunger in his eye.

Next we're duty company,
It's work to make us hard
Collecting meager rations
Or sweeping up the yard.

Our after-lunch siesta
Is spent in many ways
With dreams of steak and onions
We knew in better days.

We're wakened from our slumber
By a voice that's loud and harsh:
"Come grab your dirty washing
And to the tongs we'll march"

With shades of evening falling
There's visits we must pay
To see Bill and Harry
Who live across the way.

There's pals in other units
There's mates we'll never see
And dreams of dear old Aussie
Our homes across the sea.

The good old swy-ups going,
We brought it to this land
And though we haven't got much dough
I guess we'll land a hand.

"There go the pennies sailing!"
You can hear the boxer holler,
But luck is dead against us
And there goes our only dollar.

'Lights out' will soon be sounding
And though we all are broke,
I guess that one amongst us.
Will have a light to smoke

It's homeward to our billets
We wend our weary way,
To lie upon the concrete
So ends a POW's day.

*Anon*

## Journey Back to Changi

### Tommy 1942

POWs, that's a helluva flamin' word
And here we are, all rounded up, like a branded cattle herd.
God, it seems there's such a lot of us, confused and milling around;
Well, I hope it's all been worth it, for this little patch of ground.

Ahh Mate, I'm bloody hungry, and you're lookin' pretty thin
And these graves are gettin' shallower, and I've got no strength to fill 'em in;
All that keeps me goin' is believin' things'll change
Til then we wait behind these walls while the world gets rearranged...

Ahh Bluey, you look like Death Warmed Up, and I'm feelin' kind o' weak
And I feel I've got much more to say, but it's gettin' hard to speak;
There's so much I could've said and done, but it seems I won't get the chance
Got caught up in this changing world, Ahh, what a merry dance.

Yeah Mate, I know I'm goin'; but I don't want to really leave
And I don't want 'em thinkin' I wore my heart upon my sleeve;
And can you ask 'em, when you're home again, were they really only bluffin'?
And ask 'em for me will you, Mate, did we go through this for nothin'?

### Bluey 1992

Well, I've come back here again, old Digger,
And so many years have passed
And things ain't really changed that much
They've just moved on too fast

But, you and your grave, well, you're still here,
A symbol of past mistakes,
And I see those old words that we scratched there:
'That's Life' and 'Those are the Breaks'.

Ahh Tommy, old Mate, these thoughts take me back
And a thousand things pass through my mind,
Like the Wire and the Walls that kept us caged up
And the Conflict that makes people blind

And those ghostly old shadows of mates long gone now
With my eyes closed I see 'em once more,
And I wipe out the memory of skeletal men
And recall how I'd known 'em before.

And you, Tommy Brown, I remember you then
And how you thought that we'd both live forever,
What a cruel twist of Fate, when we lost you, old Mate
And this place seemed a long way from heaven.

Yeah, I remember, old friend, when they captured us then
And how we thought that somehow we had failed,
And we dreamed of the day we'd escape in some way
From this hellhole they called Changi Jail.

Oh Mate, I can't linger there, those thoughts lead to despair
And the question you asked, I can't answer;
"All for Nothin'" you said, and we both hung our heads
As we listened to Fate's hollow laughter...

*Requiem 1992*

Well, the crowds gathered now, once again there's heads bowed
And soft words raise those ghosts from the past,
And while memory's tears fall, to that sad bugle call
We pray your Soul's resting at last.

And while I'm standing here, silent, with head bowed,
Trying hard just to hold back my tears,
I can still hear the words to a song
Sayin' 'Thanks for the Gift of the Years'.

And Hey Tommy, old son, when my time's finally come
And, I think we'll meet up before long,
We'll recall better times and forgive 'em their crimes,
And I'll teach you the words to that song...

*Les Mellet*
*AIF Cemetery*

## *Untitled*

There's a plot of land that's tendered by their comrades by the score,
   In which they've buried Diggers who died while Prisoners of War;
They were every bit as gallant in their sufferings through disease
   As the men who fell in battle 'gainst the swarming Japanese.

The men who died through shot and shell have made their names immortal
   But those who lay and waited death went quietly through his portal;
A flag draped body, stretcher born toward the grave is ferried
   The Last Post sounds o'er Changi Camp: another hero buried.

For surely though his end was quiet and far from the muskets rattle
   He gave his life to the cause for which his comrades died in battle.
So when in peaceful times to come we turn to thank our Maker
   Just say a prayer for those who lie in Changi Camp, 'God's Acre'.

*Anon*

# Chapter Six
# Peacekeeping

## *Yugoslavia Lost*

I feel sick at humanity's naked truth
(Though humanity may be too kind a name)
For a people who blithely wound and claim
Vilification and purity for their youth.

Time has not repelled their hate
Nor distilled the witching brew
Of ancient tensions born anew
To demand a people repatriate.

Time shall surely quell their tears
The anguish, the wounds, the pain,
But time knows festering sores remain
Weeping freely from the ears.

Pity them their bloody ear
That prevents strong screams from sounding near
But pity not their eyes that hear
That see and lust with passion clear.

Yesterday's history holds no lesson
That has not yet been heard nor learned
The page long read then overturned
Quill dipped in blood, a new page begun.

*Tony Anetts*

## *Our Life*

The blokes are out on the Cease Fire Line
Thinking of home and the girl left behind,
Of cold ale and beaches and sun shining free
Of the land of their fathers where they'd rather be.

It's a place that they think of to help pass the time,
For time there's a plenty as they go through the grind
Of daily patrolling out there on the front
Between Arabs and Persians, the tanks and the grunts.

Life at the front can be boring and dull,
Except for that moment, the break in the lull,
When time is compressed in a cold bead of sweat
And your heart skips a beat and you think of things yet

To be done with your wife or your family at home,
And you question your presence and yearning to roam.
Australia is home and it's where we should be,
But the war is not over and we're not yet free,

So we'll finish our tour with a skip and a jump,
No more to Iran with our swags will we hump,
But travel again to our homeland and wife
And get on with that thing we've forgotten – our life.

*Anon*
*UNIIMOG*
*(AWM PR 00431)*

## *I Have*

I have driven crowded streets where people mill and stand
Dodged through rack and ruin and a beggar's outstretched hand,
    I have seen sights of shockingness, of open poverty
    The resulting devastation of a people's anarchy,
I have smelt the stale aroma of filth, death and spice,
The stagnant pools of squalor fed by people, dogs and lice

I have held the bony hand, of a starving, dying child
Shared a mother's anguish as her children's bones were piled,
    I have dodged rocks and missiles, thrown and aimed at me
    Used a baton to deter unabashed thievery,
I have run, sung and played, with children like my own,
Tried to understand their language and the world in which they've grown.

I have experienced a people's fervour, at the Feast of Ramadan
Watched in fascination as Muslim rites are done,
    I have been privy to the meeting of a dedicated few
    Who loathe their country's lawlessness and wish to start anew,
I have witnessed use of terror by bandits and their kin
And the subsequent denials as the questionings begin.

I have witnessed execution and the sorry stench of death
As bandits and their kind suck their last dark breath,
    I have bartered at the markets, as the locals ply their trade
    Of selling simple prayer mats, on which Elvis himself has prayed,
I have felt the sheer elation of a people's shout of cheer
Of the call of 'Australia' yelled from far and near.

I have known so very much in so short a span of days
The experiences of a lifetime in oh so many ways.

*Tony Anetts*

## Changing Tides

The old men of Bagana, Bale and Tore
Had slipped below the waters,
Were brave and proud no more.
Waves of greed and corruption
Had taken their toll through the years
No stranger saw them drowning
And no one saw their tears.

The oasis in the Pacific was paradise no more
All hope was left behind then
Washed up on some foreign shore.
Midst the currents of resentment
Drifted M16 and spears
No stranger heard them crying
And no one saw their tears.

White teeth against black faces did little to hide their pain
They hid amongst the jungle
But their hiding was in vain.
For the enemy within them
Knew their deepest thoughts and fears
No stranger felt them tugging
And no one saw their tears.

I stood in line and placed my stone
'twas a tiny thing
But thousands more they did the same
to make this place a home.
And so it was the island rose
The waves rolled back, the tempest clears
And strangers to the island
Had dried away their tears.

*L/Col Jack Gregg*
*Wakunai, Bougainville*
*11 March 1999*

## *A UNIIMOG Ditty*

If I were writing from Balmain
And pigs at last could fly
The news from here in Kurdestan
Would lack essential fire.

And Canberra isn't quite the place
To ponder in your mind
That every time you place your feet –
It could be on a mine.

Or yesterday on that grenade
That rolled beneath your feet
No risk? Well bar that little pin
It was in fact complete!

The aircraft violation
That flew low above the ridge
Was only taking photographs
And not dispersing death.

There's interest in your gas mask
As you watch the vapour trail
Your hand preparing Atropine
If that defence should fail.

The thought "Is that for me?"
Each time you hear something explode
Instils appreciation
For that rocky little hole.

And as you wonder of your mate
In sunny Khorramshar,
He's down behind a wall like you
About to kiss his arse!

*Luke Carroll*
*UNIIMOG*
*(AWM PR 00431)*

## *Silly Poem*

I'm sitting here in Persia, just wondering why I'm here,
Dreaming of home, my wife and kids and a pie and a can of beer;
It's great here at the Team Site, but it's open to debate,
With no TV or shorts or the UN cars it makes us pretty irate;
Of course we respect the laws of this rigid Islamic state,
We eat their food and so not to be rude we say it's really great;
But the first thing I'll do on my CTO is go to a place elsewhere,
Where you can drink and swear and wear your shorts
and nobody really cares!

*T. M.*
*UNIIMOG*
*(AWM PR 00431)*

## *Diggers In Blue*

Australians should be proud of their Diggers in blue,
Scattered around the world for a cause that's true,
The spirit of the Diggers surge through our veins
As we answer the call again and again.

Our standards are high which is plain to see,
And that's not small praise coming from me,
We work hard and play hard and that's nothing new
Dinkum Sons of Anzacs wearing UN blue.

The dangers are real as we toil day to day
But don't tell anyone, we'll just laugh them away;
Rifle, machine gun, grenade and shell,
Mine or UXB could blow us all to hell.

We try to take care and still do our job –
Don't tell them at home, let them think I'm a slob.
Australians should be proud of their Diggers in blue
As we strive for a concept that should not be new

World peace – blissful peace. Then let me go home
To my wonderful wife and my daughters unknown.

*Dave Harris*
*UNIIMOG*
*(AWM PR 00431)*

## *The Grunt's Confession*

'Twas Grunt, a bright young Infanteer in service of the Queen,
Who found himself in Kurdestan and held in some esteem
By members of the reptile group that goes by name of 'snakes'
About the time he played a role in letting one escape.

The walk was long and arduous on that, the fateful day,
With Grunt asweating freely as he clambered up the way.
The puffing escort followed and the LO cursed his name,
The Pasdaran all turned around and went the other way.

They made it to the junction and ensured that all was well
Then turned around and recommenced descending from the hill.
But as they passed a small green bush a sentry shouted "Ist!
I'm sure I saw a bloody snake and heard the bastard hiss!"

Said Grunt "We've got some snakes at home would make you miss the show",
And craning forward he said "Let's see how long these blighters grow!"
But yon Battalion Headquarters had different thoughts in mind,
As all right up to Colonel armed with stones of different size.

As Grunt, still quite oblivious, said "G'day there Joe Blake!"
Old Hissing Sid the Viper came aware of his mistake.
The only way to safety seemed between those bandy legs,
And off he shot toward him like an All Black flying wedge.

Now Grunt, like most young Infanteers, had some synapse delay,
It took him precious seconds as he stood there in the way.
But watching the trajectory, the angles and the lines,
He finally came to realize he was just about to die.

He stood without a motion as he watched his ending come
While most of those behind him all went reaching for their guns
When in that final second of the cataclysmic crash
Young Grunt went fifteen feet straight up and fourteen feet straight back!

He landed midst the firing squad and crashed them to the ground
The whole Battalion Headquarters went running round and round.
And somewhere in the hail of shouts and clash of rifle stocks
Old Hissing Sid the Viper reached the safety of the rocks.

It's rumoured here in Kurdestan that ever since that day
Not one Australian Grunt been bit by one Iranian snake,
And all the diggers stay dispersed against unseen attack
In case it once more goes straight up and fourteen feet straight back.

*Luke Carroll*
*UNIIMOG*
*(AWM PR 00431)*

## *The Letter*

*(This poem was written by Mike Subritzky, himself a veteran, during a train journey to farewell his son when he was posted on Operations to Bosnia in 1998, to serve with B Battery, Royal Horse Artillery.*

Dear Mr Subritzky, sorry to be a bore,
    but we're sending your son Danny to the Bosnian War.
Yes, we know you did Rhodesia, your cousin Bill did Vietnam,
    but we're running out of soldiers and we need a few good men.

Sure, your uncle Jack the Anzac, was in the Battle of Chunuk Bair,
    and Bob Subritzky caught a packet on the Somme.
But we need a few good men, to send to Europe once again,
    and we'll kit them out and send them with a song.

Cousin Fredo got a head wound in the Monte Cassino fight,
    and poor old Archi, he went crazy on the wire one stormy night.
Yes, your family's done its bit, but it doesn't count for shit,
    and when your son gets back, we'll give the lad a gong.

Now you know the bloody score, it's just another friggin' war,
    and we're off in a couple of days, to the blood and smoke and haze.
Of course your boy should be alright, unless the Serbs decide to fight,
    because the Moslems in his sector seem OK.

*Mike Subritzky, 1998*

## Dusk

Now is the healing, quiet hour that fills
This gay, green world with peace and grateful rest,
Where lately over opalescent hills
The blood of slain Day reddened all the west
Now comes at Night's behest,
A glow that over all the forest spills,
As with the gold of promised daffodils.
Of all hours this is best.

It is the time for thoughts of holy things,
Of half-forgotten friends and one's own folk.
O'er all, the garden-scented sweetness clings
To mingle with the wood fire's drifting smoke.
A bull-frog's startled croak
Sounds from the gully where the last bird sings
His laggard vesper hymm, with folded wings;
And Night spreads forth her cloak.

Keeping their vigil, where the great range yearns,
Like rigid sentries stand the wise old gums.
On blundering wings a night-moth reels and turns
And lumbers on, mingling its drowsy hums
With that far roll of drums,
Where the swift creek goes tumbling midst the ferns.
Now, as the first star in the zenith burns,
The dear, soft darkness comes.

*C. J. Dennis*
*UNIIMOG*
*(AWM PR 00431)*

## *Lights of Dili*

### *(Food for thought)*

Toward the lights of Dili, what is that you see?
Home, innocence, suffering, injustice.
Do you complain inwardly at the anguish, the pain of absence,
Or empathise with those whose indignity lays beneath shadows,
Whose blood forges a future, breaths life into a new nation?
Are you willing, able to set aside your loss, your anger,
Overcome adversity, appreciate with clarity the role you play?
Or will you close your eyes to humanity, compassion and reason,
While revelling in your own self pity and shame?
Beyond those lights, what is it that you see?

The greatest pain we endure, our ultimate sacrifice,
Is not the political bunglings or the confusion of power,
Nor the uncertainty of each passing day.
It is not another night being unable to taste normality,
Nor the drudgery, monotony or routine of each wakened breath.
The deepest pain to strike our hearts is that of absence,
Absence from our children, our families, our friends.
It is being denied irreplaceable moments in time,
The closeness and passion that family brings,
The stability, cohesion that friendship nurtures.

Whist doing battle with absence, our weapons of choice –
Commitment, loyalty, faith and charity –
Save and separate us from the rest of society.
With a language strange, and abstract perceptions of life
We transcend, conquer, all barriers to soar ultimately successful.
It is our ability to adapt, to confront challenge with determination,
To forge ahead where others would falter.
These traits are what govern our destiny, make us unique;
This moment in time is what fate has decreed
And we will as always, prevail, for it is our nature.

So if doubt, loneliness and anger consume,
Remember what it is that we take for granted,
Freedom, democracy, a right to choice and speech.
Breath a sigh of relief as you contemplate life,
The predicaments of others and the luxury of your birthright.
Appreciate that your sacrifice is merely inconvenience
When compared to the sacrifice of others less fortunate.
Stand proud knowing you served righteousness, the good of man,
Setting aside your needs, to embrace, to give selflessly,
To those whose only world is one of servitude, aggression and sadness.
And next time you are staring toward that far away isle, ask:
What is it that I see, in those far off Dili lights?

*Jim Hodges*

## A Tribute to a Kimberley Gidja Soldier

### To my nephew, Jeremy Manning

I held back the teardrops from falling
As he walked inside our front room door;
He was over six-foot, every inch a soldier,
And just come back from East Timor.

I had held him in my arms as a baby,
This Kimberley nephew of mine;
We used to share many stories together
And his eyes would brightly shine.

He had said, 'I wanna be a brave paratrooper,
Although the discipline is hard to take.
I wanna be an example to my people,
As strong as Uluru, not a fake.'

This time he brought two white mates with him
One of them also went to Timor
Under the leadership of Major General Cosgrove,
And boy, you could not ask for more.

For he earned his rank o'er in Vietnam,
And mate, I'll tell you, it's no joke.
He instilled dignity and fire in the guts mate,
And one would die for that kind of bloke.

My fine young nephew with a military hair cut
The Timorese kids, they would shout and sing.
He gave them lollies, picked them up in his arms, mate,
They loved him and treated him like a king.

"Have you been in grave danger?" I asked him.
"Yes, it was a danger we did not foresee.
It took place inside of a foxhole."
This was the story he told to me.

"One day I faced a cocked machine gun.
Death stared at me square in the face.
I said a silent prayer to my Maker,
To protect me and give me some grace.

"I did not show any fear, nor tremble,
I did not move or even cry.
When the moment of tension was over,
I looked up and thanked God in the sky.

"Uncle Ron, can you give me a Bible?
I lost mine back in East Timor.
This is part of a good soldier's armour
It keeps fear far away from the door."

His mum came from proud Gidja kinfolks,
His dad Bill, an Irish Aussie at heart.
Their love transcended racial boundaries,
They gave Jeremy, their son, a head start.

I choked in my throat when we said our goodbyes.
He was a Kimberley man through and through.
Yet, he left bridle and saddle, to take up his gun,
A brave soldier and real Aussie mate, it is true.

A great example he is to his own people
His own countrymen thought he was great,
Yes, he is a might fine Australian
And a real dinky die Aussie mate.

So, to all Aboriginal youth in Australia,
You can train in the Navy, Airforce or Army.
May Jeremy Manning's life be an example
Of helping people in all lands to be free.

*Ron Williams*
*Aboriginal War Historian*

## *Mighty Lady*

A warship never sleeps, never tires, never weeps,
But lives and breathes with the life of the present,
Pulsating with the souls of a distant past.
Her heartbeat, her voice a constant companion,
To those who served before and to those who will again.
She is a mystery, an enigma a challenge,
She is many things to many men;

A tired mistress who requires painful attention,
Demands respect, dictates loyalty, commitment.
To those who serve, her repayment in kind, her thanks,
Is that of drudgery, long days and empty nights,
Loneliness, absence and weary confinement.
Unforgivingly harsh and a true task master,
She is a tired mistress who will give no quarter.

A beautiful lady, who shines through  trials and tribulations
Keeper, protector of righteousness,
Of value, moral standard, ideals.
A symbol of nations, a wonder to behold,
One which exemplifies honour, typifies pride.
A chariot, a conduit for faith and hope,
A beautiful lady who encompasses all things noble.

Her life's blood, sailors, give her magnificence,
Each with their own unique manner, character,
Different creeds, beliefs, ideals and history.
Melded, bonded, thrust together as one,
With a single goal a single purpose and direction,
To ensure that she breathes, achieves,
The greatness that destiny has bestowed upon her.

She has been, and will be, many things to many men,
But for me she stirs consciousness, conflicting memories.
She has been my home, my prison, a sanctuary, a trap,
The source of joy, pain, passion and anguish.
I know I will never escape her profound impact, her hold,
For years with her have moulded perceptions,
Have etched changes within my heart, upon my soul.

A surge of affection will always flow through my veins,
As I reflect upon a brief moment in time,
When my service was dedicated to her life.
The tides of change will never dull or wash away
Those years of bitter-sweet memories.
And my heart will always resonate with mixed emotion
As I look back toward her from destiny's distant path.

So when she reaps vengeance with feminine wrath,
Or you feel the sting of her unforgiving demeanour,
Remember what it is to sail within her,
What it means, signifies, to be a part of that life blood.
Take pride, take comfort and solace, from the knowledge
It was your commitment, your strength, your passion
Who gave spirit to a mighty lady of the sea.

*Jim Hodges*
*6 October 1999*

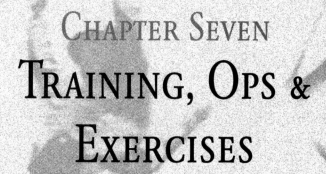

# Chapter Seven
# Training, Ops & Exercises

## *Air Hours at the Ops Cell*

There were air hours at the Ops Cell,
The word soon flashed around,
Let's stop some road-moved rations,
And air-drop them to the ground

We need a bit of ADE
And space on Caribou
To set this lot of tucker
Adrift from out the blue.

Our OPSO was an air drop man,
Full bottle on that score;
We put the plan into his hand
To make it doubly sure.

All was booked and ready made
When Mate, you wouldn't credit it,
Again the hand of HQ came
And turned it all to – .

Instead of a few, well planned drops,
'Twas all turned on its head;
"Let's take the entire ration break
And drop the lot instead."

The Wombats and the rigging crew
Then did a double take –
To break and pack this mighty stack
A sleepless night would make.

The hours came and slowly went,
The sweat in rivers poured
Until at last, the word was passed
"She's set to go on board!"

The ink had hardly time to dry
Upon the message pad
When alteration followed change
And the blasted lot went bad.

Confusion reigned, the air turned blue
The OPSO threw a fit,
But just remember one thing lads,
There's training value in it.

*Capt. Don Buckby*

## *Duties*

There are many minor ailments
That plague a man through life,
To some it is their station
And others 'tis their wife.

And even carefree soldiers
Have a reason to complain,
I mean the many duties
That follow in a chain.

Some of them are easy
But most of them are bad,
They must think I like them,
I find it very sad.

If they're ever under strength
And need a couple more,
They pounce with pure enjoyment
On five-five-eight-three-four.

It may be company runner
Or picquet in the town;
They may need a glamour guard,
So my name goes down.

Now I've touched a tender spot,
It always makes me swear,
And even baldy headed chaps
Try to tear their hair.

When they post the duties
I'm always on the list,
Even though my turn is past
My name is never missed.

I soldier on without complaint
But inwardly I moan:
Of the many duties,
It's guard that makes me groan.

The hours aren't excessive,
Just eight in twenty-four,
But when the ordeal's over
In health I feel quite poor.

I'm always so tired
That I can't even speak,
If they wouldn't wake me
I'd slumber for a week.

But when they blow reveille,
I must rise and shine
And prepare for daily training,
For we parade at nine.

*Raymond John Colenso*
*(AWM PR 00689)*

## *The Coming of the Beast*

It's a lonely winter evening
The air is cold the moon is high,
All the nature is passive now
There's not a star in the sky.

Tucked away in your bag it's pleasant there,
The warmth you try to keep;
Last man creeps up to your vehicle
It's your turn not to sleep.

Up watching, cautiously waiting,
You hope it will come through the night,
If it does it will mean relief
And end the unknown fright.

You know it's out there somewhere
Watching with eyes open wide,
And if it does reveal itself
It'll meet the friends by my side.

Suddenly the darkness rules
As the moon is blinded by a cloud,
You're thinking, "this is the moment!"
As the insects laugh out aloud.

Sounds are easily picked up now
The creaking from nearby willows,
And through the canopy of the trees
A relentless, icy wind blows.

Uncontrolling shivering overpowers you now
As the wind keeps getting colder,
There's still no sign of it yet,
The night, still it grows older.

He will come, you know full well
That he will visit tonight,
But it's still lurking in the shadows,
You pray quietly for the sun's light.

Your friends are waiting silently
To meet it, like it or not,
When it comes they'll scream at him
Their barrels will glow white hot.

Your shift is nearly over, soon you'll go
When your watch says that you can,
And creeping up to the next vehicle
You'll wake the next tired man.

Back in your bag you'll sleep warm again
Until the morning's feast,
But before then you'll rise again
For the coming of the beast.

*Cpl. M. J. Walburn*

## *Time at the Bay*

Whilst you've got your feet up
    I'll ask you not to disperse,
Stick around and I'll intrigue you all
    By reading you rhyming verse.

A few weeks ago we left Townsville
    For there were Army games to play,
So down the coast we travelled
    To a place called Shoalwater Bay.

Now I know some may not like it
    But I think it's good for a change,
And anything's better than bumbling around
    For a couple of weeks at High Range.

We travelled down on buses
    It's a poguish way to deploy,
After a thousand and one truck stops
    We met up with the rest of the boys.

Churchy, Dyso and Danny,
    Blacky, Willy and Bish,
They'd only been there for a couple of days
    But a beer and a babe was their wish.

Immediately we were into it
    And over the Bay we did roam,
After a couple of days we were settled
    The Bay was our temporary new home.

Elanora, Landsbury, The Glen
    These would all be places we'd see,
Raspberry Vale and Mount Alec
    A Polygon and a Lemon Tree.

We bashed across country as usual
    I don't know how many trees we mowed,
And how many times did we drive up and down
    That boring old east-west road?

Mount Tilpal, The Plains and Razorback
In these sectors we left our mark,
They were our AO's we called them
Vivaldi, Mozart, Beethoven and Bach.

The days and nights were hectic
We didn't have time to scratch,
Just when we thought we could all flex out
We were into a blue-on-blue match.

Troop rivalry is always a good thing,
I can't really tell you who won,
But I can tell you this one thing is true –
A lot of callsigns from Two Troop got done.

After this we went down to Camp Growl
To fix the cars that were maimed,
And I don't know why they call it that
Maybe by lesbians was it named.

A live-fire stint came soon after,
We gave them a mighty good whack,
But the only trouble about this is
Figure-eleven targets don't shoot back.

We travelled back home on buses again
We filled all the truck stops till
(and to the delight of everyone)
We arrived back home in the Ville.

I don't know if it was a success
But I can tell this to you all,
Being out scrub for a couple of weeks means
More money to piss up the wall!

*L/Cpl M. J. Walburn*

## *On Exercises*

*(A soldier's view)*

To think that I have come to this:
In the bush and off the piss,
A place of dreary temperance
Surrounded by incompetence;

Confusion reigns while havoc rules,
Methinks we are controlled by fools;
It makes me fearful of our fate
(And you thought Woodstock was a rock show, Mate!)

*Capt. Don Buckby*

## Canungra

Canungra is a hateful place,
Of all camps most detested,
And those who do not pass this way
Can count themselves most blessed.

We hate the Sergeant Major's voice,
We hate the endless hurry,
We hate the ceaseless tearing 'round
And getting in a flurry.

We hate the bayonet like the deuce,
We hate the river crossings,
We hate the march down to the creek,
Just for to do our washing.

We hate the raucous clanging sound
Of cart tyres hung on string,
Which wake us up at early morn
E'en long before birds sing.

But yet there's something in the place
That sort of, kind of, holds us –
It may be in the comradeship
Of those who are around us.

It's not a rest home to be sure,
Nor yet is it a picnic,
But though it's very hard on us
There's something makes us stick it.

The food's not bad, there is no doubt
About it, all the credit
Is to the cooks, the way that they
Can manage to prepare it.

Of course there's not too much to get
But who has time to eat it?
We hardly get a taste of it,
When 'bang' – it's time to beat it!

I will admit it's interesting,
And also educating,
Each day a change in 'syllabus'
Helps make it to our liking.

The treks we do are really fun
If one is young and healthy,
But if one's spirit is not in it
Then all is gone for nothing.

Of course it's hard, the guns and packs,
No matter just how careful
We are to make them light, they just
Get heavier every minute.

The ground we cover in each march,
Up hill and down to valley,
By jungle track and over fields,
Is really most amazing.

I'm not a very striking chap,
Five-foot-three is my limit,
So when a six-foot leads the way
I soon drop back to rearward.

I struggle on, my head bent low,
There are no signposts pointing
The footprints on the dusty earth
Are all the signposts needed,

Until I come at gathering dusk
To where two tracks are crossing,
The prints can go full three ways here,
I must be most discerning.

I made my choice and on I plod,
Though somewhat hesitating,
But then of course I'd talked with God:
'Twas His way I was taking.

Then after having climbed a tree,
As high as I could get,
I saw some lights not far away,
On which my sights I set.

Thus struggling on, I found a track,
'Twas well defined and friendly,
No 'Wait a Whiles' upon this path,
They'd met the old machete.

When back at camp and DP One,
Work parties now the fashion,
There's talk of going further north,
Which generally is the order.

But soon it will be o'er at last,
Canungra long forgotten,
Then what we'll meet we do not know,
And some not even caring.

*Pte. W. J. Baker, NX 139320*
*Canungra, 1943*

## *Canungra's Way.*

Tramp, tramp, tramp, morning noon and night,
Over mountain, hill and valley,
Through the scrub and fern-lined gully,
Over rocks and sandy patches,
Hands and faces marked with scratches
Trying to make jungle fighters –
    That's Canungra's aim.

"Left right left," ringing in one's ear,
Up at six and off we gallop,
Double quick time down to river
Wash and shave and back for breakfast,
Gulp it down, no time for sitting,
And no chance whate'er of quitting:
    That's Canungra's way.

"At-tention!" through it all we go,
Or "Port Arms" rifle inspection,
"Shoulder Arms, we're going marching,"
"Stand at ease" or "just stand easy,"
Everything to be done neatly,
Shoddiness is not the fashion
    Up Canungra way.

One, two, three, changing arms by numbers,
Lesson five will be on Bren gun,
Name the parts and reassemble
Making sure that parts are all clear,
Pull the bolt back, press the trigger;
That's the way that things are done here,
    Up Canungra way.

"Pay attention here, that man on the right,
You will tell us weight of Owen,
How to hold when it is firing,"
Number four will then dismantle
Telling us a cause of stoppage."
All of this they try to teach us,
    Canungra's own way.

Day by day this is what goes on,
Maybe we will turn out soldiers,
Each a credit to the tutors;
Maybe time will all be wasted,
We, perhaps will ne'er go over,
But for me my choice will never
    Be Canungra's way.

*Pte Jim Baker, NX 139320*
*Canungra, 1943*

## *Accidents*

Statistics prove that accidents with military trucks
Are getting far too numerous, they're mounting up and up
So that they're causing grave concern to us and police force too,
And really men, I'm sure you'll say, it's just the same with you.

We're proud of GT116 and all it means to us,
We're proud of you who do their job without a lot of fuss,
Each truck and man within this camp is needed every one,
The job you're doing reg'ly helps knock out Jap and Hun.

You say, "I only drive a truck around suburban camps,
Or carting timber, stone, or muck – that won't Jap ardour damp!"
My boy, we're each and every one just one tooth on a gear,
Yet one tooth being broken off may prolong war a year.

When trucks o'erturn, the fire brigade and police must burn up juice
To see the truck does not catch fire, be ruined for other use,
And workshops men must leave their jobs, perhaps important too,
To take out towing truck and gear to bring your wrecked 'bus' through.

A man or woman may get hurt, who work in factory,
Employed in making shells or tanks for our boys overseas.
So you can see that accidents, it matters not how small
They be, the fact remains that they affect us, one and all.

So if we all will do our best
To drive more carefully,
We'll have 'No Accident Month' I'm sure
And happy we will be.

*Pte Jim Baker.*
*NX139320*
*116 Aust. Gen. Trans. Coy.*
*Marrickville NSW. 31 August 1942*

## *Victory of the Sands*

Now the 1st Brigade quoth the old story
How they marched from Tel-El-Habar
Of the four thousand men who started
And the two hundred who got there.

But the 16th Brigade claims the laurels
In the terrible Grecian campaign
How we marched ninety miles over mountains
Non-stop through the snow and the rain.

But the pages of history don't mention
One march that we'll never forget
'Twas a march through the Sinai desert
Brought about by an officer's bet.

Now a course was laid down at places
There were clocks to check on our paces
And home was the camp football ground.

Number 8 ran the distance in fine style
Captain Coslet sat down with a grin
Told his boys that they now had the bag tied
And the laurels were safely within.

But he reckoned without Johnny Blarney
And his team who would follow him through,
Though they weren't very brilliant at drilling
They had what it takes to get through.

They started off smoothly and happy
With Fogarty setting the pace
The prize was a skinful of Aussie –
Little wonder they made it a race.

But the sand up 'Tomb' hill was cruel
And we lagged as we climbed that long slope,
Ronnie William kept heaping on fuel
And his cheery voice brought us new hope.

We passed '61' with two seconds to spare,
Our leaders had gained second wind,
Joe Shaw and Tom Dixon were gasping for air
With Doug Stewart dropping behind.

Jack Blarney sang *Old Tipperary*
Young Webber sang *Mother McKee*
George Stephenson's old puffing billy
Was a fair imitation of me.

Young Shorty said goodbye to dinner
As the winning post came into view
And I thought of Tom Rigg and Pat Edmonds
And the trouble they took with the stew.

George Wickham came out in his scanties
Capt Baird cheered us on with his hat,
We raced in with a two-minute margin
And every man flopped on the mat.

Now if men want to bet in their mess room
Let them bet on the day it will rain,
Desert marching is exclusive to camels
And I'm damned if I'll try it again.

*Anon*
*(AWM PR 00526)*

## A Digger

Carry the claymores
Carry your pack
Carry the radio –
All on your back
Carry your rations
Carry your tent
Carry your clothing –
Sorry you went
Up hill and down hill
Over the ridge
Sleep in the Ulu –
Make your own bridge.
Walk-talking softly
Listen and sign
Eat what you carry –
Watch for a mine.
Give us a break sir
Stop for awhile
Have you ever seen
A CSM smile?
But you change...
Polish up your boots
Polish up your belt
Silver star and brasso –
It's the best you've ever felt.
Fall in at BHQ
Check your hat's on straight
March off in the evening
To guard the old camp gate.

*Margaret Gibbons*

# Chapter Eight
# Units

## *We Were the 46th*

We were the 46th.
We went to a war that was worlds away,
Why did you go you say?
We went for king,
We went for country,
But most of all we went for our pride in ourselves.
We're all gone now,
We are no more,
But in the photos and text within, we are reborn,
We live again.
I can see Rollie Touzel,
The Country Boy from Cudgewa,
I can see Alf Willison,
The City Man from Melbourne,
The blue collar and professional alike.
I'm with them now,
With the mates we left behind.
No more are we in the stark madness of Pozieres,
The mud, ice, and the death at Flers,
Or the unbroken wire of Bullecourt,
Where I held a shattered mate's hand as his young life ebbed away,
I looked him in the eye and told him he'd be just fine,
I lied.
This was the nightmare I lived,
'Till my own life had ended its day.
I was one of those who came home,
To my family, my children;
They were all precious to me,
But they couldn't understand the difference within,
The pain, the anguish,
The scars of my time could never be healed as those that are physical.
Look at the photo,
Can you tell who I am?
I'm everyone,
A member of the 46th,
An anonymous infantry soldier,
The salt of the earth,
As much as we were from different walks of life
And different parts of the land, we were as one, we were a family:
WE WERE THE 46TH!

*Ian Polanski*

## *On the Breaking up of 116 AGT. Company, Marrickville*
### *(With apologies to Banjo Paterson)*

There was movement in the unit, for the word had passed around
    That the 116 GT was moving out,
And the rumours spread like wildfire, from the cookhouse to the 'shop'
    'Til no-one really knew just what was what.

The Sections all were grounded, not a truck was allowed out,
    The transport office quiet like the grave,
But 'Workshops' kept on working, true, with very little zest,
    Each man concerned with thoughts his skin to save.

"We're going all to Burma," was the first thing that we heard,
    Then each one came his little tale to tell.
"I heard this from the Major," or, "Up in the orderly room,"
    But the truth is, no one is allowed to tell.

The men stood 'round in batches, each one speaking, quiet like,
    Like mourners speaking of a friend just gone,
And so it was in figure, for the unit really had
    Ceased to exist in name, though not in form.

The Workshops trucks were ready for their journey further north,
    With all the inside nicely fitted up,
By Sgt Oby and young Dave, with Monty looking on,
    And S. M. Griffo dodging in and out.

The 'Moresby limp' was evident amongst quite a number there,
    Myself and Bill Grey both had it bad.
Old Stanley Noakes was suffering from 'Central Aussie cramp',
    While others tried to make out they were glad.

Old George Nerney did not care at all where he was sent,
    As long as it was somewhere near a pub,
While Alfie Weymark sure would die away from smallgoods shop
    Because he couldn't stomach Army grub.

The 'Pommy Lout' was shoutin' out and making lots of fun,
    Well, so were all the rest of us, for that,
Each one concerned with covering his feelings from the rest
    And hoping that the move was not to come.

Our Storeman 'Drumstick Baker' managed to get very ill,
    And to the hospital was straightway sent,
But fitter 'Billy Gibson' had to stand a lot of things,
    Wondering where his last two bob had gone and went.

One consolation was that we had not much work to do,
    A very rare thing for us,
It gave us time to get our foreign orders all cleaned up,
    With no one spotting us to make a fuss.

Old Jake got out to Salvage just in time, the lucky cow,
    Although I don't suppose we'll need him where
We're going, cos it never rains out in that dry old desert land,
    So windscreen wipers are not needed there.

Billy Mose the Welder is sure to like it over there,
    No rain to spoil his days off, so to speak,
But Bollins, well I don't know how he'll manage without Mum,
    Not seeing her for weeks and weeks and weeks.

There's 'Happy' Howard, Ronnie 'Hot', and Jimmy Latham too,
    And 'Draughty' Bill from Section 25,
And not forgetting 'Aussie', he's the dreamy Sergeant man,
    On bottled stuff he mostly seems to thrive.

Then there's 'Champion J.' and Godden, writing letters by the score
    And 'Ding Dong' Bell and 'Bunny' Guerin too,
And silly Carrapiett fooling 'round the whole day through,
    'Tho' better mate one never need wish for.

A few more names and then the list is just about complete,
    With Raymond Ford, the carpentering man,
And 'Bluey' Atkinson and 'Kingy' Clem the Storeman Sarge
    And 'Tinny' Wetzler, Poker playing fan.

Of course there's 'Mother' Evans, we must never forget him,
    Though often through the day he is unseen,
And 'Mac' who's always reading, and his Sergeant 'Bricky' Brad,
    And Harry Douglas – not a bad old bean.

The 'Staff' – we'll ne'er forget him, like he often forgets us,
  I mean when jobs are being handed out,
And D. M. Dunk and 'Gilly', who seem really very keen
  And Bruce and 'Robbo', both just marching out.

There's Sgt King who is away just now in Melbourne town,
  But will be back again with us some day
To show us how to time a Ford, or fix a gearbox up,
  Or change a plug the right and proper way.

Then there's those of whom we'll often think, who are not with us now,
  Like old Ralph Haken, 'five minutes to go',
And 'Scotty' Duncan, good old toiler, not a bad old stick,
  And not forgetting poor old cranky Joe.

There's one thing that we'll ne'er forget, no matter where we be,
  On desert sands or South Pacific isle,
When we are tired and hungry, or resting in the shade
  Or playing cards, or idle for awhile,

And that's the ladies – regular as clockwork did they come
  Each Sunday with their loads of scones and cakes,
With smiles and pleasant words of cheer to help us on our way,
  And army life monotony to break.

*Pte Jim Baker NX139320*
*30 January 1943*

## *The Salvage*

On active service not dismayed,
Who is this Unit on parade?
None other than the Salvage crowd,
Shoulders back and heads unbowed.

"Attention there!" "Stand at ease!"
Your gallant 'Fuhrer', you must please.
He stands commanding your regard,
His gun attached, "On guard!" "On guard!"

'Note book' Hall looks slightly hurt,
'Gas' Cunningham is on the alert.
'Shields' wants to put you on the peg,
'Barrett' is immovable – don't pull his leg.

And there's dark Durack full of sin,
With P. T. Gatherer so still and grim.
A post for Walker would be a small cost;
Skinner and Hampton appear to be lost.

Dalton and Plummer sometimes run the show.
Maclean as far as words has a wonderful flow;
There's young 'Tich' Wilson the Unit's noise
And criminal Smith, one of the boys.

The 'Woorooloo Ram' with his short arm is there,
And 'Transfer Charlton' so fat and fair.
'Megaphone' Foley can sometimes be heard;
The 'Limping Scuttler' is a bit of a bird.

There's Private Plant of the 'Wailing Wall'
And Lanky 'Fields' with his nobs and all;
The Dunlops brothers can give you a pain,
Gabell looks on in sarcastic vein.

There is also our youthful 'Bantam Howard'
And overrated Ovens who looks a bit soured.
Rudkin there our spoiler of food,
'Whispering' Willis stands in pensive mood.

There's 'Gambler' Power small and hairy,
And 'Little' Fitch the Unit's fairy.
Plus little Kent who talks with beer,
Of steady Iredell you never hear.

There's 'Two-Ton Tony' with all his might,
Lench, Hartnett and Phillips are pretty quiet
'Goggle Eyed Merry' stares with defiance,
Collins and 'Two Up' have sworn an alliance.

McDonald looks glum, his temper is short;
McKenzie, junior recruit, has come to report;
Summers the card fiend, is going to the dogs;
James looks ashamed of his friends the 'Wogs'

"Attention! Attention!" "Stand at ease! Stand at ease!"
'Tis the call of the Salvage, a sort of disease.
"Will you take my punishment, or have a Court martial?"
You must say the Fuhrer is fairly impartial.

*Sgt John Patrick Hampton*
*9th Aust. Div. Salvage Section*
*(AWM PR 00759)*

## *Song of Tobruk*

They brought us, from Australia to fight the Nazi Hun,
Who're once more on the Warpath, well equipped with tanks and guns.
They shoved us into Libya where, the guide book says, it's grand,
But forgets to mention little things, like flies and fleas and sand,

Tobruk was chosen as the place for us to 'Strut our Stuff'.
Old Jerry soon besieged it and began to treat us rough;
He dropped a kindly hint or two as to how we soon would cop it
Advising us to turn it in, forget the war and hop it.

Now being mad Australians we just didn't take the drum,
So he sent his diving Stukas and made things dam well hum;
A few blokes took the final count, and some joints got knocked about,
But the damage done, as Tommies say, was really "Bleeding nowt!"

He keeps on raiding with his planes, drops bombs and booby traps,
His soldiers sometimes make a move, and the lads have front line scraps,
But months have passed, he must admit, it seems we're here to stay
Till the Springboks come to join us, marching up from Bardia way.

And when we're back at home again and all this strife is o'er,
Some silly is sure to ask, "How did you win the War?"
You can look the bloke right in the face and pat the baby's curls,
Say "We defended old Tobruk, where there wasn't any girls."

Of all the Units we have here, there's one we'd like to toast,
They're always up to something, but you never hear them boast.
It's good to hear them working, with reverberating crack.
We dip our lid sincerely to – the boys of the Ack Ack.

*Sgt John Patrick Hampton*
*9 Aust. Div. Salvage Section*
*(AWM PR 00759)*

## Never Beaten

*The following verses were written by Cpl Manning of B Company while his company
was in occupation of the forward post during the period when they suffered heavy
casualties from enemy shellfire. The Latin,* Nunquain Victus *or 'Never Beaten' is
the motto of the old 48th Battalion of the first AIF.*

They were drawn together by some master hand,
    Who chose them somehow throughout the land
And flung them into the melting pot,
    Where for a time they were as men forgot.

Now some there were who knew quite clear
    They were there for all they held most dear.
Others had come for what they'd see,
    And others after some wild spree.

Then came a time when tempers were tried.
    We were mucked about 'til we could have cried,
And we mocked and jeered at *Esprit de corps,*
    Saying, "What the hell do they take us for?"

At last we heard of the blue and white
    And what it meant in the world of fight;
Tales were told of the men who'd worn it
    And with what pride and glory they bore it.

We listened to men who had gone before
    Of the tales they told of the last great war,
Wondering how we could stand the test
    Of measuring up to the Nation's best.

Then was the time we got the idea
    Of something that rose above mere fear
And felt the stir of a strange new pride
    In things we used once to deride.

Then came the day we were waiting for,
    When we saw the last of Australia's shore!
But still we were a polyglot crew
    And what we'd do well – no one knew

We landed at last, in Palestine,
    And if all thoughts were the same as mine
We had the idea we were a garrison mob,
    Not thought worthy of a real man's job.

Then came orders. We were due for a shift,
    And you could feel our spirit begin to lift
For the news got round we were moving west
    Going, perhaps, to our first big test.

We finished up on the Libyan plain
    And thought once more we had to train,
And then they found us jobs to do,
    Which could have been done by an infant crew.

At last we were moved by the powers-that-be
    From a resting place by the still blue sea;
We had camped, for a breathing space,
    In what, to us, was a damned good place.

Then rumours came: Things weren't so hot
    For-our ancient foe had us on the trot.
We were moving back – or so they said –
    Though then we thought the war was dead

Back we were going, and going quick,
    For Jerry's tanks were pretty slick;
This was the time we'd been waiting for,
    "At last," we said, "We're in the war!"

Back and back and still back we went,
    'Til we wondered what our bosses meant,
And strength and endurance were needed now
    For sleep was a thing that was snatched somehow.

Although we went through a little hell,
    There was something born which repaid us well,
For we learnt what mateship really meant
    And knew 'twould last where e'er we went.

The backward rush was stopped at last.
　　Outside Tobruk we were told, "Stand fast!"
And there we were – untried men
　　Waiting for something beyond our ken.

We lay all day under the torrid sun,
　　There was our baptism of fire begun.
We learnt the whine of the screaming shell
　　And some suffered more than they will tell.

But to cut and run never entered a head
　　Although we saw our mates lie dead,
And all of us made a determined vow,
　　We'd avenge their deaths on the Hun somehow

For a week or more there we stood,
　　Although he flung at us all he could,
And flat we lay on the stoney earth,
　　While his planes and bombs tested our worth.

Then came the day when his plunging tanks
　　Charged up and down our meagre ranks,
And we knew when they had passed
　　We'd take all he'd give and still stand fast

But best of all, there in my heart,
　　The feeling that I was at last a part
Of a band who knew that they were a crowd
　　Of whom their Fathers might well be proud.

*Cpl Manning*

## *You Have Served Us Well*

DDG 38 you entered my life
    in Boston USA;
Thirty-four years ago I joined you
    on your commissioning day.

We were proud young sons of Australia
    Three-hundred-and-thirty-three strong,
And as the band played *Waltzing Matilda*
    we embarked from the dockside throng.

They named you *Perth* after another
    who now rests in a watery grave,
You had a proud tradition to follow
    established by men so brave.

I recall your baptism of fire
    when we were called to that Asian war,
Of how your guns thundered in anger
    toward a troubled shore.

San Som, Dong Hoi and Cua Sat
    are names that drift in from the past,
In those northern 'Sea Dragon' waters
    you forged a reputation that was to last.

You still carry the scars of that conflict
    from the hot metal that punctured your skin,
Old shipmates on their chests wear coloured ribbon
    but tend to hold those memories within.

I knew I could not serve in you forever
    and in life's journey we ventured apart,
Many thousands subsequently joined you
    and maintained you as 'State of the Art'.

You have nurtured a number of heroes
    and there were larrikins that I knew,
You've been a source of pride and frustration
    to the twenty-seven who skippered you.

I have returned for your last voyage
    as your remaining days are but few;
Soon you will enter your final harbour
    and they will take your name from you.

The wind plays a sad tune in the halyards
    but your heart beats strong through the deck,
And I sense the presence of your old sailors
    as I spend this quiet moment to reflect.

Soon the wake will not surge from your quarter
    nor your routines be run to the bell;
It's now time to say "Stand easy old friend!"
    for I know you have served us well.

*Jack Aaron*
*(Ex POQMG)*

## *HMAS.* Warramunga

For grace and speed she had no par
Across the oceans deep
And on her we, who traveled far,
Adored her striding sweep.

From flaring stem to thrusting screws
And every plate between,
Her purpose spread its warlike news
Wherever she was seen.

A gentle shepherd she indeed
Or fearsome as a lion,
A friendly sight to all in need
Those others of her scion.

Seen from above, her clean slim lines
Was target made to miss,
Well worthy to those slanting eyes
Of anticipat'ry 'Hiss-s-s-s'.

With agile swerve and greyhound speed
Her crew all well prepared,
She welcomed each assailant's deeds
With snarling fangs all bared.

Her bristling weapons aimed on high
Defied their birds of war,
Hurling skyward flak and fire
A deadly reaching claw.

Her probing prow sought out the Jap
Defying all his cannon
To wipe 'Australia' off the map
And rename it 'South Nippon!'

She braved each storm and shed each green
Flung from the briny main.
She swam the tropics like a Queen
In calm, or hurricane.

From North to South and back again
Wherever she was sent,
Her handsome hide oft showed the strain
But served with fierce intent.

She carried all who served in her
With confidence and strength –
No comfort, ours, in any berth
Along her spartan length.

She wasn't just some 'Lady Fair'
Although her lines were such
For she was but a 'Dog of War'
Without the 'Midas Touch'.

We love her still, our mem'ries bright,
Her every action marked,
Till we are gone far out of sight
We'll live the love she sparked.

*L. (Tarz) Perkins.*

## Destroyer

A gallant little ship sails the sea today,
Fighting for old Aussie and paving the way
For liberty and freedom
We know will come one day.

Her name is *Warramunga*,
A tribal ship by class,
Manned by young Australians,
Who will stand up till the last.

So hats off to the ship and men,
May she ride the sea and foam,
And God guide them back to the ones they love,
Back to home sweet home.

*Leading Stoker F. J. 'Shags' Turner*
*1943*

## The Warramunga

The Warramunga is a destroyer
Built at Cockatoo;
When the shakedown trials are finished,
She'll do close on forty-two.

Then whether we sail the Indian
Or the beautiful blue Pacific,
What we've got for Tojo's boys
Is something just terrific

Three twin four-point-sevens
Backed up by twin four-inch,
If the enemy comes within our range
They are sure to feel the pinch.

The A. A. boys are watching,
Waiting for the day
That one of the Japanese bombers
Would fly across our way.

The torpedo men are waiting
For the detector to get a ping
So they can drop a water bomb
And teach those Japs a thing.

We are like the Aboriginal tribe
With a mission to fulfil,
So to keep up their motto
*Warramunga* 'hunt to kill.'

*A. B 'Happy' Fellows*
*1942–3*

## *Never Forget Them*

Through day and night our brothers marched
To a long-off desert town,
In a last ditch effort from the Allies
To bring the enemy down.

As they charged against the Turks
Their desperation was hard not to see,
In the trenches and behind the guns
The scared Turks, they did flee.

Although the task seemed impossible
The town they took that day,
Victoriously they raised the flag
Before the sun went down.

All these men are gone now
Their experiences left in the past,
But as long as there are blokes like us
Their memory will always last.

Other units in the Army today
To find their roots they've tried,
Most of them have nothing near
What we've got 'Cavalry pride'.

So remember what they did,
These men you've never met,
Echo it through the generations
So that no one will ever forget.

*L. Cpl. Michael Walburn*

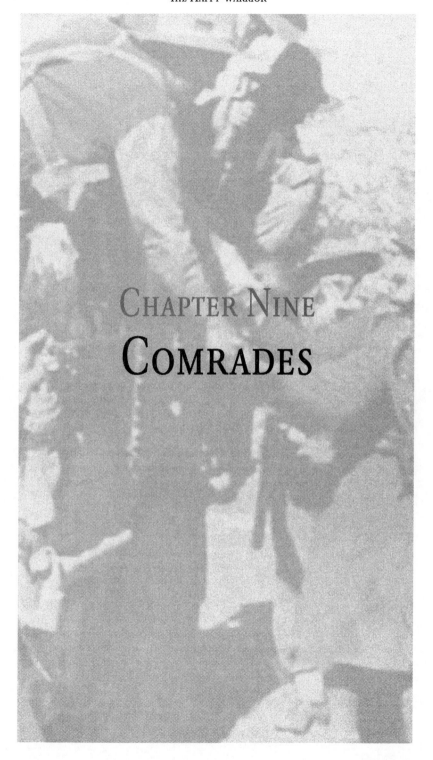

## Chapter Nine
# Comrades

## The Fuzzy Wuzzy Angels of the Owen Stanley Ranges...

Many a Mother in Australia, when the busy day is done,
Sends a prayer to the Almighty, for the keeping of her son,
Asking that an angel guide him and bring him safely back,
Now we see those prayers are answered on the Owen Stanley Track.

Though they haven't any halo, only holes slashed through the ear
And their faces marked with tattoos and with scratch pins in their hair,
Bringing back the badly wounded, just as steady as a hearse,
Using leaves to keep the rain off, and as gentle as a nurse.

Slow and careful in bad places on the awful mountain track
And the look upon their faces makes us think that Christ was black,
Not a move to hurt the carried, they treat him like a saint;
It's a picture worth recording, that an artist's yet to paint.

Many a lad will see his Mother and the husbands see their wives,
Just because the Fuzzy Wuzzies carried them to save their lives.
From mortar or machine gun fire, or a chance surprise attack,
To safety and the care of doctors at the bottom of the track.

May the Mothers in Australia when they offer up a prayer
Mention these impromptu angels with the fuzzy wuzzy hair.

*Sapper Herbert Beros*
*(AWM PR 88 019)*

## *...And the Answer by an Aussie Mother*

We, the mothers of Australia, as we kneel each night in prayer
Will be sure to ask God's blessing for the men with fuzzy hair,
And may the great Creator who made both black and white
Help us to remember how they helped to win the fight.

For surely he has used these men with fuzzy-wuzzy hair
To guard and watch the wounded with tender loving care,
And perhaps when they are tired with blistered aching back
He'll take the yoke upon Himself and help them down the track.

And God will be the Artist and this picture He will paint,
Of a fuzzy wuzzy angel with the halo of a saint,
And his presence will go with them in tropic heat and rain
And he'll help them tend the wounded in sickness and in pain.

So we thank you Fuzzy Wuzzy, for all that you have done,
Not only for Australia, but for every Mother's son;
And we're glad to call you friend although your faces may be black,
For we know that Christ walked with you on the Owen Stanley track.

*Anon*
*(AWM PR 91 061)*

## Crosses

Each life has its crosses,
and a soldier has his share
From a trip across the ocean, to that envied *Croix de Guerre.*
There are crosses by the sensor, far too many so it seems,
There are crosses on the letters from the girlfriend of his dreams,
There are crosses worn by heroes who have faced the storm of lead,
There's a cross when he is wounded and a cross when he is dead.
There's a little cross of mercy
that very few may own,
To a soldier it is second
to that of God alone:
It's a cross that's worn by women,
when we see it we believe
That we recognize an angel
by the Red Cross on her sleeve.

*Private Tommy Gray*
*1941*
*(AWM MSS 1562)*

## Praise to the Nurses

*(Written whilst a patient in 2/2 Hospital)*

You may talk about the Anzacs over on Gallipoli,
You may talk about the heroes of Tobruk,
You may praise the Royal Navy and the Air Force thrown in too,
I know their gallant deeds would fill a book.

There's the fuzzy wuzzy angels too, who've had a lot of praise,
Of course they deserved it - every one,
The AWAS, and of course the WAAFS, and all the rest of them,
Can each have written to their names, "Well Done!"

But what about the Red Cross nurse? Are they not heroines too?
If ever a band deserved the title they
Have earned it every day they served,
And sometimes without thanks or even smiles to help them on their way.

From dawn of day, 'til dark of night, with never ceasing care,
They tend to all our endless wants and needs,
With smiling face and tender touch and pleasant words of cheer,
Their very presence breathes a note of peace.

Though often feeling worn and tired and sad at heart as well,
They gamely carry on their ceaseless task,
Concerned with others' comfort and their peace of mind as well,
Are they not Heroines? ALL of them, I ask?

*Pte Jim Baker, NX139320*
*Moratai NEI, 1945*

## *Young Shannon McAliney*

It is hard to describe to the uninitiated
The unity and spirit that our Army has created.

For the Army is a family, where to serve is to belong,
Where bonds are everlasting and friendships made are strong.
For us to lose a mate is akin to losing family
And today I lost my brother – young Shannon McAliney.

I heard tonight of Shannon as the CO paced the floor;
It soon became apparent this was ground not trod before,
For all our previous patients had been black not white of skin,
My stomach felt uneasy and my calm was paper-thin.

I watched with trepidation as his stretcher hurried past
Hoping against hope that tonight was not his last;
The mere presence of the CO and the grey haired RSM
Turned me sickly cold, for these were very busy men.

I cannot describe the bitter feeling or the empty hollow pain
When I heard the long count start up, then quieten down again.
Angry and frustrated, my nerves felt tightly strung
At the death of Shannon McAliney, who died so very young.

You know, I never knew young Shannon, couldn't tell him from another,
Yet Shannon McAliney was and is my brother.

*Tony Anetts*

## *Barley, Wheat and Rye*

I'm just a lonesome land girl, my home is miles away,
I'm away here in the outback and working hard each day.
Ploughing, digging, sowing, to help the food supply,
Growing barley, wheat and rye.

We, of this women's service, raise our voices high:
"Come on girls and join us, give the Land Army a try!"
And when the war is over, you can proudly cry:
"I helped to feed the country with barley, wheat and rye!"

*Anon*
*(AWM PR 84 286)*

## Australian Women's Land Army

From their homes of peace and comfort, from the city's sparkling lights,
To the bush of toil and hardship with its lone and silent nights
Come the daughters of Australia, set to take whate'er befalls,
Glad to cast aside the ball gown for the patriot's overalls.

And they plough and sow and harrow, and each one pulls her weight,
They get up very early and knock off very late;
They're doing man-sized missions as they've never done before,
Which is no small contribution to the winning of the war.

'Mongst the paddies, pigs and pumpkins, 'midst the cabbages and beet,
In the freezing winds of winter and the summer's scorching heat,
As they battle choking dust clouds and plod through slush and rain,
They are fighting too for Victory and their toil is not in vain.

Suntanned, strong and healthy, they are feminine and dear,
They're the mothers of tomorrow, and Australia need not fear
While she fosters daughters like them, marching boldly with her sons,
To steer the plough triumphantly while her brother mans the guns.

They are fighting a silent battle on the front behind the front,
And their combat – just as vital, though it's girls who bear the brunt.
Smeared with grease and grime of tractors, clad in dirty overalls,
Unsung heroines of warfare, answering to their Nation's calls.

And the watchword on their banner they, in Freedom cause, unfurled
Is, 'The hand that guides the tractor is the hand that feeds the world!'
The first round of the battle goes to their men who fight,
While those fair and silent workers continue day and night,

On the farms and in the dairies, on the outback station runs,
Those girls with grit are needed just as much as men with guns.

*Sgt S. Clark. RAA*
*(AWM PR 84 286)*

## To "Bobby Tobruk" "The Dog"

He was only a stump-tailed poodle
    He had no pedigree,
He was born in a Libyan dust storm
    Near an "Itie" RAP.

He'd do his share at line guard
    And share of piquet as well,
And never a crime had Bobby
    And never an AML.

He saw his share of fighting
    And fought like a soldier too
For we taught him concealment and cover
    In the barracks of Mersa Matruh.

He barked on the plains of Olympus
    And fought in the thick of the van
The boys of C Company loved him
    And voted young Bobby a man.

For Bobby was born to battle
    Though with none of a battler's luck,
And he who dodged dive bombers
    Had to die 'neath an Arab truck.

So we gave him a soldier's funeral –
    It was all that we could do –
For Bobby Tobruk was a cobber of ours
    And helped us see it through.

*Anon*
*(AWM PR 00526)*

## Black Anzac

They have forgotten him, need him no more,
He who fought for his land in nearly every war;
Tribal fights before his country was taken by Captain Cook,
Then went overseas to fight at Gallipolli and Tobruk.

World War One two black Anzacs were there,
France, Europe's desert, New Guinea's jungle, did his share
Korea, Malaya, Vietnam again black soldier enlisted –
Fight for democracy was his duty he insisted.

Back home went his own way not looking for praise,
Like when he was a warrior in the forgotten tribal days;
Down on the Gold Coast a monument in the Bora Ring,
Recognition at last his praises they are starting to sing.

This black soldier who never marches on Anzac Day
Living in his Gunya doesn't have much to say,
Thinks of his friends who fought, some returned some died,
If only one day they could march together by his side.

His medals he keeps hidden away from prying eyes;
No one knows, no one sees the tears in his old black eyes –
He's been outcast just left by himself to die,
Recognition at last black Anzac hold your head high.

Every year at Gold Coast's Yegurnbah Bora Ring site
Black Anzac in uniform and medals a magnificent sight
The rock with Aboriginal tribal totems paintings inset
The Kon-iburnerri people's inscription of LEST WE FORGET.

*Anon*
*(AWM PR 91 163)*

## To a Comrade

In this time of dreary waiting
Many happy hours were spent
Sharing all our fun together
Taking jokes as they were meant.

Now our joyful days are over
Fate decrees that we must part
But the memory of our friendship
Gives us all a cheerful heart.

So where'er your travels take you,
And whatever friends you make,
You'll know you've lots of comrades
And a friendship none can break.

*W. P. Toffin*
*(AWM 3 DRL 3527)*

## *The Sailor*

It isn't in the papers, so you do not always know
  Where to find him, so just address your letters 'care of GPO'
Today he isn't where tomorrow he may be,
  For yesterday he's somewhere and the day before at sea.

You can see him in a bar room, and groggy on his feet,
  You can see him slowly stagger up the middle of the street,
You can see him with his missus and baby in his arms,
  You can see him with a sheila or a girl of doubtful charms.

You can see him when he's cockeyed drunk and out upon a spree
  But you never seem to realise the time he's been at sea,
Where he's keeping middle watches for days and days on end;
  It isn't any wonder that it drives him round the bend.

When the great Pacific rollers come crashing o'er the bows
  And the ship shakes and shudders, then slowly forward plows,
When there's thunder in the turbines and the shaft begins to scream
  And you're called a stupid idiot if you lose a pound of steam.

So it isn't any wonder, when his ship arrives in port
  That the sailor only wonders the fact that time is short,
So he takes whatever's coming and lets his morals slide
  For you never know tomorrow if you may cross that great divide.

When you're dead and soon forgotten and no one tolls a bell
  If you never get to heaven, why not try for hell?
For at least you know what's coming and really couldn't care
  As you are sure to have some cobbers, stoking fires, with you there.

*R. J. Sturdy*
*HMAS ARUNTA*

## *Polly*

At nine o'clock, our Nurse signs on,
To watch us through the whole night long,
And when we are safely in our beds,
Lightly up the ward she treads.
A kind smile here, a helping hand,
We all agree she beats the band.
All the night she's at our call,
With cups of tea and toast, and all,
Then at 6 a.m. she'll grin and say,
"Good Morning, Boys, it's a bonzer day!"
And even though things may look black,
On all our cares we'll turn our backs,
For Nursie Dear has shown the way,
And so from all the boys we say,
"Thank you, Polly!"

*Ward 8, 2/12th AGH, Warwick*
*Anon*
*(AWM PR 88 019)*

## *Smilin' Thru'*

Though fate has been unkind to us with sickness and in pain,
It takes the kindness of the nurse to bring us health again;
    Her smiling face so cheerful, with radiance aglow,
    I'll praise her work unending wherever I may go.

No words that I can utter with justice half express
The gratitude I'll always feel, the depths you cannot guess.
    The kindness and devotion bestowed in Mercy's cause,
    Deserves the highest praise of all – a round of loud applause!

No doubt they have their troubles (who hasn't some these days?)
But they never show they have them, dispensing kindness many ways.
    There's one just here as I'm writing, who is always bright and jolly,
    And the first prize I would surely give to one whose name is Polly.

So Australia is indebted, and the soldier thankful too,
To the sisters and the nurses, with their motto 'Smilin' Thru'.
    Farewell I'll soon be leaving, you've done so much for me,
    For others in their illness and Australia generally.

*A. M. McDermott*
*(AWM PR 88 019)*

## *Merciful*

On a pedestal I place her high, so kind, so pure, so sweet,
Doing her duty nobly well, in her uniform so neat.
Tending the wounded and the sick without the slightest fear,
The Red Cross Nurse, she stands alone – we hold her very dear.

To the noble cause of Mercy. she has dedicated her life,
With the gentleness of a Mother and the sweetness of a wife.
Nothing a trouble to her, the bravest thing God made,
So loving, kind and gentle, but yet so unafraid.

The soldiers of the battlefield, who know her real true worth,
They respect her, and they love her like nothing else on earth.
She has tended them in dire distress, in misery and in pain,
Saved many from a soldier's grave, not once, but over again.

This pen of mine cannot record, all the Mercy I have seen.
But the Red Cross Nurse is God's Own work, Humanity's Queen.
So I wish her all the very best in God's care I leave her now,
Knowing that He who made her, every blessing will endow.

*A. M. McDermott*
*(AWM PR 88 019)*

## *A Prayer of Thanks*

The night is dark and dank and drear,
I toss upon my fevered bed
And softly comes on soundless feet
An earthly angel to my head;
And over my burning brow her hand
So soft and cool in sweet caress,
A healing touch that soothes my pain
With loving care and tenderness.
God bless 'The Rose of No Man's Land',
Who guides me through my night of pain,
And keep her safe throughout the storm
Till peace dawns bright and clear again.

*Anon*
*(AWM PR 00526)*

## The Last Anzac

They buried Doug Dibley today,
a fine old gentleman who died in his sleep,
at Rotorua on a hot December afternoon.
No warrior's death for him on Walker's Ridge,
where the poppies fed on the blood and frozen dreams
of good young men from Wellington.

A day's leave and a seven-year-old son at my side,
we bore witness as six tall infantrymen in service dress
raised him high from the gun carriage,
and quietly marched his flag-draped casket to eternal rest
among the trees and hills of his beloved Ngongotaha.

Volleys fired and mournful bugles call,
we shall not see his like again,
no more grow old as yet no more remain
with living memory of that time,
when machine gun and bayonet did their awful work,
and Anzac boys closed with desperate Turk,
among the gullies and crumbling ridges
of a foreign coast that was Gallipoli.

Remember this day my son,
remember this hour and this place,
for here and now they bury this Nation's last lament,
to a time of King and Empire.
And the poppies on the ridges grow,
and the scrub thorn in the valleys thrive,
and the memory of young mates who died
we sod this day with Trooper Dibley.

*Mike Subritzky*
*1997*

## *By The Way*

When the fire's burning bright
And my pipe's drawing right,
When the war's passed by many a day.
Once again in my mind
Many faces I find
　Of the chaps whom I met by the way.

They were friendly, these blokes,
With their songs and their jokes,
And helped when the world was darn grey,
So I hope that the fates
Have been kind to these mates,
　Splendid chaps whom I met by the way.

They've lent me a hand
In dust and in sand,
In fashion I ne'er can repay,
And in war's strife
When you fear for your life –
　You thank God for these chaps, by the way.

Thank you mate for your cheer,
It's the knowing you're near
That helps a man through a bad day,
For when trouble looms nigh
You will answer the cry:
　Noble friends whom we met by the way.

*Anon*

## *We thank You*

Thanks, boys, for the peace you helped to keep
In this fair land that has not known,
The agonies of ruthless war,
Save those who for the absent weep.
Yet, smiling through their tear-stained eyes,
They thank you, too, for what you bore
Through weary years, not for the praise
You hoped to get, but freedom's cloudless skies
That they might be forever more
The very joy of living ne'er forgot.
And so with deepest gratitude we say,
"Good luck, God bless you all, and thanks a lot!"

*Anon*

## American Tribute to the "Desert Rats"

The roads are clogged and dusty as the trucks go rolling by
With loads of weary soldiers with a twinkle in their eye.
The trucks are coming eastward for to give the boys a rest,
And I tell you all in Cairo, each one deserves the best.

There are Sikhs and husky Tommies, and Aussies tall and thin,
And the Scotties and the Tank Boys with berets and brown skin;
Still many other soldiers are coming down this way,
And I ask you all in Egypt, to give them thanks today.

For not many weeks behind us, old Rommel made a boast
That he soon would be in Cairo and that his friends would toast.
But these weary lads before you, with dusty clothes and gun,
Are the ones that freed all Egypt and kept Rommel on the run.

So raise your glasses highest and give a mighty cheer,
For the boys who won the battle and saved what all hold dear!

*Anon American*

## When "Black" is "White"

While Australia fears invasion and war knocks at our door,
　　the AIF is fighting back not far from Aussie's shore.
On the island of New Guinea, where the mountains kiss the sky,
　　and the Owen Stanley Ranges take their share of all who die.

Through a tough, infested jungle on a lonely native track
　　our boys are gamely marching on; some know they'll not come back.
From Moresby to Kokoda, through mud and splashing rain,
　　they cut their way through jungle, your freedom thus to gain.

So let your prayers be for them, as you pray to God each night,
　　to give them strength and courage to win the fight – your fight;
And whilst you're praying for them, pray for the native, too,
　　those angels without haloes, who're dying too, for you.

We met them first at Moresby, then on the jungle track,
　　those fuzzy headed angels that we all thought were black.
We classed him as a nigger, we thought 'white sense' held lack,
　　this tawny Papuan native, we called him 'boong' for black.

Unrecognised his presence, his company we would shun,
　　he seemed far from our equal and his colour caused us fun;
But when it came to battle and bloodshed on this isle,
　　boong showed that he was white – we learned to love his style.

And with our sick and wounded, no mother could do more
　　to ease a loved one's suffering than the boongs did on this chore;
From the tangle of the jungle he bore our wounded through
　　many miles to dressing stations: Boong, we owe to you.

We thank you little brothers; in this tough and bloody fight
　　We're proud to have you with us – you've taught us 'black' is 'white'!

*Bill Curnow*

## Red Shield Angels

*The Fuzzy Wuzzy Angels* is a poem you well know,
It will always be remembered no matter where you go;
But there's other blinking angels where ever you may be
They're the men who give you comfort – the boys of the 'Sally' Army.

I remember that great battle on the hills of Shaggy Ridge,
You would hear those welcome voices, "Like a smoke?" or "Have a drink,
Dig?'
The Red Shield is a byword, two words which mean so much
To the boys who are in there fighting: "The angels are with us!"

Even in the midst of battle, e'en 'mongst tremendous din,
You will always see that banner with the words on it, HOP IN
No matter where the fighting, no matter where you are
You have always got that feeling that the Salvos are not far.

Their work is not just the Army when you turn to them in strife,
They're always there to help you, even back in civvy life.
In the courts where men do battle for freedom for a time,
They know they have a backing, and it doesn't cost a dime.

So I'll close this little poem with all the highest praise
For the men of the Salvo Army, and their deeds in war-torn days.
May God bless and keep them till better days are known
When we all can cry together "Australia, free land, our own!"

*Colin Rap*

## *It's Ours*

The battle raged unceasing
With bursting bomb and shell
Both dead and wounded lay about
Amid this earthly hell.

Then through the smoke of battle
We saw them standing by –
The Red Cross plain for all to see,
We heaved a heatfelt sigh.

The wounded soon were loaded,
We wished them best of luck,
We blessed the driver and his men
For their courage and their pluck.

Back to the 2nd/9th Field Ambulance
Where willing hands stood by
To mind the wounded, soothe their nerves
And see they did not die.

Day and night these gallant men
Worked on for hours and hours
And when a shell burst near they'd say
"Don't panic boys it's ours!"

No words of praise are high enough
To give these boys a name,
But through it all the 2nd/9th
Stood by and played the game.

*Anon*

## *Our Mates, the Yanks*

I have a mate or two among the Yanks in good ol' US of A,
'Mum' and I have visited once or twice and despite a few differences,
We're so much alike that mutual respect
is built into their "Hi!" and our "G'day!"
Our differences relate to 'lingo' and lifestyle
but we have pulled down most separating fences.

In our oft' offensive tagging we often call them 'Tanks',
Not because they're mobile, iron-sided and vulnerable,
'tis better than 'Hey! You!'
And it is kinder than 'Septics', besides it rhymes with 'Yanks' –
We like to have them visit so we can stir a pot or two.

The 'laid back' pace of American sport and the aggressive pace of ours,
Accentuates national attitudes of 'steady as she goes!'
and an urgency to prove the point,
So side by side we go, as we have through many tours,
And our friendly rivalry has often led to partying that really 'rocks the joint'.

Whether you stroll the Boulevards of Hollywood
and drive the 'crazy' freeways of LA,
Or sail 'cross Sydney's Harbour and try to cross the 'coat-hanger' in peak,
You'll share the traveller's highs and lows of leisure and delay,
And comparing both experiences you'll agree that there's a common streak.

They say that wealth abounds in good ol' US of A and that every man is
rich,
And that we'll have to 'pull our socks up' if they maintain the pace,
But I've seen the poor in LA and New York
and watched them make their pitch
As they do in Sydney, and other Aussie towns, so it's national wealth *per capita*
that keeps us in the race.

The Yanks are patriotic, proud and sometimes rather loud,
While Aussies have a gutsy, arrogant and rebellious stance,
Yet we have a similar determination to remove every dark and gloomy cloud,
Yanks and Ockers, together, are a formidable barrier
against potential foes that prance.

Our soldiers train together now for, united,
we've fought and bled when things were really rough,
The Yanks joined in the fray in World Wars I and II
and turned the tide when we were on our knees,
So we helped them out in little 'dings' in Korea, Vietnam and the Gulf,
I guess that's the price of brotherhood,
we have to stand together so that all can feel the breeze.

We've taken our place upon the international stage,
and gained quite some respect,
Mother England gave us birth and showed us how and where to stand,
Uncle Sam is our big brother but we need not hold his hand,
he expects us to be direct,
We are all one, a strong united family, and the world – it likes our brand.

Now we struggle to cut parental ties with dear old Mother England,
For we feel a need to take the final step to nationhood,
To have a very special flag to unify our pride and represent our land,
The Yanks have 'old glory', John Bull the Union Jack,
and ours will be as good.

As we, again, stand up to face the world, let us give thanks to 'Mum',
And clinging tightly to our Anzac heritage,
go out with courage to a future shining bright,
And to our bonded mates, the Kiwis', add the beat of the Yankee drum,
We'll march the course of freedom so that liberty, through courage,
might give the world its light.

*Bill Phillips*
*1997*

## *Kiwis*

The Kiwi is a little bird and kinda cute the girls do say,
But 'tis the symbol of a nation that lies across the way.
It has inspired New Zealand's people and filled their hearts with pride,
And Aussies, too, are proud of them
    for we always stand side by side.

When we became a nation and were asked to stand and fight,
For the freedom of captive people, little Kiwi brother fought with all his might,
And we stood together to challenge all aggressors to throw at us their best,
We bled, we died, we cursed 'til victory it was won
    and we stood the mighty test.

In peace they play all sorts of games still challenging the entire world,
And this little bloody Kiwi will ne'er concede defeat no matter what is hurled.
We sometimes knock their 'All Blacks' flat and belt them at the wicket;
But back they come – they won't lay down –
    that cursed little bird ahiding in the thicket.

Rebellious and rugged these oceanic people have shown that they don't give a stuff,
For aggression or pomposity I guess it's in the water, which can get mighty rough.
Aussies and Kiwis proudly earned, together, the title 'Anzac',
So don't ever pick a 'blue' for it's not just a title
    earned at Gallipoli or on the track.

I must admit I'm puzzled, an insignificant Kiwi would surely inspire the least,
The Poms have a rampant lion (though it's not a native beast),
We've got an old man roo and an emu (neither takes a backward step),
But a little tiny Kiwi – it must be just a joke
    but it sure does give 'em pep.

They've got a long white cloud, and heaps and heaps of sheep,
Then there's snow and bubbling stinking mud and mountains fairly steep,
And there's an accent for which we tease them heaps,
They come and pinch a job or two
    and our pollies do the weeps.

If the Kiwi were an emu or little brother cassowary I could understand,
But a cheeky flightless bird that's nocturnal is hardly grand.
I've oft been told to watch my tail but a Kiwi doesn't have one,
The way the Kiwi's fight it's probably been shot away
　　or he ties it in a bun.

No matter how I rave or puzzle I must admit to admiration,
For there's a rugged proud determination that is akin to the spirit of our Nation,
And they've fought tenaciously for other people's freedoms and did it with a grin,
That takes a lot of spirit and I love 'em,
　　it makes me feel a twin.

Hey, Kiwi! May I shout a word of warning as we compete again,
Don't get under our emu's feet for he'll treat you with disdain.
We hope you come in second for we like to win our games,
So we'll do our best to beat you
　　and we'll shoot you down in flames.

Yes! Across the mighty ocean hidden by the long white cloud,
Is a nation of our brothers of whom we're mighty proud,
And we'll stand together always, whether it be in peace or war,
But why a bloody Kiwi?
　　It still sticks into my craw.

*Bill Phillips*
*1998*

## *The Sapper*

Just an ordinary sapper
Neither debonair or dapper,
A simple kind of bloke it's good to know;
Maybe over fond of liquor
Still there's no doubt he is a stickler
And he'll go where any other man will go.

He may be a cranky blighter
But, fair dinkum he's a fighter,
He's always ready when things are tough;
Every time our mob advances
He is there to take his chances
And he sticks it until the foe has had enough.

To consolidate positions
He is there with demolitions
He just loves to play around with dynamite,
And at night he's on barbed wire
Somewhere out there, under fire,
Ever ready to be mixed up in a fight.

In your peaceful contemplation
When you're praying for the Nation
And you ponder on the dangers that are past,
Don't forget he's worth attention
For the roll of fame will mention
That he did his duty squarely to the last.

*Anon*
*(AWM PR 00526)*

# CHAPTER TEN
# ON REFLECTION

## Elegy Written in a Country RSL
### (With apologies to Thomas Gray)

A bugle sounds the end of Anzac Day
The limping Diggers head off home for tea,
The General's strut his stuff – he's earned his pay –
And silence hands their memories down to me.

Twilight on the stone sits slow and cold
The last rays of sun provide a crown,
Some galahs make one last sortie bold
Then any noise disturbs and earns a frown.

There's just one Stone about to tell the tale
Of all the local heroes called to war,
And all the mums and lovers wan and pale
When told that they would see their loves no more.

Then later in the bar of the RSL
Old Diggers tell their tales and memories,
Their luck to survive that bitter tortured hell
That took the lives of so many Aussie boys.

It wasn't really all that long ago
That soldiers, sailors, airmen played that scene,
While politicians argued to and fro
And we are left to guess what might have been.

But Diggers who came back recall their mates
Their future dreams and hopes not soft or loose
Their plans complete in detail – e'en the dates –
When once back home and they'd be free to choose.

Remember Jack? would put the world to rights
And put to shame the present politicians
And Bill who took a brush to all the sights
Some paintings were like Boyds, some like Titians.

And Phil was to write about the outback
The reader caused to smile or shed a tear,
And Sam who'd sing a song for all in concert
But now he won't 'cause he was shot that last year.

A new age philosopher was our Mark
To rid the world of pain was Markie's goal,
But he drowned in the sea – down deep and dark –
And his death is sure to leave a gaping hole.

So, sad to say, they will not have their day,
They gave their lives that we could now have ours
Yet we both squander life and waste the day
Too busy by far to even smell the flowers.

They had a vision for this land of ours
Once shared by all the people of our land,
Forgotten in our busy business hours
Or buried under mounds of trivial sand.

## The Epitaph

If you stop by to read this now and then
And ponder on the ones it's placed here for,
Then when you've finished say a loud 'Amen'
And gently smile and grieve for us no more.

The future, no longer ours, but now it's yours
Bequeathed to you – it is our parting gift;
Don't look with envy to some distant shores
But make a blessing that will give our souls a lift.

Make of this land the 'heaven on earth' we dreamed
Let not our pains and deaths have been in vain
Bring to life those dreams and all they seemed
And in that future – there we'll meet again.

*WO2 Paul Barrett*

## *Toad's Party*

You were mentioned at the table, as they passed around the Port,
They were talking of Terendek and Vietnam
They had known you in the 60s – At Serikin, where the rats
Lived beside and all around you at The Fort.

Where the rations came by plane and star pickets fell like rain
And beer was hot – But Indos must be caught.
You all wandered in the Ulu
With your rations on your back.

Crossed the border, and were miles away from home
When young Andre caused a panic,
So you raced back up the track,
But Terendak wasn't far across the foam.

When you came home to Australia you kept practising your skills
At Tin Can Bay and Ingham – lots of fun!
Then you climbed aboard the *Sydney* and across the China Sea,
you sailed to stop the Commos on the run.

And you felt the bullets flying, while Alex lobbed grenades
And the fight was often over in a flash.
Then you gathered up your gear, sometimes trembling with a tear.
And you wondered why you did it – not for cash

Back home in '68 you were moving at a rate
To Townsville and High Range –
The Strand and Louth's. And you lived the local life,
And you found yourself a wife.

But you did it all again!
with a different group of men
With Len and John and Pat in 71.
At the Horseshoe and Vung Tau you were there to show them how,
To do the job – and still – to stop the Commo Run.

And we talked till after midnight as we sat among the plates.
And we wondered where you went and what you've done.
Since the time you shared together – with the friends you'll have forever –
You were mentioned at the table
By your Mates.

*Margaret Gibbons*


## *Great Day!*

I see him at reunions and he smiles and says "Hello!"
    Then he sits and talks with mates who do the same.

And I wonder what they're thinking as they sometimes gaze away
    To quieter, darker corners from the game.

Are they thinking of the paddy fields, or tall denuded trees,
    Or grass so high and hot you cannot see?

Perhaps tears, or lonely longing for family and friends:
    Self pity – that's something you won't see.

It's time to go till next year, he pauses at the door.
    "Goodbye!" he'll say and quickly looks away.

The tiny tear that twinkles in his eye, he tries to hide,
    And his parting word is usually "Great Day!"

*Margaret Gibbons*

## *In October*

I see soldiers when they're marching
   I see soldiers when they walk
I see soldiers when they're laughing
   I see soldiers when they talk.

And I like to stand and watch you
   when we gather on the Tweed,
And perhaps just more than anything
   this may be what you need.

Just to get your thoughts in order
   just to stop and think awhile
To find a friend you have forgotten
   helps you walk another mile.

So come back again to Twin Towns
   talk and laugh and meet a friend,
For that weekend in October
   means our memories don't end.

*Margaret Gibbons*

## *After the March*

Unpeopled streets, swept clear
As by a flood;
Here lies confetti – gay,
But mixed with mud.
Bright streamers strew the ground
In tangled heaps
Like weed cast on the sand
When the sea weeps.
And in an office door
Stand, here and there,
Small tearful groups of girls
Just stand and stare
Into a future suddenly made bare.

*Marjorie Larcombe*

## *Remember the Green Parrot?*

Telok Anson, Tanjung, Tokong -
Ipoh, Nasi Goreng,
Aussie Hostel, Golden Sands –
Nothing ever boring.

Drinking in the Hong Kong Bar,
Lasah, Lumut, Naafi,
Koyli, Jocks and Ghurke too –
Sometimes even Taffy.

Up the sharp-end
In the Ulu, Sandy Croft and curry.
Merle could feed a hundred men –
No one's in a hurry.

Makan, Tiffin, Pappodams,
Whiteaways and Minden,
Tiger beer and Lucky Strikes –
Oh boy, but you were thin then!

Charlie Brock's old monkey,
A trip to Alor Star,
Gambling at the Garrison,
Haggling in Bazaar.

Chin Peng on the run again,
Taiping, Hong Kong Bank,
Forward scout for Claude this week –
Who can we all thank?

Endless hours of tramping jungle,
Aching backs and tired feet,
Snatch some sleep at Tanjung Bungah,
Fit in some time in Chulia Street.

Your back still aches on Anzac Day,
Your sight is getting dim,
But your eyes search all the ranks
Looking for that special 'Him'.

The one you used to laugh with,
The one who was your mate,
You haven't seen him lately –
And you hope it's not too late.

*Margaret Gibbons*

## *Colours*

We stood at the Ho that first summer's morn,
Hearts bursting with pride, tears welling inside,
Thoughts of back home and how far we'd come,
The pipe it was shrill in the crisp air still.

We stood tall that morn and first saw her rise,
Our Ensign she's white, inspiring, bold and bright,
There's been so many others have stood here before,
And watched glory rise, up into southern skies.

It's the start of her day hoisted up slow...
All hands salute... let's give her a show,
On her way up, the red white and blue,
That chord in our hearts will always ring true.

As she reaches the top, the silence is great,
Australia's White Ensign – she'll do me mate!

*LSMT Scott Bayley*

## *The Sea!*

The sea! That vast, majestic plain
Of foam-flecked wave and windswept rain,
And howling gales that bend the brain
And fill brave men with dread.

The sea! That sparkling crystal pool
Bedecked with phosphorescent jewel,
Where dolphins play the merry fool
And Neptune makes his bed.

The sea! That final resting place
For sailing men of every race,
Where seaweed shrouds are commonplace
Among the grateful dead.

No grave for me, nor crypt, nor tomb,
Nor roaring furnace in curtained room,
But Nature's cool and watery womb
Is where I'll lay my head.

*Ron Baker*

## *Remember*

Remember, Australia, now peace bells have rung
And Victory's song have been joyfully sung,
Remember the blood that was shed for this land;
Forget not the courage so noble and grand.

Remember, Australia, when birds sweetly sing
And nature's soft blossoms are glories of spring,
As trees gently sway in the light laughing breeze;
Remember the battle to keep gems like these.

Remember, Australia, those brave men who fell,
Whose lives ebbed away in a valley of hell.
Remember their children, and others loved dear
And give them a future to face without fear.

Remember, Australia, the brave who return,
The wounded, the war-torn, you must never spurn;
Remember these men, and discharge your debt well,
Secure and in comfort, be sure they all dwell.

Remember, remember, forever, these sons
Who flung back the foe with a thunder of guns!
As free soil you tread, and on beauty you gaze,
Remember, Australia, remember always!

*Cpl S. George Van Staveren*
*September, 1945*
*(AWM MSS 1560)*

## *Return from the Unknown*

*On the planting of trees near Rockingham RSL dedicated to fallen Rockingham Soldiers.*

He was young and loved the earth's green places,
Sea in the sun, gardens under rain,
Old trees, long roads, the loveliness of children's faces,
Orchards in blossom, wind on rippling grass,
Dappled skies and all wild things.

Then came a war from half a world away,
And he who saw the world through happy eyes,
Gave up his heritage of quiet play.
He bade farewell to family
And went forward into the unknown.

So plant a tree that it might grow,
Strong and straight with muscled bough,
A tree to say to passers by:
Don't shed a tear and please don't cry,
For once again Rockingham's my home
And midst these trees I'm not alone...

*Lt. Col. Jack Gregg, RA Inf*
*Rockingham, 16 October 1999*

## *Bataans' Plaque*

Ulverstone is the place they met
    on the north Tasmanian coast
Just to show and not forget
    the deeds of Bataan with a toast

A plaque was laid in the park
    for all who came to see,
It was lit up in the dark
    and showed what used to be.

A destroyer of the tribal class
    which served in war and peace
And set a standard unsurpassed,
    a prestige that would never cease

Now some are grey and old
    and others have passed by
Bataan's deeds will still be told –
    the plaque will never die.

*Herbert M. Boys*

## *The Men of Yesterday*

Along our coasts the cannons roar, our towns are all alight.
And drums they roll and bells they peal to call the men to fight.

But where are the men all trained for war their country to defend;
We have the men, but all untrained, it would be fatal these to send?
From country farm and city street, with hair that's turning grey,
They form once more in steady ranks, the Men of Yesterday.

As they march their thoughts go back to battles long ago,
As side by side with comrades old, they face a nearer foe,
And bursting shell and battle dust block out the light of day,
For grimly fight and grimly die, the Men of Yesterday.

And quicker still the reaper swings and each sweep a full swathe takes
As the foe with deadly fire, those thinning ranks he rakes;
And wider grows those widening gaps, before that hail of lead,
Till few are left to face the foe besides the dying and the dead.

But now is heard the tramp of feet in the lull of battle sound,
And dying men their rifles grasp to fire a final round.
On they come that marching host and charge into the fray,
And through those shattered ranks they pour, the Young Men of Today.

Rank on rank their still forms lie with faces cold and grey,
No more they'll hear the glad larks sing or see the break of day;
Behind those lines the women sing and children are at play,
And perhaps at times they give a thought to the Men of Yesterday.

*G. S. Laslett,*
*OB Flat, 1940*

## *Friendship*

Friendship is the golden chain
That nought on earth can sever,
The passing years roll on in vain
True friends are friends forever.

*Anon*

## *Reflections*

Let our thoughts go back to the Unit's birth,
    Of the time that has passed since then;
Of the heroic deeds that have proved our worth,
    And shown us as fighting men.

Let us dwell for a time on the present day,
    With its trials and hardships so real,
Of the various setbacks that come our way
    Which we tackle with courage and zeal.

Let us look to the future with confident mien,
    To the battles that yet must be fought,
With courage and team work the world has not seen –
    We'll prove we weren't formed for nought!

*G. H. B.*

## *Here Again*

Your name is here again,
Resting quietly in the trees,
With the flame trees and the brush box
And the tiny native bees,

With the grey gum and the iron bark
And whispering Bribie pine,
The crows ash and the black bean,
Silky oak and turpentine.

Magpies calling in the morning-
Butcher birds and curlew fly.
Lilly-pilly's soft pink colours-
Bloodwood reaching to the sky.

The flagpole stands and watches.
May the trees grow straight and tall
And the sheoaks murmur softly:
"Thanks for answering the call."

*Margaret Gibbons*

## *Glimpse*

Hold on to freedom despite the price it costs,
Take heart in your failures, despite all you have lost.
Hold out for memories of the times spent in the past –
   Close your eyes and wish for me, I'm coming home at last.

Tired bones and weary legs have travelled me so far,
But strike the light on the old front porch and leave the door ajar.
These legs have still some miles to roam,
    Today I'm coming home.

I feel just like my father was looking from a distance,
Stretching out to bridge the gap, but I always find resistance.
To only hear your voice so sweet from the end of a telephone line,
   It echoes in this broken heart, and pleads to turn back time.

To carefully rearrange the photos as time ages your face,
To carefully construct the albums to ensure you're not erased,
To have to ask for details which should never be forgot,
   To justify the guilty thoughts and lie that I have not.

To wrestle with emotions and fight back salty tears,
The flood of these emotions which signify the years.
These years are ones of fulfilled dreams, but darkened with regret,
   Of a selfish motivated man with promises not kept.

I long for days of undue stress, a time when I'll retreat,
A time when family surrounds me and life seems so complete
When I can make amends for all the years I've been away –
   Leave that candle burning please, I won't be home today.

*Pte J. Harris*
*19 May 1998*

## *Sad Song Calling*

There's something about that sad sound,
That haunting sound when they play *The last Post*
You can feel something deep in your soul
As tho' you've been touched by a ghost.

    Yeah, there's something about that sound,
    Close your eyes and you're drifting away
    And without really knowing just how
    You are standing on Suvla Bay.

And around you there's the Dead and the Dying
Lonely shapes of the victims of War
And you suddenly find yourself crying
As you hear that sad bugle once more.

    'Tis a song that was born of a sadness,
    'Tis a song we too often repeat
    As we call to all those who've departed
    When old soldiers and memories meet.

It's a sound that drifts over the trenches
And it weaves thru' the tall jungle trees
And it whispers "Sometimes we are beaten
But we'll never be brought to our knees."

    For the song touches all with a spirit
    And reminds us how fragile we are,
    And while our minds may feel memory's wounds
    It's the heart where we're bearing the scar.

That song is the sound of the Fallen
And the wind blows it 'cross foreign lands
From Milne Bay to the green fields of Flanders
To the dust of El Alamein sands

    And the wind takes it 'cross seas and oceans
    To the places wherever men fell,
    And caresses the ghosts who are resting
    And its song touches all those as well.

And the sound follows trails they have trodden
Calling those that the jungles retain
Waking Sandakan Death Marchers, sleeping,
Then returns home to those who remain.

And for those who still march every April
It will call to their spirits as well
And for those who stand watching, and wondering
Touch their hearts with the stories you tell

Leave the gaps in your ranks when you're marching
They'll be filled, tho' they see no one there
Play *The Last Post*, and send its song skyward,
And the last note will hang in the air.

For there's something about that sad sound
That haunting sound when they play *The Last Post*
You can feel something deep in your soul
As tho' you've been touched by a ghost...

*Les Mellet*

## *The Battle Ground*

With Diggers' blood in foreign mud, and flies and stench and gore
And the wounded scream and the rest just dream, of life before the war,
And the twang and whine of the bullets flying, and the machine gun's deadly tap
And smoke filled air and a sense of despair, and the mortar's lethal clap.

Day after day 'til no one cares and no one thinks to stop,
And night after night we continue to fight and kill the cream of the crop
Ten thousand a day we waste good men, we snuff their youthful life,
Then we do it again and again and again in this terrible useless fight.

The Sergeant's back is broken and the Corporal long since dead
The soldiers' eyes are sunk right back in his bandaged blood-stained head;
The medic sits in a sludge-filled pit with a bullet in his heart,
And the coward cries as the hero dies, his body ripped apart.

And no one knows where the boundary goes or who is shooting who
And the world's a mess and you hope at best that you'll manage to see it through.
Well the years long past from that war at last, I made it out alive
And every year we march and drink beer to those who didn't survive.

But the dreams still come and the scars never left, and I'm missing an eye and an ear,
And the sight of young men in greens with a gun, still strangle my soul with fear.
But I guess I'll get by just living a lie and I'll see it through 'til the end
But my heart and my mind are shattered inside, and my soul can never mend.

*Ron Wilson*

# CHAPTER ELEVEN
# DREAMS
# OF HOME

## *Thoughts of Home*

I've just come in off duty
And I'm feeling rather blue
    So the best thing I can think of
    Is to drop a line to you.

Writing seems to cheer one
Makes a man remember home
    And often makes him wonder
    Why he commenced to roam.

Now if by chance they get me,
Should put me out of gear,
    I'll go out like a Briton
    Like you would have me, Dear.

But in the meantime while I live
When the bombs and cannon roar
    I'll pray with all my heart, Dear,
    That we will meet once more.

And when the boys come sailing back
To great Australia fair,
    Among the smiling happy band,
    Here's hoping I'll be there.

*Lt Alfred William Salmon*
*(AWM PR 00297)*

## *For Honour and for Her*

Somewhere a woman, thrusting fear away,
Faces the future bravely for your sake,
Toils on from dawn till dark, from day to day,
Fights back the tears, no heeds the bitter ache;
She loves you, trusts you, breathes in prayer your name,
Soil not her faith in you by sin or shame.

Somewhere a woman – mother, sweetheart, wife –
Waits betwixt hopes and fears for your return;
Her kiss, her words, will cheer you in the strife
When death, itself, confronts you grim and stern.
But let her image all your reverence claim
When base temptations scorch you with their flame.

Somewhere a woman watches, thrilled with pride,
Shrined in her heart, you share a place with none.
She toils, she waits, she prays till side by side
You stand together when the battle's done
O keep for her dear sake a stainless name,
Bring back to her a manhood free from shame!

*Anon*
*(AWM PR 91 104)*

## *Dear Mother*

*Dedicated to my mother, Winifred Colenso*

Weep not Mother darling,
Drive away those tears,
You think I'm still a baby
But I'm older than my years.

Now that I've joined the colours
I must go away
To help my fellow countrymen
In the coming fray.

For many years you nursed me
And kept me fit and well,
If I thought it would help you
I'd gladly go through hell.

Do not be despondent,
For I hate to see you blue,
No matter where I travel
I will always think of you.

As the person who has loved me
And reared me with fond care,
Your son can't be a shirker,
He too, must do his share.

As much as this does grieve me
To go away from you,
I must do my duty
As you would wish me to.

Although I know it hurts you
To see your son depart,
I can but assure you,
That you'll always own my heart.

*Raymond John Colenso*
*(AWM PR 00689)*

## *Mothers Day*

Australians are in action
In Libya and in Greece,
While some are in Malaya –
As yet, they're still at peace.

Again the name Anzac
Is known throughout the world,
It's these sons of heroes
Who keep our flag unfurled.

To Hitler they're a menace,
These lads so brown and tall,
The way they wield their bayonets
Forms a solid human wall.

But to mothers in Australia,
These men are only boys –
They remember them as babies,
Playing with their toys.

Men or boys it matters not,
Whichever they may be,
Their mothers will be waiting
And watching at the Quay.

The sons they nursed for many years
Are fighting far away,
They who kept them fit and well
Now – can only pray.

Mothers Day comes once a year,
This time it brings regret,
Many children's photos
Are ribboned: "Lest we Forget."

But others bring back memories
Of men who strive and fight
To protect their mother's safety –
This will shall conquer might.

*Raymond John Colenso*
*(AWM PR 00689)*

## *When*

Many of the wealthy men,
In business all their lives,
Often have to travel
Overseas without their wives.
They know upon departure
The date when they'll return
To their families in the country
Of the waratah and fern.

But men who join the AIF
Know not when and where
They'll see the faces
Of their loved ones free from care.
They're fighting for a right to live,
For peace from racial hate,
But for many of the heroes
Peace will reign too late.

I left my wife and baby
By Sydney Harbour's shore
To go and join my comrades
And put an end to war.
My curly headed baby boy
Is much too young to know
That his father couldn't stay behind –
I simply had to go.

If the war lasts many years
There will be the danger
That David will not know me,
He'll consider me a stranger.
Pearl, my wife, will teach him
To hope and pray for peace;
She knows that I cannot return
Until this war does cease.

*Raymond John Colenso*
*(AWM PR 00689)*

## *Thoughts*

When the still of night is creeping
My thoughts return to home,
To far and distant Sydney
Whose streets I once did roam.

    The loved ones I have left behind
    Are brought quite near to me,
    The sacred gift of thinking
    Forms a bridge across the sea.

Visions of the future
Help to aid my lonely heart,
And the noble art of writing
Plays a most important part.

    To make a life-like image
    Of the ones I left behind,
    It prevents the threat of boredom
    From preying on my mind.

Discomforts are forgotten
When my thoughts commence to stray
To the many happy moments
Before I sailed away.

    My lonely heart is sated
    By the thoughts of friends who wait
    For the deliverance of mankind
    From these days of strife and hate.

*Raymond John Colenso*
*(AWM PR 00689)*

### Dreams

When I left Sydney Harbour,
Its calm blue waters deep
Became a graven image
To haunt me while I sleep,
And remind me of my homeland
Many thousand miles away,
Of the womenfolk I left behind –
Oh! How I rue that day!

When I left my Mother
And sailed across the blue,
I also left three sisters,
There was a girlfriend too.
Every night in slumber
I meet them all again –
How I curse when 'wakened
By steady pouring rain!

In the early hours
When my eyes are closed in sleep,
I hear their voices speaking
From across the ocean deep.
In my mind we're happy,
Our hearts are free from pain,
There is no room for Hitler
For it is peace again.

Each day I long for nightfall,
When I will dream once more
Of my friends and family,
Whom we are fighting for.
If my life was halted
Then turned back a year or more,
My choice would not be altered –
I'd still he here I'm sure.

*Raymond John Colenso*
*(AWM PR 00689)*

## *Homecoming*

The chaps all line the forward deck,
Their eyes are shining bright,
Hearts are light and happy
For we'll be home tonight.

We've sighted Sydney Harbour
And the beaches and the shore,
The troops are all returning
From victory and from war.

Once more we'll be united
With the folks we left behind,
The faces they remember
With heavy marks are lined.

No longer are we carefree,
We're not the lads they knew;
We changed from youth to manhood,
Our minds have altered too.

Sights we shall remember
Until our dying day
Have made us sober-minded
And taught us how to pray.

Perhaps our loved ones' welcome
Will help us to regain
The carefree hearts we left behind
Before the Nazi reign.

The ship is in the Harbour,
The wharves are now in view,
Despite their smiling faces
Tears keep coming through;

For now they're very happy,
From far across the foam,
The men they love so dearly
From war are coming home.

The ship has dropped the anchor,
We'll now be getting off
And mingling with our kinsfolk
Waiting on the wharf.

The faces I have treasured
I now can plainly see,
Uplifted hands are waving
For they have sighted me.

Now stop your shoving, Digger,
There's no need for a crush!
Many times we hurried
But now you needn't rush.

What is that you're saying?
Oh, yes! I can hear,
I was merely absent
From those whom I love dear.

In dreams I often travel
To the land I know so well;
In sleep I find much comfort
Despite the shot and shell.

Pleasant dreams, old cobber,
On watch I'll take my turn;
'Though while awake we quell it,
Our hearts for home do yearn.

*Raymond John Colenso*
*(AWM PR 00689)*

## *Thoughtless Phrase*

Have you never felt the danger of your child's small, trusting face,
That unshakeable belief that in your words they place?
The momentary mayhem of a madman's blood-red haze
Is nothing to the damage of a careless, thoughtless phrase.
For flesh and bone can heal themselves, to good as was before,
But a wound to heart or spirit is forever fresh and raw.

*Capt Don Buckby*

## *My Boy*

My boy lays there before me on a pillow fast asleep,
His brow is clear and perfect, his rest is sweet and deep.

No tears of disappointment have left their bitter trace,
No lines of fear or worry yet mar his lovely face.

I sit and think, as fathers do, what kind of man will he be?
Brave, loyal, straight and honest – not at all like me.

I pray he's not a coward, a murderer or thief,
Just a good man with the courage to pursue his own belief.

Enjoy these days my Son, they fly faster than you know,
And then upon life's cruel streets will be your turn to go.

And I cannot walk them for you though I would that that could be,
No, I'll watch you from the distance that must be enough for me.

Watch, as Fortune weaves her fickle spell and alternates 'tween joy and hell,
And forces strength to compromise, and takes her price to make you wise.

But I shall be not far behind you should you stumble, slip or fall,
I will ever be close by you – all you have to do is call.

*Capt. Don Buckby*

## *Christmas.*

*Written in 1945 at Moratai N.E.I. and sent to his children.*

The boys and the girls are all happy today,
Because they know Christmas is not far away.
The Jackasses laugh and the other birds sing,
Knowing that Santa has something to bring
To you and to me, if we've been very good,
And helped our dear mother as much as we could,
Who works very hard, without any fuss,
To make Christmas pleasant and joyous for us.

*Pte. Jim Baker*

## *My Love for You*

There is no hour that passes by
But some sweet thought of you
Shines like a lamp of love on high
To light my whole life through.

The day is long but at its end
My prayers for you I say
That God will guard and bring me back
To ever with you stay.

*A.W. Curran*
*(AWM 3 DRL 3527)*

## If

If these thoughts have never crossed your mind then let them do so now,
That this world would be a better place, if only we knew how:

How to look beyond the strictures of self, and self alone,
How to take a stand against a wrong, not cowardly condone;

How to foster in our children a feeling of their worth,
How to teach them that there's more to life than pursuit of wealth and mirth:

How to teach them of the diffrence 'tween the body and the soul,
And that both need to be nurtured to make a person whole;

How to not impose upon their childhood to make them grow too fast,
But to offer them the wisdom of the errors of your past.

*Capt. Don Buckby*

## The Lure

From the emerald heights of Atherton to the brown of Townsvilles's plain,
The lure of Northern Queensland calls me back to her again.

I clutch my coat close 'round me 'gainst the southern winter's chill
As the vision comes to haunt me, of the sun off Castle Hill.

Jostling cheek by jowl, through the raucous urban sprawl,
I crave that sweet serenity, a placid cane field tall.

As thoughts of brilliant coral reefs are drenched in winter rain,
Ah yes! the lure of Northern Queensland calls me back to her again!

*Capt. Don Buckby*

## November Jacaranda

If there's one sight to glad the heart of expatriate Queenslanders
It's the brilliant purple blooming of November jacarandas,
For to whatever far-flung corner of this nation they may roam
This annual explosion reminds them of their home.

In sleepy, dusty hamlets, bustling cities, towns and farms,
Their gnarled and darkened limbs dispense their bell like charms
And though they're not confined to the land above the Tweed,
Its humidity and sunshine seems to make a bigger breed.

As we make our steady progress down the twisting track of life
The small things of our childhood prove a refuge from its strife,
A sight, a smell or sound can recall a better time
When life was still all mystery, no trouble, strife or crime.

Jacarandas are the herald of the end of winter's reach,
A symbol of the coming of long days upon the beach,
A relaxation from the stresses of the frantic daily race –
They're reminders of the days of a kinder, gentler pace.

And when finally I find my way back north where I belong,
When the pull of home and family at last becomes too strong,
I'll take my ease upon some sun drenched back verandah
And drink in the purple glory of November jacaranda.

*Capt. Don Buckby*

## *Twilight*

Twilight falls upon the City of the Hills,
　　Moist heat gives way to evening cool,
Bright colours melt to muted shades
　　As light upon the tropic foliage fades.

Light points twinkle on the sides of hills,
　　Child voices cease, only carnage remains:
Bikes in driveways, toy soldiers left to stand
　　On guard, night is come to Brisbane's backyard.

She has not changed, dear city of my youth,
　　Still lush and green, languid and serene
She seems unkempt 'gainst the ordered south,
　　Yet cares not, full knowing of their envy.

Yes, I love her still! She calls me,
　　E'en after all these years away,
One beckon of her tanned brown arm
　　And I would leave all, to bring us Home.

*Capt. Don Buckby*

## *Australia*

Australia, land of sunshine and rain,
The country of our birth which we hold dear,
Ne'er shall you feel the tyrants yoke or chain,
For you will fight, and fighting know not fear.

*Anon*

## *Give a Thought*

Have you ever wondered what they think
In Blighty, day by day?
Have you ever wondered if they say a prayer
For you, while you're away?

    Let me reassure you,
    They give us all a thought
    To those who have not yet returned
    Who went away and fought.

Do you ever give a thought to those
Amidst their strife and cares?
Do you think to say each night
Just one or two small prayers?

    You will find that life goes better
    When everything seems blue
    If you give a thought to those who wait
    So patiently for you.

*A.W. Curran (?)*
*(AWM 3 DRL 3527)*

## *Before it is too late*

If you have a grey-haired Mother
In the old home far away
Sit down and write the letter
You put off day by day;
Don't wait until her tired steps
Reach Heaven's pearly gate,
But show her that you think of her –
    Before it is too late.

If you have a tender message
Or a loving word to say,
Don't delay and forget it
But whisper it today.
Who knows what bitter memories
May haunt you if you wait?
So make that loved one happy –
    Before it is too late.

We live but in the present
The future is unknown,
Tomorrow is another day
Today is all we own.
The choice that fortune lends us
May vanish if you wait,
So spend those life-long treasures –
    Before it is too late.

Those tender words unspoken,
That letter never sent,
The long forgotten message,
The wealth of love unspent;
These things will ease the burden
From a heart about to break,
So play the game and be a man –
    Before it is too late.

*A.W. Curran*
*(AWM 3 DRL 3527)*

## Thy Wife

She is sitting by the fireside
The kiddies are at play,
She's thinking of their Daddy
So many miles away.

When will she get a letter?
When will she see his face?
When will he be among them
In his accustomed place?

His chair is in the corner,
His pipes are in the rack,
She looks towards his pictures
And prays "God please send him back!"

The kiddies may grow rowdy,
But she won't wear a frown;
Her man just said keep smiling
And she won't let him down.

And so for love of Daddy,
Who's miles across the foam,
She joins in with the kiddies,
To make it 'home sweet home'.

One day he will be there with them
Then life will be serene;
She's only just a soldier's wife
But every inch a queen.

*Private Charles Antill*
*(AWM PR 00036)*

## *Millgrove*

There is a town I am thinking of always,
  A town where the tall trees grow.
Where the Yarra flows peacefully onward
  Beneath the shadow of Mount Little Joe.
It's a town where the evening shadows
  Cover the valley in a deep purple glow,
A town where one train comes in daily
  And life remains tranquil and slow.

Dear old Millgrove, I have left you –
  Although I left you not for fun,
But to keep you quiet and peaceful,
  With a well oiled ack-ack gun
So that you will never hear the big guns
  Bark their defiance at the Nipponese,
So that you'll never be lit up by fires
  That start when they drop incendiaries.

That's why I'm here in a disease-laden land,
  A land of dust and mosquitoes and flies,
Where troops march along the shell-torn roads
  And fighter planes zoom in the skies,
Where the drone of the bomber planes mingle
  With the whine of each high-powered shell
And falling bombs make your spine tingle
  When they scream like the inmates of hell.

Yes Millgrove, one day I'll be returning
  And when I step off your once-daily train,
I will want to see home fires burning
  And hear birds singing freedom's refrain;
I want to see tall gums tinged golden
  As they sigh in the setting sun's rays,
Then I'll know that I've done my duty
  To the town of my child-hood days.

*Bdr Sydney J. Lynch*
*March 1942*
*(AWM MSS 1557)*

## *My Mother's Smile*

Alone with my thoughts on a tropical isle
As the sun sinks low in the west,
A vision appears with an angelic smile
And I pray that the sun never sets;

For the smile is that of my Mother
None other has such tender care,
And I know she is thinking of me over here
While I'm thinking of her over there;

And today is the day God has given
In remembrance of one who's so dear,
And as time passes on may He grant me
An increase in my love every year.

*Bdr Sydney J. Lynch*
*(AWM MSS 1557)*

## Dad O' Mine

Midsummer day, and the mad world afighting,
    Fighting in holes, Dad o' Mine,
Nature's old spells are no longer delighting
    Passion-filled souls, Dad o' Mine,
Vainly the birds in the branches are singing,
Vainly the sunshine its message is bringing,
Over the green-clad earth stark hate is flinging
Shadow for shine, Dad o' Mine,
    Shadow for shine.

No one dare prophesy when comes an end to it,
    End to the strife, Dad o' Mine,
When we can take joy and once again bend to it,
    What's left of life, Dad o' Mine.
Yet for one day we'll let all slip behind us,
So that your birthday, Dad, still may remind us
How strong yet supple the bonds are that bind us
Through shade and shine, Dad o' Mine,
    Through shade and shine.

Leagues lie between us, but leagues cannot sever
    Links forged by love, Dad o' Mine;
Bonds of his binding are fast bound for ever,
    Future will prove, Dad o' Mine.
Your strength was mine since I first lisped your name, Dad,
Your thoughts were my thoughts at lesson or game, Dad,
In childhood's griefs, it was ever the same, Dad.
Your hand round mine, Dad o' Mine,
    Your hand round mine.

Strengthened by shadow and shine borne together,
    Comrades and chums, Dad o' Mine,
We shall not falter through fair or foul weather,
    Whatever comes, Dad o' Mine.
So in the years to be when you grow older,
Age puts his claim in and weakness grows bolder,
We'll stand up and meet them, Dad, shoulder to shoulder,
Your arm in mine, Dad o' Mine,
    Your arm in mine.

*Lt E.F. Wilkinson, M.C.*
*(AWM MSS 0671)*

## Soldier Boy

Soldier Boy gone to war,
To fight and die on a foreign shore,
My blue-eyed boy I do adore,
I fear you're coming home no more.

Soldier Boy in jungle green,
Of blood and dying I do dream,
Heart of my heart please be alive,
When next my letter does arrive!

Oh Soldier Boy, so long away,
God keep you safe each breath I pray!
Dearest one, your letters seem
To be so few and far between.

Oh Soldier Boy so brave and true,
I cry each night my love for you.
Oh Soldier Boy, love of my life,
Please come home to your loving wife!

*Greg Brooks*

## *The Setting Sun*

As I sit and watch the setting sun,
In its fairest tropic splendour,
My fondest thoughts are carried back
To Mother, kind and tender.

The romantic times I've spent with her
I remember with delight,
For the setting sun reminds me
Of my lonesome one tonight.

When twilight comes with its million stars
And the sunlight rays are retreating,
They seem to kiss the hills goodnight
As we did when last meeting.

And so my prayer tonight is for my loved one lonely
And may the setting sun, in its beams of life and beauty
Spread its sunny rays upon us two
When Australia's done her duty.

*D. Greene*
*New Guinea, 25th November 1942*
*(AWM PR 83 217)*

## *Desert Evening*

Night falling and the stars
    Peek out upon the stones and sand.

*Cassiopeia* and the *Little Plough*
    Twinkle in a cloudless sky
    And the sun sinks in a flaming glow.

Our thoughts turn to that other life
    Of trees and flowers and lawns,
    And memories of our dear ones far away
    Crowd before the lonely mind.

A distant murmur, broken beat
    Of bombers, going on with fell intent
    To blast and burn and harry.

Men like us who dream of home
    In the evening's quiet peace.

Streaks of light and flashes
    Dull thuds and boom of bombs
    Which fall upon a fort and bring
    In the quiet peace of eve
    A grim realisation of uneasy life
    Which brooks upon this desert.

Bare, aloof, unfriendly,
    Full of hidden things inimical to men.

And besides the dreams of pleasant places,
    Of parks and streams and cosy houses
    Filled with happy children,
    The spectre of a hungry beast,
    A beast of prey which strangles one
    With thirst, torments with flies,
    And hides amongst the rocks
    Poisonous things, snakes and scorpions.

And yet again there are timid things of peaceful mood,
    Frightened hares and graceful gazelles
    Affrighted by our rumbling tanks
    And so, our evening dream of home
    Is shattered by grim thoughts.

We turn and stoop into our desert home
    Dug deep, of stones and sandbags,
    And there upon a box or petrol tin
    Sit around a makeshift table
    And drink our ale or good old Scotch
    And forget it all – perhaps?

Soon we bid goodnight.

Creeping to our lonely beds
    Not unhappy, yet missing all those things we love.
    The job is to be done;
    We can endure it all
    Till that great day when
    We shall be home again.

*B. M. Laird*

## *Airmail Palestine*

"Praise God from whom all blessings flow,"
The Padre said. Row on row
The rusting hymn books in the sun.
Flickered, were folded, thin as one.

A thousand voices stirred the air were silent,
Heads were bent in prayer.
Above the Padre's voice we heard
An engine drone, just like a bird.

With silvered wings we saw the plane
Above the sandhills out to sea,
Heading with mail to Galilee.
And in the clouds we saw again,

Our homes, the noonday shimmering sun
On the farm, beach and station run.
The stock knee-high in summer grass,
The shearers nodding as we pass.

Each stand: the silos crammed with wheat,
The sheep dogs panting in the heat,
The breakers curl, the lash of foam,
The aching, taunting thoughts of home.

"Praise God from who..." and each man bows
His head to thank his God who sends,
Half way across the world, the mail,
Who deems those engines shall not fail.

But that they bring across the sea,
The mail, to his own Galilee.

*Anon*
*South Australia*

## *In our Great and Wonderful Country*

We have beauty from the hills to the sea,
Like the waves on the oceans of our coastline
In our great country
We are free

We cast our thoughts to the early Settlers,
Who came from many other distant lands
To make our Country their homeland
Where the hard toils were done by hand.

When we travel through our great Outback,
Where the cattle sheep and brumbies graze,
With the closing of a beautiful day
It appears that the whole world is ablaze.

'Neath the blue sky in the Bushland
The big gums stand as with pride
As they show their admiration for our Country
And for the Stockmen in Australia who ride.

The Stockmen are up at break of day
As they do in the great Outback,
Riding their horses to the big round up
Far off the beaten track.

We have our spacious farmlands
With acres of golden grain;
Nearby are the herds of cattle grazing
Feeding after the falls of the wonderful rain.

When we travel to our great south-east,
Where the beautiful pine trees grow,
We can see more beauty of our great land –
It is a sight that we all know.

The beautiful City of Adelaide,
Surrounded by parks and trees,
With gardens of beautiful flowers,
The freshness fills the breeze.

*Sid Buckingham*

## *Leave the Panels Down*

The little grey house had a lonely look,
There wasn't a soul around
But we saw as we crossed the shallow brook
That the slip rails lay on the ground.

We rode in up to the kitchen door
For the stock might take the track,
But a woman said with a weary smile
"My boys are absent many a mile,
And we'll leave the panels down awhile
To wait till the lads come back."

And over our southern, sunny land
The same great thought holds true,
From the timbered hills to the parching sand
And the wide green stretches too.

All the boys who've done their bit,
Though many a pal we'll lack,
Whether they come from bush or town
Will know they'll find the panels down
To the hearts they left, and the love will crown –
The day that the lads get back.

*Lt S. D. Leslie*
*(AWM 2 DRL 435)*

## *They Also Serve*

We've poems to our heroes and the deeds that they have done,
And though their wreaths of laurel are begrudged to them by none,
There are braver souls, I'll warrant, far from trench or North Sea foam,
In the Women of the Empire, in the girls who stayed at home.

They were with us when our transports left our shores two years agone,
In spirit torn and anguished with the sons who they had borne,
They were with us at the landing – that immortal April Day –
And the lads who rushed the beaches bore no braver souls than they.

They were with us at Cape Helles, with a father, husband, son,
With the weary years of waiting for their loved ones just begun;
Ne'er a man fell backward stricken, but the bleeding wound he bore
Was felt by someone waiting on some far-removed shore.

They had no glow of battle such as spurred us on our way,
In a wearying inaction they must pass away each day;
No torment, hardship, hunger, no heat, nor thirst, nor cold,
But they who waited learned it, and felt with us fourfold.

And some have felt the passing of some beloved soul,
Where shrapnel cracked above us, or where Jutland's waters roll;
And some are waiting, waiting with anxious weary brain,
And fearing, praying, hoping with dull soul-searching pain.

Then here's my tribute to them, high or lowly, rich or poor,
The Women of our Empire who have helped us win the war;
To mothers, wives and sweethearts, from every mother's son,
To the Women of our Empire from the 'man behind the gun'.

*Lt S. D. Leslie*
*A. A. Pay Corp AIF*
*(AWM 2 DRL 435)*

## Safe and Well

When you're suckin' at your pencil
And you don't know what to say
When you wish the bloody censor
Hadn't seen the light of day,
There's always one small item left
Considered good to tell
It doesn't take much writing,
    "Dear Mum, I'm safe and well."

The tucker may be 'onkus',
The water pretty crook
You haven't had a drink of beer
Since Wavell took Tobruk,
You've been up before the skipper
For being AWL.
But take your pen and write it down:
    "Dear Mum, I'm safe and well."

You may have beard the Jerry bomber
Come screaming overhead,
And it wasn't very pleasant
To be dodging lumps of lead,
When you're lying in the trenches
'Midst hail of shot and shell
You still have time to send a line –
    "Dear Mum, I'm safe and well."

A grey haired Mother standing
Beside an old bush track
Waiting for the mailman
For news of soldier, Jack,
A smile lights up her worried face
With beauty words can't tell
As she reads the dear familiar words:
    "Dear Mother, I'm safe and well."

*Anon*
*(AWM PR 00526)*

## Soldiers' Dream

Leaning on my rifle
As I do my two hour shift,
Not very regimental
But my thoughts can't help but drift.

And I dream of my home town
And the girl I left behind,
The days we spent together
Keep running through my mind.

I see fair Sydney Harbour
And the happy carefree throng,
The ferry boat to Manly
And surfing all day long.

The rocks and hills and mountains,
The miles of sun drenched plains,
While golden fields of wheat await
The coming of the rains.

Someday I'll stop my dreaming
Of that far land far away,
For I'll be in fair Australia:
I'll be home to stay.

*Anon*
*(AWM PR 00526)*

## *Untitled*

When this cruel war is over
    And I'm starting home once more
I can see you waiting, Darling,
    On the good old Aussie shore.

When I go to sleep, my precious,
    In dreams your face I see,
For I live in hopes and memories
    For you're all the world to me.

As I go on down life's pathway
    In struggles, war and strife,
I'll be back again, I hope, dear
    For you're my own sweet darling wife.

*Dvr W.T. White (?)*
*(AWM PR 87 175)*

## *An Old Faded Picture*

There's an old faded picture hanging on our wall,
It's ancient paper mottled with no print left at all,
The scene is of lost days, with beauty that's still,
Of a tank on a stand, plus a lone windmill.

The mill has a shroud of hard red rust
That matches the colour of the local dust,
Now the tank is empty, the stand is rotten,
The water trough gone, and all but forgotten.

But the scene wasn't always of rust and of still
For once they were shining the tank and the mill,
As they worked together by day and by night
To man and beast a most wonderful sight.

Now there are many memories but very few lingers,
The rest run away like sand through old fingers;
There's an old faded picture hanging on our wall
It's ancient paper mottled. with no print left at all.

*Tim Lawrance*
*20 August 1990*

## *Forgetting*

Forget You ? Well perhaps I may
Forget the very charming way
You smile, and then perhaps I might
Forget your eyes, your walk, your height.

Somehow I even may forget
The way you hold a cigarette
So carelessly, and who can tell
I may forget your voice as well.

With nonchalance and *sans* regret
All these things I might forget,
But the task too difficult to do
Would be forgetting – I Love You.

*Cpl M. M. Carroll*
*(AWM PR 00544)*

## *Our Parting*

In this land so hot and sultry
With its rain and heavy dew
With its tin and rice and rubber
Here I sit and dream of you.

I often see you as we parted
How you smiled to hide the tear,
How you played your heart with courage
How I loved you then, my dear.

I tried to hide my feelings
With a carefree jovial air —
You must have thought me heartless
And that I ceased to care.

But just behind the reckless smile
I fought a bitter fight,
I felt the pangs of parting
As you did, Dear, that night.

I felt the tempter at my side,
To me he spoke quite clear
He said "The price you're asked to pay
Is costing you too dear!"

But if I had but turned my head
And "Yes!" to him had said
Unworthy of you I'd have been —
'Twere better I were dead.

I know you miss me every hour,
For me each night you pray,
I know you long for my return
Though long and rough the way.

But if to you I cannot come
With honour, head held high,
I know you will remember me
Our love could never die.

So as I think of you each night
I pray with all my heart
That we will reunited be
When we have played our part.

*Jimmy Dickinson*
*2 AASC AIF Malaya*
*Killed in action 14 February 1942*
*(AWM 3 DRL 6768A)*

## *Take this Message*

Take this message to my Mother
Far across the deep blue sea
It will fill her heart with pleasure
She will be glad to hear from me.
How she wept when last we parted,
How it filled her heart with pain
And she said "Goodbye, God bless you,
We may never meet again!"

Take this message to my Mother,
It is filled with words of joy
Tell her that her prayers are answered
God protects her little boy,
Tell her to be glad and cheerful
And pray for me where'er I roam,
And ere long I turn my footsteps
Back toward my dear old home.

Take this message to my Mother
It is filled with words of love,
If on earth I ne'er shall see her
Tell her we shall meet above,
Where there is no hour of parting
All is peace and love and joy.
God will bless my dear old Mother
And protect her absent boy.

*Anon*

## *There's a Land They Call Australia.*

There's a land they call Australia,
It's a land we love so well,
For it's there we learn to soldier
And Britain's Army swell.
    And often times when we're abroad
    Our thoughts will surely turn
    To Aussie, good old Aussie,
    In our hearts you'll brightly burn.

From this land they call Australia,
For twelve months now or more,
I've seen their bright and happy faces
Leave for a distant shore,
    The flower of Australia's manhood.
    With a job of work to do
    Leave their loved ones far behind them
    Just to help old England through.

From this land they call Australia
I've seen them come and go;
I've seen 'em fat and forty,
I've seen 'em just sixteen or so.
    Some were at the last one
    And they're to the fore again,
    For they're off again to this one
    Just to see if war's the same.

From this land they call Australia
To my mates I've bid adieu;
Pals you'd give your life for
'Cause they'd do the same for you:
    Tom and Jack, Frank and Bill
    Gosh, you know them too?
    They left their jobs and wives and sweethearts
    'Cause they were Diggers through and through.

And this land they call Australia
Some will see no more,
'Cause they gave their lives, their very all,
Like their fathers did before;
    But to their mates and pals whose luck has held
    There's a debt you have to pay:
    So see you stand up to your task
    In the same Australian way.

And when this war is over
And Hitler's met the fate he's earned,
We'll meet again in Aussie,
Those of us that have returned,
    And we'll stop and think a moment
    Of the mates and pals we loved,
    In the highest bloomin' possie
    In their last Camp up above.

*Will Handley*
*(AWM PR 85 205)*

## *Just a Dream*

I dreamt that I was home last night
And peace was here once more,
What a thrill it was to set foot once again
On dear old Aussie shores.

Gee! back home again! it was hard to believe
With Port Melbourne just the same,
I vowed right there on the wharf, they could keep all their wars –
I'd never leave Aussie again.

They were there in their thousands to meet us,
Cheering and screaming like hell,
And I turned to my mate on the boat rail and said,
"Boy, isn't this swell!"

Then I sighted Mum, and the rest of the family,
The tears just streamed down my face,
For the day that I dreamed of at last had arrived
And I longed for her loving embrace.

Then they let down the gangway;
The crowd with excitement went mad
The greatest moment of my life was here at last:
"My Mum! My Dad!"

They showered me with all sorts of questions
About places I want to forget,
For the war was over for me at last,
And by hell there were no regrets.

Then we left the scene of excitement
With its happiness, laughter, and tears
And made straight for Young and Jackson's,
Where we knocked down several beers.

The bar was full of laughter
As the boys told their narrow-squeak tales,
With a big pot of Carlton in one hand
And their foot once again on the rail.

At last we arrived at the home town
And a lump sort of grew in my throat,
She's the same as the day we waved her goodbye,
As we left on our way to the boat.

Then the band struck up on the station,
In a sec I was out of the train,
There were handshakes, streamers, and shouting
As they welcomed us home once again.

Then I pushed through the crowd on the station,
Through the gate and out on the street –
Then I felt someone tap on my shoulder,
"Wake up Dig, it's your turn on the beat."

*Will Handley*
*(AWM PR 85 205)*

## *My Father*

What were his thoughts as he lay in his bed,
His only part visible, his grey, ruffled head;
He could think of today, and also the morrow,
Of lots of laughs, or a little sorrow.

He could have been King,
But he wasn't in line,
Instead, just a man –
Upright and fine.

*Tim Lawrance*
*28 May 1989*

## *You*

You are the wind that fills my sails,
The star that guides my way,
The oasis in this desert,
The smell of the forest after the rain.

You are the stillness of dawn,
The brilliance of its shafts of light,
You are like the dew in the morning that sparkles,
You are my bay for the storm that I'm in.

Your hair is like the flowing golden sand,
Your eyes reflect your nature: gentle and understanding,
Your mouth invites my kisses every time I see it,
Your skin is smooth and delicate like that of a peach.

The way you move is like the calming of the waves on a tropical shore
You give me sanctuary, happiness and, yes, that damn smile!

*Capt. Danny Lea*

## *A Letter from Home*

When you're sitting in your dugout with your chin upon your hand
And your thoughts are ever flitting to that golden, far-off land,
When the dusty wind is blowing, and all is grit and sand,
What's the thing that bucks you up and makes you feel just grand?
    A letter from home.

When air battles are araging and all is noise and din
And you're feeling tired and dusty, and just about all in,
Your hand goes to your pocket, gropes and finds the thing you seek
And you read it over once again, though you've had it for a week:
    That letter from home.

When the air is full of Stukas, and the bombs are dropping fast
And the ack-ack guns are blazing and the Spitfires roaring past,
And the Navy's guns are booming out, bombarding from the sea,
When you reach the base you're heading for, you wonder if there'll be –
    A letter from home.

So don't forget to write to him, he loves to hear the news,
And it's sure to cheer him up and drive away those blues;
It's better far than any leave he's likely to obtain,
Please do remember, get your pen, and write him once again:
    A letter from home.

*Anon*
*(AWM PR 87/062)*

## Storied Trails

The dust swells from the sun-drenched road
    And billows in the bush scented breeze
'Tis the same torn track the sundowner strode
    To the tune of the wind in the trees.

It winds ever onward and over the hill
    Through the gums and gullies and all;
It passes the shack and the silent mill,
    Which oft saw the sundowner call.

Gone is the man with the dog at his heels
    And friendly greeting for all;
Along the old track sounds the piper's reels
    And the brazen war bugle's call.

Where his camp fire gleamed at night
    'Neath the clear and starry sky
Myriad lanterns twinkle bright
    And a sentry paces nigh.

Comes the stamp of marching feet
    And the suntanned ranks swing by,
Three by three with ringing beat
    That causes the dust to fly.

The mirages dance on the road ahead
    And nary a man but feels
That he is treading the steps of one long dead,
    The man with the dog at his heels.

*Anon*
*(AWM PR 87/062)*

## *To Cairns*

Immortal Cairns, gem of our northern seas!
Living green is found on every side our tired eyes to please,
Young peaks thrust proud heads to sapphire-tinted skies
And sparkling rivers downward flow to where the sun doth rise.

Oh, balmy spot! where winter's icy finger ne'er can reach,
Where southern sleet cold and snow are not;
Miles of waving cane nod soft heads in the lazy, friendly breeze
While red-roofed cottages nestle safely under Queensland's lovely trees.

On thy eastern side in rolls the great Pacific o'er
The coral barrier that ever rose from ocean floor;
Here the lordly sun each day spreads his golden fruitfulness,
Enriching thee, immortal Cairns, gem of our northern seas!

*Ernest H. Graham*
*(AWM PR 82 056)*

## *To Queensland*

Oh, loveliest of all our states
The fairest jewel in Federal Crown
Set in sapphire seas,
Guardian from our enemies in tragic days like these!

Land of rugged mountains,
Rich in timber wealth,
Wherein the deep, wide river
Crocodiles wait in stealth.

There miles of waving cane
Nod their head in friendly breeze,
Golden corn grown tall as fence posts
Fringed by Queensland's mighty trees.

Herds of browsing cattle red,
White and charcoal black.
Graze happily, contentedly
In this wonder state's outback.

Well-bred Merinos
And sturdy Corriedales
Live upon the stations
Filling sovereigns into bales.

Birds of gorgeous plumage,
Fish of every hue,
Bask in your golden sunshine
Amid the skies of blue.

Oh, Queensland in the brilliant future
Which, for Australia we can see,
Thou shalt lead the states in glory
To a great prosperity!

*Ernest H. Graham.*
*(AWM PR 82 056)*

## The Chicago of the West

Oh Dubbo, thou hast grown from tiny acorn
To mighty oak tree green,
While five-and-ninety years have passed
Beside Macquarie's silvered stream.

Along the willow-studded banks
Where now a large white bridge doth stand,
Many a hardy pioneer camped
Before selecting out his land.

Six busy lines of shining steel
Radiate from out your pulsing heart,
Where only yesterday many bullock teams
Had place to make their start.

Powerful locomotives,
The giants of the road,
Now carry Dubbo citizens
Into Sydney's mighty fold.

There wheat, the king of all the grasses,
The food supplier in our land,
Rises tall and strong and golden
Over all that eye can span.

Over Dubbo's tree-clothed mountains
And rich but dusty plains
Sheep roam almost unmolested
Until shearing season reigns.

Then wool, our cloth supplier, pours gold into many bales.
Oh Dubbo! the finest, busiest town in all the west,
With many beauteous treasures
We know that thou art blest.

In the dim and distant future
When other towns shall fade,
I know that thou shall blossom into greatness
Perhaps becoming the Metropolis of the West.

*Gnr E. H. Graham,*
*Cairns*
*(AWM PR82056)*

## *Our Wild Orchid*

Have you seen our wild orchid, with fragrance not,
 It's found in the most secluded spot
On the floor of our bush; it's seldom seen,
 For it's ever so tiny, with sparse foliage of green.

And when it does flower, the joy it can bring –
 But remember it's Autumn and never the Spring,
With its colour of brown, on a two inch stem;
 It's hands and knees, to discover them.

So if you are lucky and look quite steady.
 I think you'll find that there's one ready
To be looked at and studied, and left well alone.
 For our tiny wild orchid, the bush is its home.

*Tim Lawrance*
*27 April 1981*

## *The Australian Scene*

An azure mass of mountains and the swiftly flowing stream,
This thin veil of the cascade sparkling out among the green;
The tall giants of the forest holding proud heads on high
And the silken strands of whitened clouds as they go passing by.

The brilliant pools of coral where pretty fishes swim and twist and turn,
And the radiant orbed sun on the placid ocean burns;
Miles and miles of black soil plain, dotted with many sheep,
And tiny cosy cottages nestling beneath the mountains steep.

Giant snow gums of our mighty Alps, their stark white figures show,
And winding western rivers down to their ocean flow;
Exotic orchids spread their colours in the darkest jungle depths,
And the red, raw sand of inland over our broad brown land is swept.

You may have any country in south or northern clime.
But our love for dear Australian Scenes shall endure for all time.

*Ernest H. Graham*
*Rocky Creek, June 1944*
*(AWM PR 82 056)*

## *My Mum and Dad*

From the earliest age I can remember, their love and their care and concern,
They showed me the beauty of nature and all of the things I should learn.

They taught me to know good from evil, they taught me to do right, not wrong,
They taught me to hate the devil, and to praise our God in song.

I'd think of the parents of other kids and wonder, with a sense of pride,
Why God, so generously, bestowed on me the best Mum and Dad worldwide.

Although I failed to appreciate them (growing boys have other things on their minds)
My own kids (and grand kids) have taught me the breadth of their love's not outshined.

From the smallest of things in the nursery to the biggest decisions I've made
Their influence always to guide me will help me to make the grade.

I am no giant or genius of science or art or fame,
As a good man I hope to be remembered and never to bring them shame.

And now as they bask in their autumn, they can look back and feel content
Their children they raised free and happy, which I'm sure was God's intent.

And when they meet our maker, surely high on the list of St Pete
Mum and Dad's name will be highlighted: 'Reserved – to sit at God's feet'.

For certain, in doing God's wishes, as parents they have excelled,
Nothing less than the highest honours, for the duties they've done so well.

In this day and age, unaccepted, for grown men to express their love,
But for them I would make this exception, for the sake of heaven above.

For I'd tell God that he has no worries, nor concerns for these parents of mine,
Their work is a constant example – as parents, their names will shine.

To say "I love you" is simple, and it doesn't seem so much,
Just three little words in English that, hopefully, God's heart will touch.

There is no end to this poem, with gratitude in every line
For their love will go on forever – forever, till the end of time.

*WO2 Paul Barrett*

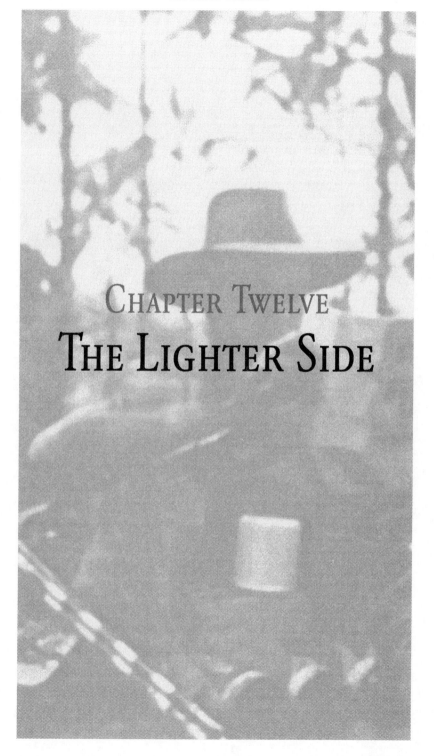

CHAPTER TWELVE
# THE LIGHTER SIDE

## *Just Another Aussie*

If he's tall and tanned and strong
And wears a careless grin
That's a 'come on', for the smarties –
He always gets them in.
And if he wants to bet you
Anything, medium, small or big,
You'll know he is an Aussie,
Better known as Dig.

If some well-known speaker
Is to lecture on the air,
And at that time they broadcast
The hounds are chasing a hare,
And you see a fellow switch on
To the dogs, well you can twig
That he's just another Aussie
Better known as Dig.

If the guns are roaring
And the enemy is in sight
He will plough right through the bloody lot
And ask you for a light.
For drought and dust and danger
He doesn't care a fig,
Cause he's just another Aussie,
Better known as Dig.

Whether it's in Egypt
Or any place inferior,
An Aussie is an Aussie
With plenty of interior.
He'll grin and he will bet you
With his mouth half full of cig,
And if he loses he will say:
*Mahfeesh*! good on you Dig!

*Anon*
*(AWM PR 00526)*

### *Untitled*

Only one more marching order
Only one more sick parade
Only one more kit inspection
And of that we're not afraid.

When this bloody war is over
Oh! How happy we will be;
We will tell our Sergeant Major
He can go – to Werribee.

*Bdr S. J. Lynch*
*(AWM MSS 1557)*

## *A Day at the Office*

Have you ever been in an Orderly Room
And studied the Clerk's routine?
No! then come along to the 48th,
Here is the opening scene:

It's situated near a stream
A number of miles from Lae,
It's not exactly an artist's dream
But here we'll stage the play.

Have you ever seen an aviary
With a gable roof on top?
Yes? We'll nail a sign 'A Office' up
And that's where we play shop.

The time is almost nine o'clock
The Sarge knows what to expect,
The Adj walks in with piles of bumph,
And the usual "type this next".

The sun climbs up in the heavens,
The minutes go fleeting on,
The little Sergeant heaves a sigh
And yells for Tonk and Don.

Faint murmurings are heard nearby
Then voices speak without,
And in they walk those clerical guys
With a "what's all the panic about?"

Don looks spruce with his whiskers off,
Every day it's considered too cruel,
Grizzles our Tonk with an injured air
"Why Don, you've broken the rule!"

Down they squat as they heave a sigh,
Says Don "it's time for a smoke."
They roll their fags with a studied grace,
And Tonk starts to crack a joke

The Sergeant gives a disgusted look
For the joke is really taboo,
He rummages around the various files
And finds them something to do.

An oath from Tonk as his screwdriver prods
Into the back of the old machine,
As he backs the spacer and thumps the bar
And tinkers with parts unseen.

Don sets to work with the roll on his knees,
And marches men in and out,
He checks the strengths of Company rolls
And his pen starts scratching about.

When Saturday dawns so bright and fair
There are Field Returns to do;
The Sgt struggles with figures of men
And thinks them all bally-hoo.

Work proceeds at a steady pace
Till the typewriter seems to be stuck;
The Sgt peers o'er the typist's shoulder
And finds he has overstruck.

He says to Tonk "Don't spare the rubber,",
ays Tonk "Looks good paper to me."
But at him is thrown an eraser,
For the Returns the Old Man must see.

Time goes on the work eases off,
Some letters the boys start to pen.
Don writes some pages to Mother
While Tonk ear bashes to Gwen.

They say to the Sarge about tea time
"You've worked us to death all day,
You can pull your silly-gig head in,
We're giving the game away!"

And so the curtain closes,
On the overworked! happy! three!
Each day is the same in the Orderly Room –
Come again some time and see.

*GB*

## *The Ninth Div Grand Final*

'Twas the day of the football premiership
    The Ninth Div final grand
When the 48th met the Cavalry
    Way up on the Tablelands.

The Tricolours were the favourites
    With better form as a guide,
Although the gallant Blue and Whites
    Are a never-beaten side.

And they proved it so, at the epic end
    Of a game that will never die
When they won the match with a well-earned goal
    Ere the final bell rang nigh.

From the start it looked the cavalry
    Would take the ridge hands down,
For playing in a flawless style
    They put the Blues to ground.

High marking safe and brilliantly
    To dominate the air
With driving kicks, from end to end
    They triumphed everywhere.

For though the 48th strove hard
    Their run to grimly stay,
They could not match the brilliance of
    The Cav's grand open play.

Goal after goal they rattled on:
    Again, and yet again,
The 'Troopers' scored to shade the Blues,
    Who battled on in vain.

(Or so did seem) till came half time
    When of that break in need
The '4-bar-8s' were six goals down
    Oh! what a heartbreak lead.

But few have known just really when
    The 48th were beat,
For when their chance looks at its worst
    They're hardest to defeat.

And once again it proved this day
    For fighting grimly back
The Blue and Whites came back to win
    Upon a hopeless track.

Right through to 'lemons' hard they held
    The dashing Cavalry
As inch by inch they slowly gained
    With dour tenacity.

Yea (spite of all) at 'lemons' still
    The Cav by four goals led,
Full well the '4-bar-8' men knew
    The task which lay ahead.

So when the final term commenced
    Straight from the starting bell
The Blues went in to do or die
    And played the game like hell.

Though hard the rattled Tricolours
    Tried everything they knew
To stem the tide; relentlessly
    Surged on the 'White and Blue'.

Time after time into attack
    With telling drives they came,
And paralysed the Cav's defence
    By closing up the game.

With deadly kicking, true but sure,
    Their score crept upwards slow –
Three points behind, a goal to win –
    Five minutes left to go!

Then ere the bell rings Smithy marks
    A few yards out of goals,
"I hope he gets it!" "May he miss!"
    Implore some thousand souls.

As midst a silence deathly still,
    His screw-punt neatly spun
Between the sticks: comes cheering shrill –
    The 48th had won!

*Anon*

## *Much Ado About Nothing*

The 48th is in disgrace for robbing an Itie nob:
Some rascal snatched a Colonel's watch, worth about two bob.

It surely was an awful deed; in the Army it's just not done,
And I suppose until they find it, no victory can be won.

They've looked in all the pawn shops from Alex to Aleppo
But not a sign can anyone find of that imitation 'Sheppo'.

Kit inspections have been held, they've questioned every man,
Tried various ways to dig it up, but b – d if they can.

To find Scirrocco's timepiece is more important than the front
All the best brains in the Army are joining in the hunt.

They're trying hard to find it and I've a strong suspicion
I wouldn't be a bit surprised if that was Churchill's mission.

The search goes on from day to day; morning, noon and night,
But seems the old wop's done it in – the watch has gone alright.

Perhaps some joker wogged it and went out on the shicker
And that would be the proper thing to do with that old ticker.

For I'll tell you my opinion of all this bloody rot,
They could stop this cranky racket if that Itie mug was shot:

For I don't suppose they questioned him or looked in his valise
For the food those Dago b – s took from starving kids in Greece.

I don't suppose they asked him, who took our comrades' lives,
Took away those good Australians leaving sorrowing kids and wives.

No, they'll see that he is comfortable and treat him like a toff,
While the people home are paying us to kill the b – s off.

*Anon*

## *Army Pay*

I'm but a bloomin' private,
One of the simple kind,
It's not that I'm a moaner,
But there's something on my mind;
    Even if you think me thankless,
    I still must have my say,
    I find that I am always broke
    With a dollar for my pay.

It's not that I am sorry
That I joined to win this war;
My pocket is always empty,
I'd like a little more.
    Nearly all Australian soldiers
    Have their pint of beer each day,
    I find I can't afford it
    On my paltry army pay.

Perhaps you'll say I knew it
When I volunteered to join,
And I only have myself to blame
For any lack of coin;
    And to be quite truthful,
    I don't regret the day
    That I signed on the dotted line
    To work for army pay.

The way I use the rifle
Causes quite a fuss,
They say I must be cross-eyed
And I couldn't hit a bus;
    My shots all miss the target,
    From the bull they're far away,
    But I line up with the marksmen
    For my paltry army pay.

When we have a route march
My feet both ache and pain,
To make conditions perfect
It always starts to rain.
 The pack gets very heavy
 And makes my shoulders sway,
 I stagger back exhausted
 To get my paltry pay.

I look back with amusement,
When I, a raw recruit,
Marched around in circles
In a brand new khaki suit.
 Although those days are distant
 And I have sailed away,
 My income hasn't altered –
 I'm on the same old pay.

*Raymond John Colenso*
*(AWM PR 00689)*

## Nil Illegitimi Carborundum

We knew he was a wrong 'un when he got on to the ship,
For he had no dignity at all and gave us all the pip
When he handed out our telegrams like an awful office boy,
And by his manner acted as if he gave each child a toy.

Then he started on the tannoy. God! How I hate his voice
"Pay attention everybody." He'd be hung by public choice
When he speaks his futile rubbish and we laugh behind our hand,
As it's only through senility he got his scarlet band.

His idea of being a Commandant is to keep things hush, the drip,
As he would be quite depressed if we were happy on the trip.
He only says, "You can't do this," he never says you can,
Which is only just what every girl used once to say to man.

He said "No leave at Freetown," which didn't matter much,
But the same thing said at Capetown had quite a different touch.
"There is danger on the small boats, as the weather is so rough."
But when it calmed next morning the airmen called his bluff.

Those that hadn't left the night before to buy things for their wife
Took the waterboat for Capetown to have some fun and strife;
The Old Boy nearly had a fit and 'Staff' warned all concerned
That any sailor who broke ship would quickly be interned.

But this only caused more laughter and decided all the boys
To go and see the Capetown Folk and taste the city's joys;
Even Royal Naval Sailors, who seldom flout the law,
Joined the happy throng in hundreds and with cheers pulled for the shore.

So the Navy still can take it, leave I mean, not tyrant stuff,
And their thumbs went to their nostrils at the Commandant's cheap bluff;
In the meantime the old blighter, who found he had no power,
Crept in shame into his cabin, where he moaned for hour on hour.

So a happy trip was stonkered by a blurry bureaucrat
Just a silly senile fellow, who will get a bowler hat,
For we've warned the old War Office and Australia's got the tip
That no Aussie troops will travel with this CO on a ship.

If Captain Bligh was Commandant, we'd have known just where we stood,
But now we just get mucked about and know nothing that we should;
We'll soon forget because of all the fun we've had together,
So 'Here's to' home and those we love in sunny Aussie weather.

*Anon*
*(AWM PR 83 198)*

## "If"... A Version for Land Girls

*(With apologies to Rudyard Kipling and in appreciation of England's Land Army.*

If you can keep your feet when snow still lingers
And paths are skating rinks of solid rain;
If you can pick wet sprouts with frozen fingers
And fill two trugs, unheedful of the pain;
If you can force each tired and aching sinew
To lift you from your warm and cosy bed
And sally forth without a morsel in you
To misty mangled field or gloomy shed;
If, with a cheerful face and lips unpouting
You can dig potatoes from ice-cold mud;
If you can call until you're hoarse with shouting
For cows you thought were calmly chewing cud
And track them down at last in someone's garden,
Employed in crushing beetroots in the ground,
Then humbly beg the hostile owners pardon
And drive them home without an angry sound;
If, when you're scything grass, you find there lying
Sickles, shears and other worn out tools,
Things that chip your scythe and send you flying,
Left there by knaves to make a trap for fools,
Yet never lose your patience for a minute or
Though your sun-baked head is in a whirl –
Yours is the earth (and the insects in it)
And ... what is more ... you'll be a saint, my girl.

*Anon*
*(AWM PR 84 286)*

## *The Lass's Lament*

No use looking bloody coy,
Can't even catch a bloody boy,
Life is robbed of bloody joy,
Oh bloody, bloody. bloody!

When this bloody war is won,
Perhaps we'll get some bloody fun,
Been living like a bloody nun,
Oh bloody, bloody, bloody!

Tired of talking to bloody ladies,
Of what the latest bloody shade is,
They can go to bloody Hades,
Oh bloody, bloody, bloody!

Waiting round for bloody letters,
Knitting piles of bloody sweaters,
Better if the Nazis get us,
Oh bloody, bloody, bloody!

*Anon*

## My Old Brown Hat

It hasn't got roller brim, it shows no shiny nap,
It sports no fancy ribbons, just a weather beaten strap;
It never swanked around the block to give the girls a treat
It's not the kind of nifty lid they'd stand in Collins Street;
It's nothing like the jumping jack you wear with evening dress,
It was never foaled by Woodrow, and it never heard of tress;
You wouldn't call it just the juicy onion for the play,
Nor the thing to hook a clue with on the bridge on Henley Day;
    It would be a hellish compliment to call it homely brown,
    But it's one side's cocked up handsome when it isn't hanging down;
    It has served through forty climates up from Collingwood to Leith,
    And it fits the frosty dial that is grinning underneath
    It's stopped a brace of bullets (it has also missed a few)
    It's my dingy, dinkum cobber, for I've never liked them new,
    So cut it out, and never think a bloke has got a rat,
    When he says "I love you like I do MY OLD BROWN HAT".

We was hell and all in Cairo, where our notions of the law
Was mostly wrote with knuckles on the population's jaw;
And coming up one evening – there were three of us – and gay,
I bumped a filthy nigger in a dirty alleyway;
He slung opinions round him with a shocking lack of tone,
So I handed him a hefty one across the dizzy bone.
He pulled a knife and yelled and then, with twenty seconds gone,
The father and mother of a blooming mix was on,
    We was back to wall and dicky till some cobbers took a share,
    And the sight of our old brown brims was the thing that brought them there;
    And only for me twisting as the blow came humming down,
    For this scar upon my shoulder I'd have worn an angel's crown;
    I was half an inch from heaven – twig the cut upon the brim –
    So I'll keep it, a memento, till I sing my parting hymn,
    Till the left of time has feinted and the right has biffed me flat,
    And for a halo afterwards, MY OLD BROWN HAT.

I took it out to Anzac, where I duly humped it from,
And I wore it for a diadem when fluttering to the Somme;
We found a front line sector, and we hadn't hardly come,
When Fritzie showed a sign which read 'Australians Welcome Home';
We weren't out to disappoint, we had a sense of fair,
We were grateful for the welcome, and we handed back a share;
We deal him good and plenty, and I think he understands,
There's other uses for your dooks apart from shaking hands;
    For we served Australian Cocktail (and the Cocktail had a kick)
    They were out for *dinge*, and *dicken* but they didn't get a stick,
    The papers called us Titans (and it's crook to hear the same)
    But the strange hats we wore, 'twas them that made the name;
    But I'm tipping Fritz's talent, till the setting of the sun,
    Will recall our fruity language and the nasty things we done,
    When we hooked them on the earhole, and we biffed them on the slat,
    Oh, they won't forget their intro to the MY OLD BROWN HAT.

When a bloke has had a blighty and he's fit to get about,
And a hint of London sunshine brings the London titters out;
The first thing that he'll notice, and the second too, perhaps,
Is the way the glad eye hovers on us khaki-clobbered chaps,
For they've seen it in the papers (which its name's not truthful James)
That we're Galahads and Heroes, and a hundred other names,
And it's no use disclaiming, for the paper blokes in town,
They've made our reputation, and we'll have to live it down;
    A Yorkshire or a Hampshire, or a baggy boy in blue,
    They're good and all to catch a skirt, and most of them have two;
    But the thing that snares the optic of the gushing feminine,
    It's not the haughty Guardsman with a picket up his spine,
    Or it's not the budding Captain with his little toothbrush mo,
    And I've wondered hard and often, you can search me if I know,
    If the thing that bowls them gently and that takes them off the bat,
    Is the lanky brown Australian in his OLD BROWN HAT.

The service cap is handy when a chap is going flash
And the helmet's most convenient when you're scoffing soup or hash;
But my dinkum shady brimmer, you can take your blooming oath,
Is worth ten ton of either, or a paddock full of both;
Its tint may strike you silly, and its outline make you laugh,
It's not a chic confection or a flaming photograph,
Its hang would send you pippy, and its shape would make you sore;
There's a hole or two about it, which I've hinted at before,
    But it kept the sun at Mena off my dainty little head,
    It has heard my prayers for guidance, and other things I've said,
    It has stood me for a pillow when I laid me down to sleep,
    When the earth was mostly water and the mud was four feet deep;
    And I think perhaps this reason makes us like as we do,
    They're what blokes pick us out by, and they breathe of home and you,
    Oh, home that makes me love you, and my heart goes pit-a-pat,
    How you'll greet me, when you meet me, in MY OLD BROWN HAT.

*Anon*
*(AWM PR 91 104)*

## *The Old Tin Hat*

Smart in spats is Tommy Atkins
His suit of khaki dressed,
On the Strand or Piccadilly
He can swank it with the rest.

But when out on shell-swept Flanders
Where bullets ping and spat
You will find each fighting soldier
Wears an old tin hat.

In the days of courtly gallants
When fair chivalry held sway,
Stately knights to win fair ladies
Oft would meet in open fray.

But in trench, shell-hole or dugout
Where nowadays our men lie flat,
You will find each gallant hero
Wears an old tin hat.

Fighting Mac arrayed in kilties
And tam-o'-shanter cap
To the sound of swirling bagpipes
Would fight with vim and snap.

But in these days of 'whizz-bangs',
Five-point-nine and things like that,
You will find each Jock and Sandy
Wears an old tin hat.

From the land of wattle blossom
Waratah and Kangaroo,
Bill and Jim with rousing cooee
Come sailing across the blue.

He is no parade ground soldier
And not half a diplomat,
But he looks a dinkum Digger
In his old tin hat.

Uncle Sam has lots of soldiers
(And gee whizz they are some guys)
To the strains of '*Yankee Doodle*'
They have marched where victory lies,

With Old Glory o'er them flying
Britain's foes they now combat,
And every Yankee soldier
Wears an old tin hat.

When the roll is called up yonder
And the soldier says goodbye,
Leaving good old '*Terra Firma*'
For the mansion in the skies,

When he meets old St Peter
Who is waiting on the mat
He may say when asked the password –
Why! My old tin hat!

*Anon*
*(AWM PR 00526)*

## *The Song of the Gremlins*

When you're seven miles up in the heavens
It's a hell of a lonely spot
And it's fifteen degrees below zero
Which isn't so very hot,

It's then you see the Gremlins
Green, gamboge and gold,
Male, female and neuter,
Gremlins both young and old;

White ones will waggle your wing-tips,
Male ones will muddle your maps,
Green ones will guzzle your glycol,
And females will flutter your flaps,

They'll bind you and they'll break you and they'll batter
And break through your aileron wires,
And as you orbit to pancake
Stick hot toasting forks in your tyres.

*Chaplain D. Trathen*
*(AWM PR 00218)*

## *Thanks for the Memory*

*(With apologies to the writer of the song of that name)*

Thanks for the memory
Of Wallgrove's canvas camp,
of days in mud and damp,
And sneaking in at two to find some cow has pinched your lamp.
    How lovely it was.

Thanks for the memory
Of Ingleburn and huts,
the Unit now has guts,
When every spare hour found us picking up matches and butts.
    I thank you so much.

Many a march in the moonlight,
Crawling to Camp about midnight,
An MO's parade, p'raps a blue-light,
    A night in town, without a brown,

So thanks for the memory
When Bathurst was in reach,
a night with some sweet peach,
Then twenty in a taxi but still charged a deener each.
    I thank you so much.

Thanks for memory,
Of two-up games on board,
till 'Black-Out' whistles roared,
Of getting drunk on two bob, if two bob we could afford.
    How lovely it was.

Thanks for the memory
Of lovely tropic moons,
of bully-beef and prunes,
And strolling round the prom deck in our tropic pantaloons.
    I thank you so much.

Then after two weeks water
And thoughts of a cow-cocky's daughter,
I shouldered my gear like a porter
And tramped with my load
    A mile upon the road,

And thanks for the memory
Of breakfast on the train,
a route march in the rain –
But now the trip's a memory and we're back at work again
    So thank you, so much.

*'Pic'*
*(AWM PR 00074)*

## *Untitled*

*(To the tune:- Road to Gundagai)*

There's a tent in the grass
That you'll always have to pass
Along the road to the 116,
Where the RPs are looking,
To see what there is cooking
Around the AAMWS Lines.
They'd like to catch us creeping
Up through the field,
But we know our onions
And keep well concealed,
So RP if you do ever catch up with me,
I'll give you the DFC.

There were times when you dozed
And we crept right past your nose,
So early in the morn,
After driving in staff cars
And riding in Jeeps,
Boy, if you'd seen us,
How you would weep,
'Cause you'd failed to report
All the things that you ought,
Along the road to the 116.

Now RP don't you see
That it's best that we go free
To wander as we please.
You'll never catch us,
Try as you may,
For we've been old soldiers
For more than a day
So go back to your bed.
And pull in your bloomin' head,
Along the road to the 116!

(P.S. The RP said when he caught us he would write the final verse.
It was never written!)

*Written by nurses at 116 AGH Cairns*
*(AWM PR 88 019)*

## The VAD's 'If'

If you can work all day without your make up,
Your snappy hair-do hidden 'neath your veil;
If you can serve up umpteen dozen dinners
Then wait on Matron without turning pale;
If you can wash the everlasting dishes
And then turn round and wash the trolley too.
And when your mess jobs are all finished
Polish up your hut until it shines like new;
If you can track down elusive orderlies,
And make them help you, when they'd rather shirk;
If you can run on countless errands for the Sister,
And still be up to date with all your work;
If you can make the orange drinks and egg-flips,
About the diets knowing all there is to tell,
And get the MO's morning tea, and heat the poultice.
And maybe sponge a man or two as well;
If you can take a 'ticking off' from Matron
And realize she doesn't mean it – much!
If you can bear to see your rec leave vanish,
When you thought you had it safely in your clutch;
If you can take the trials and tribulations,
The good times and the bad, all in your stride;
If you can do all this and keep good tempered,
Then you're not a bloomin' VAD
But a saint who hasn't died!

*From Ward 5, 2/12th AGH Warwick*
*Anon*
*(AWM PR 88 019)*

## *Only Wait Until You're Married*

My appearance before you may seem rather strange,
I've just come over here by way of exchange
With words of advice and good council to tell,
Likewise a warning and caution as well.

I laugh when I hear young blokes talk of their girl
With eyes bright as diamonds and teeth white as pearls,
Who think they are bliss with smiling so free
But just wait till you're married and then you'll see.

> Chorus: It's only wait till you're married my boys,
> It's only wait till you're married my boys,
> You single young men who go out on the spree
> Just wait till you're married, and then you'll see.

There is my wife's mother and mine can't hit it at all,
Whenever they meet there is a terrible ball,
It's my daughter a duke or earl might of won
Had she never met that young rascal your son.

Then the old one replies as a mother should do
They would get on alright if it were not for you,
Hard words come to blows and it ends in a fight
And the jolly old pair are locked up for the night.

Your joy is no more ended you rise in the morning
The nurse brings you word that the first boy is born;
But your mouth it suddenly has a decline
When your family increases from six to nine.

Now young ladies I hope you won't think me unkind,
If you think it's so bliss to have three on each knee –
Just wait until you are married and then you will see.

*C. T. Mealing*
*14 October 1900*
*(AWM PR 00752)*

### *The Engineers' Eclipse*
or 'The Downfall of the Duke'

Australia's Corps of Engineers
Throughout the world have known no peers,
Brave men of brawn and skill
They've proved their worth in desert sands,
In Greece's snows, and with bare hands
They conquered Syrian hill.

The scene has changed and now they're seen
In slimy swamp and jungle green
On Bougainvillean shore;
They've mastered bog and muddy ridge
With jeep, bulldozer road and bridge
A great and gallant Corps!

But came the long awaited day
Our Duke of Gloucester came to stay
A week with us at base
Then with their true magician's touch
The Engineers – from nothing much –
Soon housed his Royal Grace.

A regal bungalow abode
With mod cons *a la* jungle mode
No purist would rebuke,
Our Engineers gave of their best
To bless with peaceful perfect rest
His Grace, the Royal Duke.

And since all dukes and kings so high
Are cursed with bowels like you and I
The urgent need was seen
To build apart, alone, unsung,
Where modest vine and creeper hung,
The Duke's own bush latrine.

The Royal stomach gripped with pain
From dip and flip of wind-tossed plane
Soon made its message known,
And so behold his Royal Grace
With bulging eye and purpling face
Upon his jungle throne.

But, sad the tale, those Engineers
Had dabbled in excessive beers
The day they built this nest,
And dazed with much black-market grog
They failed to put each plank and log
To regulation test.

And so, as Gloucester strained amain,
Those timbers, undermined with rain,
Gave way with gleeful rush;
The Duke performed a backward bow
And to the startled ducal brow
Was dealt a Royal Flush.

The Brigadier looked swords of death,
The CRE drew frightened breath,
The Sapper Sergeant cried;
The Duke called for his private plane,
Flew off in constipated pain,
John Curtin groaned and died.

Which only goes to prove that though
Our Engineers beat rain and snow,
Beat sand and mountain pass,
No Engineer's plebeian brain
Could ever hope to gauge the strain
And the weight of the Royal –.

*'Black Bob'*
*Lt. A. L. O'Neill (?)*
*Bougainville*
*(AWM MSS 1328)*

## *Good Old Number Nine*

If your head is aching and your bones are sore,
And a cough tears your chest like a cross-cut saw.
P'raps it's bronchitis, consumption or gout,
Lumbago, neuritis – you're ill without doubt.

It may be the stomach, liver or flu,
The kidneys, digestion, heart trouble too;
A chill or a cold may have you in grip,
A touch of asthma or just the plain 'pip'.

A corn or a bunion may give you much pain,
It may be neuralgia or toothache again;
Rheumatics, anaemia or peritonitis,
Or only just common or garden tireditis.

Whatever your complaint, pray don't lose your head,
He cannot cure that, or a limb you have shed,
But it you have one of the aforementioned ills
The MO will cure you with Number Nine pills.

*Anon*

## *A Soldier's Dream*

He grabs me by my slender neck,
    I could not call or scream,
He dragged me to his darkened tent
    Where he could not be seen.

He took me from my flimsy wrap
    And gazed upon my form,
I was so scared, so cold, so damp,
    And he so delightfully warm.

His fevered lips he pressed on mine,
    I gave him every drop,
He took from me my very soul,
    I could not make him stop.

He made me what I am today,
    That's why you find me here:
A broken bottle thrown away,
    That once was full of beer.

*Anon*

## *The Digger*

I've dug holes fair dinkum, and dug them for fun,
I've dug them at night and beneath blazing sun.
I've dug little holes to protect infantry,
And awfully big ones for the blooming OC.
And holes for the Ack Ack, and holes for their shells,
And holes for the hygiene to bury their smells.
And holes around tents in case Stukas are seen,
And farther away for the Section latrine.
And the greatest event of my lifetime will be
When someone is detailed to dig one for me.

*Anon*
*(AWM PR 00526)*

## *The Singin' Diggers*

Now, I've bin nuts on poetry since I was just a kid,
The books o' verse I've bought 'ave corst me many a 'ard earned quid.
I've read *The Man from Snowy* an' ol' *Clancy* an' the rest,
An' Kendal, Lawson, Gordon. But of all of 'em the best
In my 'umble estimation (you might 'ave a different pick)

In a book I read by Dennis, called *The Moods of Ginger Mick*.
For Mick was jest a Digger with a dial 'ard as oak,
An' 'e writes home to 'is cobber – 'oo's the Sentimental Bloke –
An' tells 'im 'ow the Aussies sang on far Gallipoli,
An' socked it into Abdul to the toon of *Nancy Lee*.
'e tells 'im 'ow another mob, 'oo looked done-in for fair
When they stopped a damn torpedo, sang *Australia Will Be There*

An' bein' jest an Aussie kid, I sorter felt a thrill
To read such tales of glory, in these notes from Mick to Bill.
An' 'struth! I'm proud to think I 'ad a brother over there
'e couldn't sing for putty, but I bet 'e done 'is share
Of serenadin' Johnny Turk, an' later on ol' Fritz,
With snatches from the music 'all an' all the latest 'its.

Time mooches on. Our country now is in another blue,
An' this time I'm amongst the boys, for I'm a Digger, too.
I can see the same ol' spirit in the AIF today
That kept the Anzacs singin' in the thickest of the fray.
They still strike up a chorus, with a disregard for [tune]
As their fathers an' their brothers did on Sari's sandy dune.

Their songs may be more modern, an' they like a bit o' swing,
But when yer come to think of it, it ain't the songs you sing,
It's 'ow yer put yer 'eart in' it an' beef a chorus out.
Wot lets the 'ole creation know the Aussies is about
It keeps yer feelin' perky in a way that music 'as.

They sung in front of Bardia, their spirits soarin' 'igh
*We're off to see the Wizard* an' *The Road to Gundagai*
They charged across the desert with their voices goin' strong
An' wielded bloody bay'nets to the rhythm of a song.
While the tanks all danced a rhumba, an' the Brens played *Tiger Rag*
The Ities thought they'd all gorn mad, an' struck their bloomin' flag.

They chucked it in by thousands an' the boys jest roped 'em up.
An' marched 'em orf to compounds to the toon of *Tippy Tin,*
An' when they'd pass a brass 'at they would slow down to a crawl,
An' serenade the blighter with a bar of *Bless 'em all;*
While blokes with bandaged 'eads an' arms was trudgin' to Base.,
Singin' *Back to Yarrawonga* with a grin on every face.

From Solum to Benghazi, through the 'eat an' dust an' sand,
Them Aussie voices warbled fit to beat the flamin' band.
Then orf to Greece they shipped 'em jest to keep a date with Fritz,
An' though they copped it solid, in the thickest of the blitz
Yer'd 'ear some buddin' tenor, with 'is top notes all astray,
Sing about some yeller sheila on *The Road to Mandalay.*

An' later on while dodgin' flamin' paratroops in Crete
They could always raise a song when they could 'ardly raise their feet.
In Java an' Malaya, too, on stinkin' jungle trails,
They sang the same ol' songs they'd sung in sunny New South Wales.
The Jap thought they was *troppo* 'e could never understand
That singin' was a part of life in that fair southern land,

But 'e 'ad a narsty feelin' tricklin' down 'is yeller back
When 'e 'eard the same songs echo cross the Owen Stanley Track,
Accompanied by 'and-grenades an' Bren an' Tommy guns,
An' rendered by the blokes 'oo'd learnt their job while fightin' 'Uns
An' I'm game to take a bet that in another year or so
They'll be singin' *Waltzing Matilda* through the streets of Tokyo.

*Sapper Les Porter*

## *A Funny Lot, the Poms*

I went, at first, to Pommyland, to find out about my roots,
To see where mum was born and why my gran wore boots,
I found the place alright, and met a few who knew the family,
And a barber who 'used to cut their hair' but they sailed in 1911,
he was born in '23.

They said I had an accent, and possibly, I have,
but at least they understand me,
Travelling 'round this ancient isle I found a dozen accents
as I sought my family tree,
I asked a bloke directions an' when he spoke I burst into a giggle,
'Twas like the comedians and I laughed so much I caused myself to wriggle.

I went to visit 'The Downs' I'd heard so much about and down the hill I went,
I know about topography so 'twas the obvious thing to do,
and I searched 'til I was nearly spent,
Enquiring of a bloke I met, he looked at me amazed,
"Down here's the 'High street', mate, the high ground is 'The Downs'."
I won't tell you what I thought, talk about 'Down Under',
but it's like that in all the towns.

Have you walked upon an English beach of pebbles and felt the ripples
'round your toes?
It makes you pine for a decent wave
and sunshine where the blustery southerly blows,
Poms sit in deckchairs, just gazing out to sea and saying "Ain't it grand!"
For the sun came out today,
raised umbrellas on a beach is common in this land.

They eat a lot of funny food,
The Poms like offal and boiled eggs rolled up in pork,
There's lots of lard, kippers, an' cold pork pies upon the list,
but you have to use a fork,
There's cheese found in a toothpaste tube and 'fresh'
but you have to shoo the flies,
I found a baked bean pizza, and custard in a tin,
there's no luxury the Pom himself denies.

The Pom's home is his castle,
there's lots of them around, and they've all got bloody stairs,
I've been to Warwick 'n Edinburgh too, I'm photographing them in pairs,
I'm fitter now, have viewed a lot of history, and I thought it was all mythology;
I looked around for modern bits, and found some, but they present it with apology.

Their vehicles are something to behold, 'three-legged cars'
and 'Rollers' are often side by side,
While red buses and London cabs move tourists 'round with pride,
To see Harrods (the Arab Department store), Big Ben,
'The Palace' and much more,
It's worth a trip to Pommyland to take all this stuff in, tho 'tis a distant shore.

They drive on roads called 'M' and 'A' with lots of funny digits,
Their roundabouts are overgrown, cut your visibility, and give you quite the fidgets,
You hurtle round and find a lot of exits,
no time to read the signs, so you have to take a punt,
Most times you lose, so you see a lot of country,
it tests your sense of humour and often makes you grunt.

Yeah! They're a funny lot, the Poms, they lose a game and accept it with a grin,
But I've seen 'em come from way behind when
chips were down and end up with a win,
A funny lot they may be but we respect their grand achievements,
For qualities that they display are examples to all aspiring governments.

They've fine-tuned the ceremonial, which adds colour to their feats,
And with pomp and splendour they captivate the world, 'tis better than with fleets,
A funny lot they may be and at times a bit peculiar,
But a portion of my pride, it comes from there, so it makes me feel particular.

*Bill Phillips*
*1997*

## *Farewelling Ben*

There are many great days full of honour and glory
Described in our national music and story,
Days of high courage and nights of endeavour
Their memory is cherished and will be forever;
But the greatest appear insignificant when
 We remember the night we said goodbye to Ben.

Hec's on the bar counter, coont-cap on head,
Leading attempts to awaken the dead,
Bunny's eyes sticking out nastily glazed,
Visitors standing round frankly amazed,
Even Joe Courtnay let down his hair when
 We had a few drinks saying goodbye to Ben.

Macinnis whose voice is the flapper's delight
Sang several lewd songs and then Silent Night,
Rod Campbell for once got a little bit ripe
Eating asparagus while smoking his pipe,
Even the president lost balance when
 He sank sixteen gins while farewelling Ben.

Ron Wade showed a wonderfully wide repetoire
Of songs that could only be sung in a bar,
Shamus McKinlay had only a few
And then went away with something to do,
All the wise virgins sneaked home about ten
 Just when we started farewelling Ben.

The wild Colonel Q and his henchman the Scot
Found a jugful of gin and demolished the lot,
Bunny with eyes full of visions all starry
Only smiled when they poured gin on his Safari,
Now none of the three knows what night it was when
 We foregathered quietly to say farewell to Ben.

At midnight the G Staff got into its stride,
The gin kept Tom Williams a long time outside
Leaning against a palm risking the nuts
Wondering what had got into his guts
The SD bloke showed his wide knowledge of men
    By not staying long saying goodbye to Ben,

The medical men with their knowledge of drugs
Mixed up their drinks and behaved like three thugs
Jim English, Bill Morrow and sanitary cook,
Drank a whole lot of potions which aren't in the book,
It's a blessing that Charles Littlejohn wasn't there then
    On that night that his comrades were farewelling Ben.

Donald McKenzie climbed up on a rafter
Protesting that birds eggs were what he was after.
As full as a goog, he didn't last long
But fell on the floor and then burst into song;
He finished up talking to pigs in a pen
    Just as we got round to farewelling Ben.

To speak of the others, I have no intention –
The things they did are too crude to mention.
Bas Finlay for instance with never a care
Goose-stepped the bottom right out of a chair,
Still, Murie will issue another one when
    He knows it was broken farewelling Ben.

Jack Davis bunked off when a phone call came through
Demanding that Oscar see DA and Q.
The innocent writer was summoned along
To help Oscar prove we'd done nothing wrong
But the DA and Q soon forgave us all when
    We told him we'd only been farewelling Ben.

Like sharpening knives with an old rusty file
Was the voice of young Redpath after a while,
Loading the choruses all on one note
Stopping each minute to gargle his throat,
Only Denvil outsang him, the brogue from the glen
    Rose o'er the rumpus we kicked up for Ben.

There was drinking and singing and telling of jokes,
Spontaneous humour from all of the blokes,
Acrobatics and dancing and acting the fool,
While the floor of the mess was more like a pool;
Only one thing was missing that lovely night when
    We bade him goodbye – there was no sign of Ben

*Anon*
*(AWM PR 00250)*

## *AEME Lament*

This is a tale from the DME
And a tale that is passing odd,
It tells of the ways of a wondrous plan,
A method of gauging the toil of man,
And they call it 'prog' and 'prod'.

The role of workshops through years of war,
It was found with extreme regret,
Had never been truly understood
That the whole damn scheme was no damn good
And the whole set-up was wet,

The lack of planning was most to blame –
That and the lacking of charts
Which plot the course of man and hours,
Rooting the lot to extravagant powers
And listing ephemeral parts.

In early days at the start of it
The scheme was extremely crude
The work was recorded in primitive ways
Completed and out in a matter of days
And only the Wops were rude.

Later the Corps grew big and strong
And found to its great distress
The efficiency factor expressed as "y"
Of the output, cubed by the root of pi
Was five point two, or less.

Most of the keenest brains were set
To produce a suitable plot
For tracing the downward curve and then
Dividing it all by the number of men
With a constant for the lot.

Now that this hard fought fight is won
With the help of great reforms,
The forces of reasoning now prevail
By the use of graphs and sliding scale
And elaborate army forms.

Formulas now exist to find
All manner of cryptic things,
From the power percent of a driver mech
And the love life lost by a storeman tech
To the wear of piston rings.

Gone are the days of the *Laissez Faire*
When merely work was done,
Everything now is just compiled
Neatly bound and elaborately filed
And stored by the cubic ton.

Alas comes looming the five-year-plan,
And this may be a blow,
As some of the army of planning coves
And God only knows they come in droves
Will surely and sadly go.

And they'll tell the tale from the DME
The tale that was passing odd.
They'll speak of the ways of the wondrous plan
The method of gauging the toil of man
"*Mafeesh*", they'll say. "Thank God!"

*Maj W P Fooks (?)*
*(AWM PR 00250)*

### In The Workshop.

We're busy men within this shop,
We have no time to spare,
So if you want to talk or lounge,
Just kindly go elsewhere.

*NX139320 Pte Jim Baker*
*116 Aust Gen Trans Company*
*Marrickville, 31 August1942*

### Untitled

And if we wish to see the land,
As tourists we must,
No need to move around at all
It comes to us in dust.

So in the course of half a day
We see a continent –
No wonder Moses went away
With the arse of his trousers rent.

*Anon*
*(AWM PR 00526)*

## *Dingo Joe's Luck*

Dingo Joe would wax loquacious,
When for beer he used to spar,
And he told this tale one evening
To the crowd in Cronin's bar:

> I was way up in the desert,
> Chasing Lasseter's lost reef
> And had lived for months on damper
> And a bit of bully beef.

I was trampin' into Darwin
When the thort occurred to me
That I'd give a bit to sample
A refreshin' cup of tea;

> Now don't larf – though wishful thinking
> Sometimes gets you blokes down here,
> It is useless in the desert
> Where you're miles & miles from beer.

So I thort I'd boil my billy
But it weren't any good
You could search the blooming landscape
And not find a stick of wood.

> Even camel dung, the standby
> Of the traveller up there,
> Was as scarce as angels' visits –
> All a bloke could do was swear.

Some well-chosen words I uttered
W'en a brainwave seemed to come
An' I grab my old black billy
An' searches in me 'drum',

> For me bit of tea & sugar,
> For some grass went stretchin' back
> On a narrow strip wat looked like
> A deserted camel track.

So I fishes out me matches
An' I sets that grass ablaze
W'ile a north wind pushed it forward
Did it go? Oh, spare me days!

    With me billy held above it,
    O'er the desert sands I sped,
    Both me eyes were full of cinders
    An' me face was puffed & red;

Was I out of breath? you ask me –
Well it wasn't that maybe
But you'd think t' hear me gaspin'
That the breath was out of me.

    An' I thort that I was euchred
    When I reached the 'fourteen mile'
    An' I raved and cursed and shouted
    Bile – you rotten blankard – bile

But it couldn't last forever,
It had been quite a fair ole run –
She at last began to bubble
An' I knew that I had won.

    Fifteen miles or more I'd covered
    I deserved a spot of luck,
    For a bloke wat run as I did
    Can't be classed as short of pluck.

But a sudden notion hit me
An' I got an awful shock
An' I acted for some seconds
Like a bloke wat's done 'is block,

    Then I kicked that billy from me
    An' I groaned in anguish dire –
    I 'ad left that tea and sugar
    Where I'd lit that bloody fire.

*T. V. Tiemey*
*(AWM PR 00526)*

### The Boozers' Lament

We've fought upon Gallipoli
And toiled on Egypt's plain
We've travelled far across the sea
To face the foe again;
We've faced the perils of the deep
And faced them with good cheer
But now they give us cause to weep
They've gone and stopped our beer.

We wouldn't mind if they had stopped
The pickles and the cheese
They might have cut the marmalade
Or issued fewer peas,
But it's a sin to drink red vin
Or for a cobber shout
Which kind of sets me wondering
If they've cut the champagne out.

They stopped our rum, we didn't mind
While we had beer to soak,
But now they gone and stopped the wine
It's getting past a joke.
Each countenance you see is sad
Within each eye a tear,
The greatest injury we've had
Is cutting out our beer.

For you must shun the flowing bowl
And turn you from the wine,
And water drink to cheer your soul
If it should chance to pine;
And you must order coffee
When you toast the folks at home
And spend your cash on toffee
Chewing gum and honey comb.

There's microbes in the water lads
So drink it with a will
And every mother's son of us
Will jolly soon be ill.
And when we're on the sick parade
The Doctor he will cry:
"The lads, I fear, must have their beer
Else they will surely die!"

*Sgt A.M. Dick (?)*
*(AWM PR 00187)*

## *Oh! It's Nice to be a Soldier.*

Now I've joined up with the Army
It's a home away from home,
The meals are really lovely
And you never hear a moan,
For it's about this little rest home
That this tale I'm going to tell:
The Sergeant Major, he's a pet,
The Captain's really swell,
The Corporals are so nice to me,
And that's fair dinky-di,
That when this war is over
I'll just break down and cry.

*Chorus*
Oh! It's nice to be a soldier,
Soldering will just suit me!
From first thing in the morning
Till it's time to go to bed
We're digging holes and sloping arms
Till we're silly in the head.
When the canteen opens
All the boys begin to play
And by the time we get to sleep
It dawns another day.
But it's nice to be a Soldier
Soldiering will just suit me.

Now every morning on parade
You cannot hear a sound,
Especially when the Sergeant Major's
Marching up and down.
There's a morning in particular
I was a trifle late,
The Captain gave me such a look
And said "You're in a state."
Then after I saluted him
This was my sad reply,
"I took a Number Nine last night
And my God! I nearly died!"

Now they march us out like lunatics
They call it on parade,
No one tells us anything
And the boys all look dismayed.
Then off we go to the RAP
Where we hang round telling yarns,
Until they squirt a little antidote
Into our flaming arms.
Then after this is over
They take us for a march,
It's bad luck for the molly dooke
He cannot scratch his tail.

*Will Handley*
*(AWM PR 85 205)*

## *Bully Beef*

Here I sit and sadly wonder
Why they sent me Bully Beef
Why the living, jumping thunder
I should bear such awful grief?
Did I ever, in my childhood
Cause my parents grief and pain?
Did I ever in a passion try to wreck a railway train?
Have I been a drunken husband?
Have I ever beat my wife?
Did I ever, just for past-time
Try to take my neighbour's life?
If I haven't, then I tell you
It is far beyond belief
Why they sent me greasy, sloppy
Undeciphered Bully Beef
Bully Beef, by all that's mighty
Streaky, strangly Bully-Beef
I'd sooner face a thousand Jackos
Than half a tin of Bully-Beef.
Ask the cook, what's for dinner
And he'll tell you BULLY BEEF
Breakfast, dinner, tea or supper
All consists of BULLY BEEF.
BULLY BEEF, why blow me, Charlie,
I would forfeit ten days pay
If I could lose the sight of BULLY
Just for one clear gladsome ray.
YET, they send me in a parcel
Along with greetings, short and brief,
Lots of nice things, sweet and tasty
BUT, among them, BULLY BEEF!

*Tpr W. H. Johnstone (?)*
*8th ALH, AIF*
*(AWM PR 84/049)*

## *Female Invasion*

When the Munga steamed out of Sydney
    On a wintry July afternoon,
Who would have thought for a moment
    There'd be females invading her soon.

No one guessed when the Japs gave it best
    What the future held in store;
The normally sexed were not perplexed
    About a celibate year or more.

Not so our boys from the Wardroom,
    Our inspiration, to wit,
A gentlemen can't keep his end up
    Without getting his regular bit.

So you should have seen the excitement
    When the news got 'round down there,
We were taking on women and children:
    'Twould've driven their wives to despair.

Now a bright boy is Subby Jack Alway,
    Intent on making his bid
Knew the surest way to a woman's heart
    Is to make a hit with the kid.

None can gainsay that this worthy
    Didn't play his role to a tee,
'Twas only a matter of minutes
    And he had a kid on his knees.

Who knows what went on in his cabin?
    You can please yourselves about that,
But a bloke with a technique so subtle
    Won't waste time with a sniveling brat.

Now we've got a bloke name of Robeson,
    An Engineer Subby, brand new,
Who fancies himself as a lover
    We were anxious to see what he'd do.

In a minute or two from his debut
    The women were calling his bluff,
And the boys looked anxiously 'bout them
    For a bloke made of sterner stuff.

They weren't to wait long for the answer
    For presently hove into view
A real Casanova, no kidding,
    With a lover's Varsity Blue.

This bloke's a national hero,
    I'll prove it to you old chap
Didn't the Women's Weekly
    Reproduce his masculine map?

Noel Abrams (to whom I'm referring)
    Wasn't beating about the bush,
He went straight into action
    With a regular gem of a blush.

This buggered the blokes' calculations:
    "Who's going to save the side?"
They'd put all their dollars on Abrams,
    A good bet, it can't be denied.

Meantime the bookies were chuckling,
    They'd selected the pick of the bunch,
But they didn't let on to their cobbers
    The guts of their shrewd little hunch.

This gent may've been schooled at
    Eton, Harrow or Oxford, by Jove,
A regular hit with the ladies
    And not a bad sort of a cove.

Well there's no harm in him thinking it, fellers,
    When a bloke likes to get himself in,
It's a hell of a pity, admitted,
    And a source of constant chagrin.

But as long as it isn't contagious,
    Don't be a victim, my man,
Let him talk himself blind if he wishes
    And get himself in when he can.

He's got a beautiful accent
    A product of RANC,
You'll find it in most straight ringers,
    The hallmark of dignity.

Ed Dollard's the gent I'm portraying
    Number one boy in the ship,
Well equipped both in poise and in stature,
    Not averse to admiring a hip.

As most of the women were English
    His bearing was made for the job,
And his form at this critical juncture
    Was watched avidly by the mob.

He's in an enviable possie,
    The master of all he surveys,
It's impressed all the women, the sucker,
    His power in so many cute ways.

But despite his advantage as Jimmy
    Our Ed didn't do so hot,
But it wasn't for lack of trying
    He was giving it all he'd got.

Somehow these straight-ringers reckon
    They're perso-boys plus, it appears,
Take Edwards, mother perm product,
    And not very far on in years.

The blokes hadn't reckoned with Peter
    On account of his thinning thatch,
They thought that the women would shun him
    Foresaw no potential match.

The first thing that came to our notice –
  We could hardly believe our eyes –
Was a game of 'Handles' on X deck
  By jingo, we got a surprise.

Now I guess you've all seen the advert,
  Depicting a bloke with no wool
Wed to a woman who trapped him
  Just for the money – the fool.

Admitting that Peter's no pauper
  Tho' bloody near bankrupt of hair
No woman would wed him for money
  He's no bloody millionaire.

This got the boys thinking shrewdly
  "What's Peter Edward's game?"
She can't harry him for his money,
  And his thatch is a crying shame."

But, kept under observation,
  The boys discovered at length
That Pete was the hunted, not hunter –
  The lass was exerting her strength.

Then came an expert manoeuvre,
  A strategic withdrawal by name,
The woman abandoned her quarry
  In search of more gullible game.

You must hand it to Frank Sanguinetti,
  (Not a bad bloke, you'll find),
A chap with a couple of youngsters
  And a charming young wife left behind.

He didn't fall for the glamour
  Of a wench who'd be outcast in Vic,
Carried on with his regular business
  And helped any kids who got sick.

Bishop and Stormy were others
  Whose passions were not aroused,
Both likely-looking youngsters, too,
  And neither of them espoused.

Theirs was the call of duty,
  Likewise the Gunner (T),
"What is the love of a woman
  Compared with the love of the sea?"

John Coles was another non-starter
  In this Bacchanalian game,
His thought of his wife and his family
  Hung on to his unbesmirched name.

Even our Yankee Allies,
  Renowned for their womenly guiles,
Simply greeted the females with décor
  And a few irreproachable smiles.

The Doctor had the boys guessing,
  No one could quite make out
When he welcomed the femmes at the gangway
  Just what it was all about.

Was it professional manner?
  Or was he going to flout
The trust with which he's divested?
  He got the best of the doubt.

Put a query alongside Bob Wilshire,
  He wasn't seen much up on deck
Probably down in his cabin
  With a passionate dame 'round his neck.

Tough luck for Skipper Nobby:
  Whether he liked it or not,
The laws of the Navy dictated
  The bridge was to be his spot.

Rather a handsome blighter,
     Would've acquitted himself well
If given a chance like the others,
     Might've trapped an unwary gal.

So listen, down in the Wardroom,
     Why don't you take a hint:
It's the man that gets the woman –
     Don't care if you own the mint.

And though braid may look just ducky,
     It's superficial just,
It's the man in you that gets 'em,
     If get a woman you must.

Just look around the messdecks,
     And see what I'm talking about,
You'll be looking then at he-men,
     Men's men without a doubt.

So curb your sexual hunger
     Wake up and do your stuff!
And never lose your heads boys,
     Over a little bit of fluff.

*'Longfellow'*

## *Tobruk Test*

You've heard of Bradman, Hammond,
MacCartney, Woodfull, Hobbs,
You've heard of how MacDougall topped the score
Now I'd like to tell you
How we play cricket in Tobruk
In a way the game was never played before.

The players are a mixture,
They come from every rank
And their dress would not be quite the thing at Lord's;
But you don't need caps and flannels
And expensive batting gloves
To get the fullest sport the game affords.

The wicket's rather tricky
For it's mat on desert sand
But for us it's really plenty good enough,
And what with big bomb craters
And holes from nine-inch shells,
The outfield could be well described as rough.

The boundary's partly tank trap
With the balance dannert wire
And the grandstand's just a bit of sandy bank,
While our single sightboard's furnished
By a shot-down Jerry plane
And the scorer's in a ruined Itie tank

One drawback is a minefield
Which is at the desert end
And critics might find fault with this and that,
But to us all runs are good ones
Even if a man should score
Four leg byes off the top of his tin hat.

The barracking is very choice,
The Hill would learn a lot
If they could listen in to all the cries
As the Quartermaster Sergeant
Bowls the Colonel neck and crop
With a yorker while some dust was in his eyes

And the time the Signals runner
Scored the winning hit
When, as he sprinted round the wire to try and save the four,
The Battery Sergeant Major
Fell into a crater deep
And the batsman ran another seven more.

If we drive one in the minefield
We always run it out
For that is what the local rules defines:
It's always good for six at least,
Some times as high as ten
While the fieldsman picks his way in through the mines.

Though we never stop for shell-fire
We're not too keen on planes,
But when the Stukas start to hover round
You can sometimes get a wicket,
If you're game enough to stay
By bowling as the batsman goes to ground

So when we're back in Sydney
And others start to talk
Of cricket, why we'll quell them with a look:
"You blokes have never seen
A game of cricket properly played
The way we used to play it in Tobruk."

*Anon*
*(AWM PR 00359)*

## *Promotion*

"Promotion," said one cocksure bloke,
Needs personality
You tell the CO some good joke,
And earn three stripes – watch me!"

He slapped the Colonels back and said,
"Old Cock, let's have a drink!"
No stripes for him, no gold and red –
Just three weeks in the clink.

*Anon*
*(AWM PR 00526)*

## ANZAC Exchange

Sarge, I think I'm buggered,
    I'm bitten on me back,
    a bloody snake's bin crawlin' thru the grass.

So call the Medic quick,
    to give me arm a prick
    and take away the pain until I pass.

Yer mate the Bombardier,
    can have me 'ish' of beer,
    I won't be drinkin' Fosters when I go.

I've wrote me mum a note,
    and I've put it in me pack,
    she's livin' down near Kunga-munga-mo.

So tell me Aussie mates,
    youse Kiwi bloody skates,
    have caused the death of one of Anzac's finest.

And when I pass away
    don't put me in the clay,
    the bloody dingoes here are rife as goats.

What's that you bloody say?
    the chopper's on its way,
    it won't be here in time to save this Digger.

The Doc he said it's what?
    Now how did that get there?
    A tear tab from a beer can caused this wound?

Well, the pain will pass away,
    and I'll fight another day,
    but PLEEZE youse Kiwis keep this to yourselves!

*Mike Subritzky*
*161 Battery at Enoggora, 1986*

# CHAPTER THIRTEEN
# OTHER CHARACTERS

## Galloping Horses

He may have been tall and distinguished
    with full head of hair and a mo
Trim and taut and terrific
    and always ready to go.

Or maybe he's not quite so tall,
    with less hair, and not quite so trim.
He could have been bald – not quite perfect,
    but no one to question him.

Short hair, no sideburns, no creases,
    spit polish and brasso – no choice
Pace stick, measured stride, and you shuddered –
    just at the sound of his voice.

He's old now, and grey, sometimes lonely,
    but he smiles at the time that he spent
Making men out of boys for the Army –
    and he wonders where you all went.

*Margaret Gibbons*

## *At the Trees*

I saw him today at the trees,
Almost seventy now, got crook knees,
And his weight is a problem as well –
But he always has stories to tell.

He laughs while he works with his mates
As they rake and shovel and rest,
And the young ones who look passing by
Never think these may be the best.

The best of the 50s and 60s,
The best of the 70s too,
They walked tall and straight and unflinching
They were rascals and marksmen all through.

They have secrets they share when together
They have thoughts of their own none can share,
But to know just what they are thinking
You really had to be there.

You had to have lain in an ambush
Or jumped from a chopper in flight
Or waded in deep smelly water
Or said to a mate "You'll be right!"

But the work party's over for now
And he's off to his home and to 'Mum';
He values the time he spends with his mates
And he still feels the beat of the drum.

*Margaret Gibbons*

## *Old Bob*

A hellhole like New Guinea,
Which can health and spirit rob,
May have wore him down and sickened
But never bested Bob.

The years of work and raisin' children,
That seeming endless plod,
Did not to my knowin'
Show up too much bad in Bob.

That cruel blow which struck him
May have cost his pride and job
But could not make him quiet –
He was a 'goer' was our Bob.

The great occasions of my life,
Wedding's joy and death's harsh sob,
Were made sweeter or a comfort
By the presence of our Bob.

His latter years were hard ones
While cancer did its job
But never weak complaining
I ever heard from Bob

He's left us now to rest at last
Some say 'tis best – Poor Bob –
But 'tis we who are the poorer
For the passing of our Bob.

*Capt. Don Buckby*

## Tom the Barber

*This poem was written for the retirement of Mr Dennis Hardy who was known affectionately by all as Tom the Barber. Tom had been one of Defence's resident, and no doubt the longest serving (long suffering?) barbers in Sydney for forty years, mainly in the Moorebank/Holsworthy districts.*

Old Tom the barber's cut the hair of a hundred thousand soldiers,
    And passed along the soldiers' lore and tales for forty years.
He's never hurried or upset – a happy jovial soul,
    Comedy and tragedy with equal gusto told.

His shop remains the repository of memories, dreams and such,
    So little space it's hard to find the room to store so much;
Mementoes left by customers of lands and times gone by
    To continue myths and legends long after we all die.

He's also got some naughty books of ladies with no clothes on,
    He says its 'art', but we believe it's for customer satisfaction;
The customers are mesmerised, no anaesthetic needed,
    Tom snips and combs and tells his tales, his sallies go unheeded.

And now old Tom has 'pulled the pin', a well earned rest is waiting,
    He's served his time, he's done his bit, no other way of stating;
We wish him well for all his plans, contented in retirement,
    No doubt we'll see him round the traps and bleed him of his pension.

And when he gets to heaven will he cut St Peter's hair?
    Or do they have a need for such as Tom away up there?
And what about those naughty books what will the Blessed think?
    A holy penthouse version of 'Angels in the Pink'!

What will you do to fill your days now cutting hair no longer,
    A lazy day, a beer or two, or maybe something stronger?
Farewell, old friend, (as many have the right to call him such)
    For all your work and friendship – Thankyou very much.

*WO2 Paul Barrett*

## *Lionel Lyons*

In my usual verses
Sarcasm always shines,
This time I shall be different
As I dedicate these lines

    To a friend who has departed
    Into the great beyond
    And joined the wife who left him
    Thus tying the severed bond.

On every second Sunday morn
For seventeen long years,
While placing flowers on her grave
He shed bitter tears.

    He never missed attending,
    In sunshine or in rain,
    Although his every visit
    Only added to the pain.

Time, the greatest healer,
Couldn't mend his broken heart,
But now I know he's happy –
They no longer are apart.

    He was always at our meetings,
    He attended every night,
    To see him playing poker
    Was but a common sight.

He was in fact an addict
To this game of luck and skill,
But, no longer will he deal the cards,
Or ask, "How many Bill?"

No one can tell by watching
If his luck was good or bad
He wore the same expression
Whatever cards he had.

Now the Lodge has lost this Brother
And we have lost our friend
Because his life was finished
And Fate had written end.

He's rejoined the wife he loved
And side by side they lie,
By his sudden death is shown
All that lives must die.

Brothers, be upstanding,
And toast to one we love,
Although we'll always miss him
He was needed up above.

I'll ask you all to join me,
Repeat with me these lines:
"You'll never be forgotten,
Farewell, Lionel Lyons."

*Raymond John Colenso*
*(AWM PR 00689)*

## *Jungle Jim*

Where the jungle is the toughest,
Where the going is the roughest,
Bathed in sweat with face so grim
    You will find him – Jungle Jim.

Wading through the filth and mud,
He has proved he is no dud;
"Onward always" is his hymn,
    He's a tiger – Jungle Jim.

Where he goes he pulls his weight,
At rendezvous he's never late,
Though he's light and rather slim,
    He's a battler – Jungle Jim.

When at last he fades away,
(Not we hope, for many a day)
Then the angels tour will sing:
    "Here he comes – Old Jungle Jim."

*'Gibbo'*
*(AWM PR 00074)*

## *Bert of Bardia*

Bert of Bardia, back in town,
Bert of Bardia, big and brown,
Dragging a leg with a shattered knee,
Came to the bar and drank with me.

There was a mournful look on Bert,
He had the air of a man whole hurt,
And glancing down at his blighted limb
My heart was sorry indeed for him.

"Stiff luck!" I said, then it seemed to me,
That I had made a mistake, for he
With his strong half smile and his manly touch,
Declared, "Aw, it isn't that so much."

And his gaze went through that city bar
Till fixed, it seemed, on things afar,
And I knew that he saw the sand dunes,
In Libya under the scorching skies.

And I knew that in spite of the price of war,
He yearned to be back with his mates once more,
There with the cobbers he loved so well,
Fighting his way through a dusty hell.

And it cheered me to think there were other grim
And resolute sons of the soil, like him,
The type who will see the battle through,
So 'Bert of Bardia' here's to you!

*Anon*

# CHAPTER FOURTEEN
# 'THOSE LEFT BEHIND'

## War Graves on Tarakan

Will you walk with me in the heat of the day
Till we come at the crossroads on the way
Of a dusty road on Tarakan
To a scene in the scheme of the war's mad plan?

There are soldiers there in a little square
Who will breathe no more of the dust-filled air,
On the trails they died, by the road they rest
With foreign soil on each manly chest.

On the crosses which mark the arid mounds
Are the tales of courage which know no bounds
'Killed in Action' and 'Died of Wounds'
But wasted lives are war's worst ruin.

You will see mates at the graveside stand
Quietly, slouch hats held in hand
And you may grieve, as they will too,
For the hopes and dreams which will not come true.

In death these men have simple needs,
No separate tracts for differing creeds;
For the shoulders, which never were cold in life
Are together in death as they were in strife.

You may gaze at the flag which hangs from the mast
To honour the men who were staunch to the last
And fancy you hear a quiet voice say:
Australia, my country, will you repay.

Will you warm my heart, give daily bread
To the hungry mouths which once were fed
Through the sweat and toil of a fallen man
Who sleeps by the road on Tarakan,

So when you return by the dusty road
You may bear your share of a sacred load
With a pride whose flame ignited them
Will burn to the sound of the last 'Amen!'

*FO T. Latham*
*(AWM MSS 1234)*

## *White Crosses*

On the day before leave taking
From this place called Tobruk Bay
One last visit I'll be making
To that graveyard down the way

Where eight hundred small white crosses
And eight hundred sacred mounds
Show the place wherein our Heroes
Sleep the last on foreign ground.

Every white cross tells a story
With a number rank and name
Every mound is one of glory
For it holds an Anzac frame.

Each join state a space divided
[missing line]
In the square of Libyan sand
Fairest square in all the land

Every mound holds someone's Digger
Every cross a mother's pride,
And Australia's fame grows bigger
For the way those Heroes died.

Best of mates it's hard to leave you
In this sandy waste so bare
But fond hearts will not forget you
In your native land so fair.

We know not our destination
When we leave this hostile bay
But we've this determination
We will square the debt some day

And perhaps it sounds like 'hooey'
But the orders read 'No noise'
Or I'd shout one long last "Cooee!"
As a farewell from the boys.

*Pte Worthington*
*QX11656*
*(AWM MSS 1562)*

## *Untitled*

*The following poem was prefaced with: 'Lines pencilled after a fruitless search for the grave of my late beloved nephew Charles Chetwynd Currie. Killed in Action, Lone Pine ANZAC Aug 8th 15 after being wounded in the landing April 25th 15. Killed after volunteering to bomb an enemy trench – the first to volunteer from his native town.'*

Although directed to the place
    I cannot find a single trace
Of where my bonnie nephew sleeps
    For whom, poor Nel, my sister weeps;
Howe'er I try the search is vain,
    Perhaps some day I'll try again.

One of the first to volunteer
    To serve the flag he loved so dear,
Thus answering his country's call
    He freely gave his life – his all –
From home and kindred far apart;
    Unknown to flinch, that noble heart.

Weep not dear sister; well I know
    His loss must seem a bitter blow
But he to whom such praise is given
    Must find a corner high in heaven,
For none deserves it more than he
    Who sleeps so far across the sea.

But changed events and gathering years
    At length may stem a mother's tears;
Father's, sisters', brothers' grief
    Who, in these facts may find relief,
That Charlie fell amidst the brave
    And rests within a soldier's grave.

*(AWM MSS 1445)*

## *The Letter Which Came Too Late*

Fondest love and tender wishes,
From your loving Mother dear,
I hope this letter brings you
Good luck with every cheer.

We miss your kind and smiling face,
We wish that you were home
God give you strength and guidance,
No matter where you roam.

There's a chair beside the fireside,
Where once you used to sit,
A lampstand in the corner
You always wanted lit.

Your presence at the table,
We all can't help but miss,
Your boyish sort of manner
When you gave your good-night kiss.

It seems so very long ago
You kissed us at the door,
Our eyes were full of parting tears –
My son was off to war.

I pray son that God's Angels
Will guide my loving son,
And bring him safely back to me
When all this war is won.

A log burns in the fireside,
No better place you'd choose,
A wireless in the corner
Is giving out the news.

"Our bombers raided Buna,
And four did not return."
That anxious waiting Mother –
Her heart will always yearn.

*W. A. Dutton*
*(AWM MSS 1481)*

## *Honour the Brave*

On the palm-fringed shores of an emerald isle
Just north of Samari,
In shaded jungle palm groves,
From the burning northern sky.

Dusky dark-haired maidens,
With dark and fuzzy hair,
Their skin is dark and shiny,
A skirt of grass they wear.

Fragrant, scented breezes
Blow in from out the bay,
With the tang of musty seaweed
In the salt foam and the spray.

Tall and lofty palm leaves
Reach out to touch the bay,
Their leaves are long and slender
In the breeze they swing and sway.

In this tropical jaded splendour,
Along with nature's law,
You forget the past and horror
Of this world and bloody war.

But down there on those beaches,
A month or so gone by,
Men, they fought with fury
And many had to die;

To save this jungle paradise
From a foe who mars its joy,
And an island far away to south
Where once he was a boy;

To stem the rising Nippon tide
Which tried to reach our shore.
To take from us the beauty
Of the bushland [we] adore.

They fell there, bathed in glory,
Their suits of green stained red,
And now they sleep in peace and still,
A cross above their head.

They'll never see that victory
For which their lives they gave;
But we shall not forget you,
Our gallant strong and brave.

*W. A. Dutton*
*(AWM MSS1481)*


## *Vale*

Let him be
That dying eagle,
Let the flames devour his nest
Multicoloured, golden, blazing,
Like the sunset in the west.
Let him be,
While his life's sands are running
Fast unto the end
Beyond the little helping
Of his closest friend;
Pause and once remember
Smiling lips and laughing eyes,
Then turn your back upon him
While he dies.

*Pilot Officer T. L. Stewart*
*(AWM MSS 1250)*

## Shed Thou No Tears

Shed thou no tears –
This road they chose, this way of pain was theirs
Who drank the cup of bitterness
And lie in alien soil, hungering for home
From fields wherein the streams of youth ran deep
They heard the far clear call and answered
Out from the quiet places and the gentle folk
They knew and loved, and graciousness
They went and questioned not.
Thorns were their portion and their end a lesser Calvary
…weep not for them
For they have gone beyond the night and found
Quiet havens where the laughing waters run, and rest is given.
They sleep in fields of Aramanth, flow'r crowned,
And all their glory lights the hills of Heaven.

*Pte Gladstone George Harvey 'Harry' Barratt*
*(AWM MSS 1297)*

## A Grave in the Grass:

Stand to, sentry…
The dreams of the past file by,
While the buried hopes of a Mother
'Neath the kunai grasses lie.

A small wooden cross
And a tin hat mark his bed…
Salute, when you're passing, soldier,
Where a mother's dreams lie dead.

Here, where the hand of evil
Has slain the brave and good,
Pause, and pray… for a Mother…
By this little cross of wood.

*Bdr Sydney J. Lynch*
*(AWM MSS 1557)*

## *Standing By – Tobruk*

There's a row of wooden crosses in a hollow near Tobruk
    o'er a row of shallow graves hard there by the town,
And we, their comrades, say a charitable prayer
    for those brave lads who never let us down.

When the storm of battle's over and the guns have ceased to roar
    and the gentle breezes blow from in across the sea,
We'll still hear their cheery voices in the waves along the shore
    and take solace in the thought – it had to be.

They heard the 'Fall In' sounded and knew that they must go
    though on parade they soon would stand again,
Lined up for 'inspection' by the heavenly CO,
    whose Battalion can't be filled with mortal men.

There Jerry cannot bomb you or pelt you with HE
    and you're marching with the army of the brave, the proud and free;
We'll meet you over yonder, till then "Good shooting, mates!
    You've founded a tradition for the 2/48th!"

*'The Wandering Bard'*

## *Reward*

They lie in Egypt's sands, Australia's sons,
That those who love and laugh may live;
They gave unflinching to a hell of gun,
The young fair lives that duty bade them give.

And on a shifting fringe of foreign land
That undulates and rolls towards the sea,
The rows of wooden crosses starkly stand
To mark the holocaust to liberty.

But say not that this hopeless, endless place
That lifeless lies between land and sea
Has taken to its deathly cold embrace
The ashes of a burnt-out destiny.

For from those lonely, windswept, hallowed graves
Will burst the destined flame and light the way
To life and hope for countless million slaves
And set ablaze the sun of freedom's day.

*Anon*

## Vale

Oh valiant heart: purest was thy spirit,
    Nobly you went, without fear of the cost.
Eager, wherever the bravest would fear it –
    We who remain are the ones who have lost.

Yet with us still we believe that you tarry,
    One without efforts to vanquish the foe.
Long may the way be and hard, yet we carry
    Nerving endeavour, a memory aglow.

And when the guns cease their song of destruction,
    Silent the desert and peace comes to men,
We shall remember in sore reconstruction
    The brave who went forth, but who came not again.

*Anon*

## Farewell

A life of busy toil has ended,
Of effort for his country's good,
A soul that sought to do his duty
Has passed to be at home with God.

Standing on the ocean's border,
Just where the land and waters stay,
With the weight of war upon him
Came the closing of life's day.

How we miss the voice that's silent!
How we miss the form that's still!
How we know we cannot call him
From his slumber, if we will!

Farewell then, to you our cobber,
Sleeping in your quiet grave.
Eyes grow dim, but hope triumphant
Holds us fast o'er life's rough way.

*Anon*

## *Timber*

They are only a plain piece of timber
But their meaning is stately and grand,
For there's many a gallant man sleeping
'Neath the little white cross in the sand.

I often have wandered among them
And read from inscriptions they bear
The rank, the name and the number
Of one of my pals resting there.

These Diggers have died for their country –
They gave all they had in the fight
For the safety and peace of their loved ones,
A cause that must surely be right.

And when the last battle is ended
And peace has come over the land,
Let us never forget those white crosses,
In rows, in the hot desert sand.

*Anon*

## *Somewhere*

Somewhere a gun lies red with rust
And there 'midst the trampled clay
The bones of a Gunner have turned to dust
That the March winds waft away.

Somewhere a Mother's eyes are red
As she weeps for her only boy
Who sleeps at peace in his muddy bed
Somewhere by the corduroy.

*Cpl John (Jack) McHugh*
*(AWM PR 00750)*

## *Our Fallen Mates*

The battles fought are now history
And now we live in Peace,
The memories of our fallen mates
These sad memories will ne'er cease.

When we stand and face the crosses,
Each bearing one of our mates name
His Rank, Number and Battalion
Who paid the supreme sacrifice with fame.

To the families who have lost loved ones
These words come from the heart;
Their name will be remembered for evermore
For freedom they played their part.

The Boys came from the city and country
And from every walk of life;
They volunteered on a United front
When their Country was in strife.

The Officers and other Ranks march side by side
In the march on Anzac Day,
It proved what Unity will do
In the War it proved that way.

THE BATTLE'S BEEN WON
THEIR DUTY'S BEEN DONE
AND THE WORLD KNOWS OF THEIR DEEDS,
AS WE LAY BACK IN THOUGHT
OF THE GLORY IT BROUGHT
TO HELP THE WORLD TO BE FREE,
AS WE STAND AT THE CROSS
AND THINK OF THE LOSS
OF OUR MATES WE LEFT BEHIND,
WITH THE PASSING OF YEARS
WE STILL SHED OUR TEARS
FOR THE BOYS WHO GAVE THEIR LIVES:
"LEST WE FORGET".

*Syd Buckingham*

## *Bomana*

Blue sky
Green rolling hills
To mountains tranquil, stretch.
White clouds in a wide blue sky.

So quiet
So peaceful
Above the young sleepers
Resting beneath each white cross.

With each new dawn,
Their rising sons greet the rising sun
As the days march to eternity.

But they will march no more.
No more to toil along the muddy track,
No more to wonder where their track will end.
It ended here.

Thousands.
Sleeping peacefully,
Under that clear blue sky.
There, in their earthen beds,
Beneath each white cross,
As I walk the graves
And wonder
Why?

*Peter Tremain*

## *The Hardest Task*

*'The Hardest Task' was penned by a friend who had asked what was the most difficult thing that I had had to do during World War II. I told him that telling a mother of one of my mates, who had died in my arms while on patrol, how he had died had been difficult for me and remains a painful memory. Reuben penned the following poem. Bill Phillips, 1998.*

The hardest task a man could do –
I could think of some and so could you –
But one there was for my friend Bill,
Thrust on him against his will.

On distant shore to serve his King,
Taught to expect anything…
Well, almost anything.

There they saw the battle rage,
Far too much for boys their age,
Guns and mortars and wartime pranks
All took their toll on our boys' ranks.

Some in shock were very numb,
Others screamed and then struck dumb.
Then it was Bill found this lad,
His time was short, the wound was bad.

The talk was brief and tears, they glistened,
He propped him up and then he listened.
The hardest task was about to come,
His final words … "Tell Mum."

*Reuben K Fox*
*1998*

## Soldier

Build me no monument, should my turn come.
Please do not weep for me and waste your tears.
Write not my name on honour rolls of fame
To crumble with man's memories though the years.

Wear no dark clothes, speak in no saddened voice,
Seeking rare virtues which did not exist.
Just let me be, under the cool sweet earth
And sleep in peace where I will not be missed.

I ask one thing that, in still far off days,
Someone who knew me should in their daily round
Suddenly pause, caught by some sight or sound,
Some glance, some phrase, some trick of memory's ways,

Which brings me to their mind: then I shall wait,
Eager with hope, to hear them say "How great
If he were here." Then, softly at the end,
All that I ask for, just "He was my friend."

*David McNicol (?)*
*(AWM PR 00392)*

## *To Lieutenant Norman Blackburn*

*This short ode was written in tribute to Lieutenant Norman Blackburn of the 9th Division. He was killed by a Japanese sniper in New Guinea, 2 October 1943.*

Oh soldier, brave and strong,
First of proud line to fall
In distant battlefield;
Fair, tall and noble youth,
Pride of mother sweet and three sisters fair;

You went to battle with a cheerful heart.
With straight limb, steady eye
And face towards the foe,
We know you were true to Australia fair,
We know your heart was all aglow.

Let us who come behind
We who gained liberty, freedom, all,
From your great sacrifice,
Let us, our kind, let us
Oh, Norman! remember thee.

*Ernest H. Graham.*
*PR 82 056*

## Death of a Peacemaker

*In Memory of: A997234 Private Leonard William Manning, DOB 15 August 1975 –
KIA 24 July 2000, Bravo Company, 2/1 Battalion RNZIR: UN Forces, East Timor*

With the courage of youth
and in the company of his mates,
he moved forward as the lead scout
to form a ring of steel
between the oppressed people
of East Timor and banditry
loyal only to the violence
of the parang,
   – and the politics of the machine gun.

At twenty four years of age,
he was under no illusions
as to the dangers he faced
when he placed himself in harms way
and probed silently forward
to keep his fated appointment,
   – with death and destiny.

Ambushed and caught in the killing zone,
he was unaccounted for
in the confusion of sustained
and overwhelming heavy fire,
reported as 'missing' only later,
   – after the 'Re-Org'.

During the Company sweep,
his mates found him,
dead where he lay
in the heat of an Asian afternoon
weapon missing, ammo missing,
and body disfigured,
   – in the age old way.

And so in death,
he journeyed back
that sad and cold
New Zealand winter's day,
to the lush green fields
of his Waikato home
and the quiet streets,
   – of small town Te Kauwhata.

And tributes came,
and tributes glowed
as the politicians spoke,
but the tears that flowed
from his mates that day
as they bore him shoulder high
said more than all the gallant words
   – as his cortege passed me by.

To the warriors chant
and the Kuia's cry!
they slow marched through the town
and beat the drum with a solemn tone
as the left boot struck the ground,
they bore the broken body
of Private Manning upon high
to the wailing of the Kuia,
   – and the tears as soldiers cried.

His Tour of Duty's over,
and his body's laid to rest
he sleeps the sleep
of stolen youth
in the soft sweet soil
of a warrior's grave,
   – and the Rangiriri earth.

*Mike Subritzky*
*(2000)*

## *The Best Friend I Ever Had*

If you will lend me your ears for a moment
There is a story I feel I must tell,
For I'll never forget that dark morning
We marched into Bardia's Hell.

    For two weeks we'd been living in trenches
    While our guns roared by day and by night
    As they pounded the Ities' defences
    Which in turn gave us little respite.

Their shrapnel fell thickly around us
They bombed us with murderous intent,
But we stuck to our guns and we waited
For the dawn of the final event.

    The dust storms would rise and the darkness
    As dark as the midnight would fall
    And the soft sweeping sands of the desert
    Would bring us under its pall.

The trenches were crawling with vermin
Our rations were terribly light:
Bully beef, biscuits and water
One quart for a day and a night.

    With me was a bit of a stripling,
    A lad from the sunny 'North Coast',
    Who spoke of his Mother and Sister
    But never of his own deeds did boast.

We shared all together in army life
Our letters our money and all
And each one had certain instructions
If one or the other should fall.

    It was the evening before the encounter
    As the sun in the desert sank red
    That he took from his pocket a wallet
    I recall clearly the words that he said:

"Now Johnny, if I fall tomorrow
And this wallet you still find intact
Will you send it back home to my sister?"
And we shook on that last solemn pact.

By next dawn the shrapnel was flying
And bullets were falling like rain
The sun rose on dead men and dying
Out there on that shell battered plain.

We stuck side by side with a Bren gun,
We kept up a deadly tattoo,
All the sand and the dust choked the action
And we knew we had but one thing to do.

We had just reached the head of 'Death Gully' –
That place ain't a name on its own
For 'twas there that death reaped a harvest
From the seed that a nation had sown.

The shells fell more thickly around us
As we knelt and dismantled the gun
While the dust and the smoke from the battle
In a great cloud that blacked out the sun.

"Gun ready!" he shouted "Up lad,
Grab hold of your ammo and run!"
As he sprang to his feet he fell backwards,
A dead man on top of his gun.

In a stupor I knelt down beside him,
I saw that his battle was through,
That a hard cruel fate had denied
The best friend I ever knew.

I picked up his shrapnel-scarred Bren gun
With a curse for the foemen ahead,
I went onward to join in the battle
While behind me my comrade lay dead.

I thought of the Mother and Sister
He had left in his own native land
And the last solemn promise I made him
And the firm honest clasp of his hand

    The fight had grown fierce by midday
    Our advance was considerably slowed
    The D Company reached an embankment
    And took cover behind a raised road.

Our ammo supply was exhausted –
We'd lost more than half of our men –
We faced fourteen guns with bare bayonets
And five magazines for a 'Bren'.

    Now those cannons are silent and rusted
    They are pointed in shame at the ground
    While the crews of them have all been mustered
    And placed in a prison compound.

By noon on the third day we ceased firing
The battle of Bardia was won,
Then orders were given for retiring –
The worst was still to be done.

    For lying back there on the desert
    Among scores of our valiant dead
    With the soft desert sands sweeping over him
    Lay the best friend I ever had.

The sun on the fourth day was sinking
On a desert now far, far away
When two men stood silently thinking
By the grave where our dead comrade lay.

    So gently we laid him forever
    'Neath his name on a rough wooden cross,
    And we shared with our loved ones so far off
    This sadness and terrible loss.

The high Army Command heard the story
And despite all our terrible loss
They wrapped up our company in glory
And presented our Captain a cross.

So we won the first stage of the battle,
With honours we carried the day,
We rounded up prisoners like cattle
And hastily marched them away.

In a wadi where shells couldn't find us
We lay to snatch brief respite
A battalion moved in behind us
And the battle raged on through the night.

And now when the evening is falling
'Retreat' sounds so sweet and so sad
My thoughts fly to faraway Bardia
And the best friend I ever had.

*Anon*
*(AWM PR 00526)*

## *March of the 7th Division*

A ribbon of green 'neath an azured sky
As the men in their jungle suits march by
But I see them again in the mountainous heights
In the tawny semi-treacherous light.
I see them splashed with rain and mud
Broken bodies and guns and blood
Ever advancing, gaunt and lean,
An endless column in jungle green.

And too I see, as they march along
In faded green, a ghostly throng;
I hear the sound of their phantom feet
Silently pacing the sunlit street.
For them the cheers and waving flags
In their darkened valleys and mountain crags
My heart is filled with pride and pain
For the deathless band who march again

And who shall stay their fateful stride,
Can stay the flood of the flowing tide?
Their guns are broken, their deeds are done
But their standard is raised 'neath the southern sun.
Onward and upward 'tis borne along
Mine ears are filled with their silent song
And I look to hear in the years ahead
The triumphant tramp of our marching dead.

*Cpl Frank Lundie*
*2/27 Batt.*
*(AWM PR 00619)*

# HMAS Sydney

She may not come back in triumph
Of bunting or of bell,
With a victor's pride about her
As she breasts the harbour swell.
There will be no bands aplaying,
No whistle piping clear,
As she swings aside the pier.

But at midnight in the silence
When the very stars are dark
She may come again to moorings,
A ghostly phantom barque.
Though she lie in floods unfathomed,
We may seem to see once more,
Her silver shape go shining
Down the path she trod before.

Not in fury, not in peril
Of battle or of crag,
But with life-breath in her funnel
And with flutter in her flag;
And the eyes of her last company
Seeming bright and valiant yet
Ah! The iron ship shall moulder
Ere the hearts at home forget.

*Lance Fallaw*
*(AWM PR 87/062)*

## *The Last Farewell*

Some survive on the battle field
    Where others, sadly, die;
Some had time for a last farewell
    Reaching vainly for the sky.

And I wonder, how much time will pass,
    How long before I see
The hills of home, a country lane,
    Or smell an old gum tree.

Times are tough, the going rough,
    No life for man or beast,
Cold bully and biscuits hard as nails –
    At times even this a feast.

The blood and mud, heavy underfoot,
    The vermin a constant curse,
At least those alive can still complain:
    Could things ever get much worse.

Then you look at the man, standing by your side
    You hardly know him at all,
But your life may rest in his two hands
    When you hear the bugle call.

With shot and shell and bullet whine,
    Side by side we run,
Knowing not the reason why
    This battle has begun.

As we go through the bloody slaughter,
    This man-made image of hell,
There's a gasp from the man beside me
    A sad look and a last farewell.

*James D. Young*

## Remember

*The sinking of H.M.A.S. Canberra, 9 August 1942*

'Twas on the ninth of August, just after midnight fell,
The heavy cruiser *Canberra* was steaming through the swell
The night was very dark and still,
Till the alarm bells rent the air –
The enemy was close at hand
And things had to be prepared.

Then suddenly the stillness broke with a terrific bang and roar,
And a salvo of shells crashed through the plates,
And some men knew no more.
The old ship stopped, the lights went out,
She shook from stem to stern,
She listed port and lay there still,
Just off Tulagi shore.

When dawn broke, the rain was worse,
The wounded men just lying there, not even rent a curse.
A stoker spoke before he died,
"Just tell the wife, I love her dearly,
And when the baby comes along,
Don't forget to call him John."
A smile just lingered on his face,
"Goodbye old man," he said "Young John will take my place."

The word came through to abandon ship
For she was listing fast,
And as we pulled away each man looked up with tear-wet eyes
And gave three hearty cheers;
And in each heart, I know quite well,
There was a silent prayer.

*Leading Stoker F. J. 'Shags' Turner*
*A survivor*

## *The Reluctant Hero*

He was just an ordinary youngster
From an ordinary part of town,
When the National Service call up
Finally tracked him down.

They put him in a uniform
And handed him a gun,
The ungodly metamorphosis
Of this boy had now begun.

They trained him in the art of war
Said the jungle was his friend,
Then shipped him off to Vietnam
His training at an end.

There he found a different world
Learnt many things he didn't know,
How to fight a dirty war
When you can't tell friend from foe.

He learnt a strange new language
To describe a soul destroying fight,
Search and destroy, win the hearts and minds:
Would the politicians ever get it right?

Silent jungle, clammy heat
Expectation, but who knows of what,
Feeling observed by a thousand eyes
Waiting to fire that first fatal shot.

A sigh of relief passed down the line
As the 'pick-up zone' came in sight,
The choppers arrive, exactly as planned –
It's back to Nui Dat for the night.

Now he has time to think of Vung Tau
And girls in the ubiquitous bar,
Or better still, a week in Hong Kong,
On some well earned R and R.

But what of our conscript, here by chance,
Looking forward to a spell in reserve?
Those who legislated this lottery
Knew they'd never be asked to serve.

Soon back to war, as all soldiers must
To execute those malevolent skills,
To join once more in the dance macabre
In those distant, Vietnamese hills.

He didn't hear the rifle shot
They say you never do,
And somewhere in the Long Hai Hills
A young soldier's life was through.

He saw not the flag draped casket
Nor heard the Last Post call,
One of many, who didn't make it
Those reluctant heroes all.

*James D. Young*

## *Milne Bay*

In an old Australian homestead, with roses round the door,
A girl received a letter which just came from the war;
With her Mother's arms around her, she gave way to sobs and sighs
And as she read that letter, the tears came to her eyes.

Why do I weep, why do I pray?
My love's asleep, so far away;
He played his part that April day
And left my heart in Milne Bay.

She joined a band of Sisters, underneath the Cross of Red,
Just to forget a heartache of a lad who now lies dead;
Many suitors came to woo her but they sadly turned away
When she told to them the story, of a grave in Milne Bay.

*Anon*
*(AWM PR 88 019)*

## Goodbye, All

*Written by a stretcher-bearer as a tribute to a nineteen year-old country lad he found on the wire at Tobruk.*

"Yes, Dig, I've stopped it pretty bad,
    Think I've done a wing;
I'm comfortable... don't worry lad,
    You're like a breath of spring.

"A cigarette... my oath I will ...
    May prove to be the last.
You Red Cross blokes just take the pill
    Never wait until you're asked.

"I think I'm going, Nightingale,
    Just tell me as a friend
You'll see and tell her without fail
    She's with me to the end."

I held a hand that tightly closed
    Around the name he pressed
Into my palm. He dozed,
    He closed his eyes in rest.

I've heard the cheers, that sweet refrain,
    I've felt the crowd's pulse throb,
I've clasped the hand of noble strain
    I've shaken with the mob.

But back o' handshakes I'll recall
    His handclasp and his look.
His bravely whispered "Goodbye, all!"
    That still night in Tobruk.

*Pte J. Kneeshaw, QX14342*
*(AWM PR 87/062)*

# CHAPTER FIFTEEN
# SOCIAL COMMENT

## *The AIF is Calling*

From the fields of battle o'er the sea
The Diggers call to you and me:
Give us tanks and give us guns
Give us a chance to beat the Huns.
We're on this job, the going's tough,
We're out to call Hitler's bluff.

We don't know the word 'defeat'
Although we took a knock at Crete.
We had to leave some pals behind
But fate, to them, has been unkind.
We're carrying on, we'll see this through
That's if we get some help from you.

Give us your best, send us the stuff
Till Hitler cries he's had enough,
A sporting chance of one-to-one
To meet this murderous brutal Hun,
Brutal both on land and sea,
Chief oppressor of the free.

You heard of how we fared in Crete
Through lack of arms a forced retreat
Falling back against [the] grain
While paratroops fell down like rain,
Gliders, carriers, dropping tanks,
Smashing our depleted ranks.

Against such odds our chance was small
But we fought on, our backs to the wall;
Stukas made death dealing swoops
Trying to destroy our troops,
But man for man and gun for gun
We'll clean this earth of brutal Hun

And when his lust for power has gone
A peaceful world shall carry on,
A wiser Britain then shall know
And be prepared for any foe.
The lessons that this war has taught
Must not be lost for want of thought.

Let costs of war, with all its strife,
Be measured first in human life,
And when our boys from o'er the foam
With duty done come sailing home
See to it then that they're repaid:

For every sacrifice they made,
They who kept Australia free,
Have risked their all for you and me.

*Pte Albert Edward Godwin*
*(AWM PR 86 160)*


## On Army Tradesmen

A country pollie had a notion, while scraping cow dung off a boot
    To get rid of army tradesmen and save us all some loot,
"We'll replace 'em all wiv civvies, youse know how quick they goes,
    Jus' look 'ow fast they scamper when the knock off siren blows."

"So now when grunts and tankies go slogging through the bush
    Why, we'll send along Fred Nerk to help maintain the push –
Except of course on weekends (when 'e 'as a two-day rest)
    Or if 'e strikes for 'igher wages, hmm, now won't that be a pest.

Or when 'e claims for dirt and danger and for 'ard layin' too,
    Or flexes off on Fridays or takes a sickie, or a few."
(Then our pollie will relent and say "We'll keep them green instead,"
    While clouds of fat pink piglets go flying overhead).

*Capt. Don Buckby*

## *On Immigration*

We sit in splendid isolation
Indulge in high pontification
On a subject vital to our nation:
The make up of our immigration.

To question earns a racist tag
While xenophobes hold high the flag
Each cause the migrant's hope to sag;
He's on a rock, a lonely shag

One group says, maintain your roots,
The next, be Aussies to your boots,
Either choice not the other suits –
We can at times be callous brutes.

There is no answer short and sweet
No path to guide the new chum's feet;
Do you blame him then if he's discreet
And does not seek to risk defeat?

*Capt. Don Buckby*

## *On Progress*

Great blocks of glass and concrete rear up to strike your eye
And cast an ugly silhouette against the northern sky;
The Brisbane of my childhood has swiftly changed her face,
Cast off her grace and beauty to become a barren place.

Gone her shady awnings with their canvas gaily hung,
Reduced to rag and matchwood when the wreckers hammer swung;
Gone Cloudland and the Cecil, the Belle Veue and the 'Cri',
To a generation's mem'rys we bid a sad goodbye.

As a lad of thirteen summers it seemed the grandest treat
As with my mother and a brother I walked a city street
To buy a Loyal from Wallace Bishop and lunch at an hotel:
The former's moved, the latter's gone as this tale to you I tell.

Yes, our city's changed, but for the best, the pollies quickly say,
We have buildings, towers and freeways to match Sydney any day;
But Sydney had to pay the price when her building boom did start –
That vibrant, bustling city, now owns a cold dead heart.

Adelaide and Charters Towers have progressed but kept their looks,
Perhaps we should have taken leaves from those two cities' books;
Progress need not mean destruction and a crane boom swinging high
Bear that in mind when next the glass and concrete strikes your eye.

*Capt. Don Buckby*

## *Australia in the 90s*

Forlorn our youthful country stands, despair upon her face,
    The hopes, the dreams her firstborn held, all dashed without a trace,
Her population ageing, her economy in debt,
    By crashing market prices she is cruelly beset.

Cast back her mind, just fifty years, her world was smiling then,
    Through expended blood and treasure she'd escaped the tyrants' den
The grind of the depression, was a distant mem'ry now,
    While the tensions of the Cold War had yet to crease her brow.

How quickly that scene altered in a short four-decade span,
    From the years of dull indolence when Menzies was the man,
To the tumult of the sixties when the Beatles took control
    And a war in South East Asia on her young men took a toll.

Then came those seething seventies when Whitlam's men held sway,
    And the dull minds of the Liberals were brusquely swept away;
In their haste to push their program they made some awful blues
    That perhaps our children's children may yet pay off the dues

Next came the heartbreak eighties, with hard drugs, AIDS and war,
    Divisive immigration and stock markets through the floor,
Labour's men again in charge from Fraser's wasted years
    Saw street crime and inflation the cause of countless tears.

So what now for the nineties, does yet a light shine through?
    The Middle East again in flames God knows what might ensue.
If we, by chance, escape world war, we're still by troubles cursed,
    With pensions and pollution right up there with the worst.

'Tis said, the hour brings the man, pray God that hour is near,
    This Nation's close to fracture through want and hate and fear;
Our forebears in their ignorance made black men's lives a hell –
    I fear we may be doomed to share, that bitter fate as well.

*Capt. Don Buckby*

## *Australia*

In the not so distant past Australians shunned help like a curse
Now it seems there's plenty willing to live off the public purse.

Perhaps their pride burned stronger in the 'not-so-easy' days –
Has technology seduced us to seek the softer ways?

Our past abounds with stories of the will to fight and win,
Nowadays, it seems the fashion to try once then give in.

Yes, there are examples of the chanced hands that won
The Hardys and the Hancocks, and look how well they've done.

But for each who shows the spirit to put life to the test,
You'll see a thousand shirkers who accepted second best.

They're the ones who squeal the loudest 'bout the state the country's in,
The first to duck for cover should the call come to 'put in'.

Our pollies woo their voters and seek to please them all,
They avoid the hard decision lest their cushy job should fall.

They've built an expectation that the world owes us our keep,
In retaining 'middle ground' they resemble milling sheep.

But the blame's not theirs in total (insipid as they are)
The truth is, You and I have let it go too far.

We've lived beyond our means and capacity to pay
With our lazy working habits and our love of holiday

Poor product, too expensive to compete with foreign trade,
Sets our Lucky Country's future on a course of wane and fade.

The days of wool and coal are drawing to their end,
Other nations sell it cheaper and that's where the buyers spend.

Our foreign debt is mounting on the dollars daily fall,
A crushing welfare burden has our backs against the wall.

'Though it's not the loss of dollars that's the greatest tragedy –
It's the toll on our young people that every day you see.

They haunt employment centres for jobs that are not there
And each day their expectation grows a little more threadbare

It will take a mighty effort to retrieve our children's hope
But without that, with life's trials, they will surely never cope.

We regularly hear some pollie give forth his vapid spiel,
Some wishy-washy twaddle that they hope will make us feel

That they have the plan to 'make it right' and keep us 'strong and free'
But it's hard to give much credence when just 'politics' we see.

Some words that they speak give us some slight cause to hope
But they do not take them far enough to get us up the slope.

Then the Opposition side has their chance to e'en the score
But they promise nothing different that we haven't tried before.

Do they think that cheap point scoring can solve this country's plight?
This is the crucial battle that together they must fight.

One has the ear of business and one the working man
And both will be required in the drafting of the plan.

We must regain the spirit that made our Nation great
And dispel this selfish torpor that keeps us second rate.

For the warning bell has sounded and we'd better heed it's call
There may not be much time left before we lose it – all !

*Capt. Don Buckby*

# *If*

If these thoughts have never crossed your mind,
    then let them do so now,
That this world would be a better place, if only we knew how.

How to look beyond the strictures of self, and self alone,
    How to take a stand against a wrong,
not cowardly condone.

How to foster in our children a feeling of their worth,
    How to teach them
that there's more to life, than pursuit of wealth and mirth.

How to teach them of the difference
    'tween the body and the soul
And that both need to be nurtured to make a person whole.

How to not impose upon their childhood
    to make them grow too fast,
But to offer them the wisdom of the errors of your past.

*Capt. Don Buckby*

## *On Urban Ponds*

The endless, mindless clamour of the teeming, smelly street,
With the grimy, run-down hovels their symbols of defeat,

Those chains of fear and family bind fast the little man:
He stays the hapless pawn of a cruel, uncaring plan.

If he would but lift up his eyes to see the chance beyond
He'd no longer stay a tadpole in this murky urban pond.

*Capt. Don Buckby*

## A Word With Banjo

I heard a song the other day, I knew the jingle well,
They say it's survived a hundred years, but who can really tell.
Your song is but a memory for the republic of my time,
And for all your city living, you wrote a bloody good bush rhyme.

You wrote of a young Australia, that was home to sheep and bloke,
To mounted troops and billabongs and a truth not now bespoke;
You told a rhythmic story of a bloke whose luck was out,
Whose tuckerbag was finally full when three troopers were about.

Now the irony of your sad tale should not be lost, my friend,
For do we not all search and find a billabong in the end?
At least a hundred years ago, your swagman jumped alone,
He begged not for a welfare cheque, nor pension card, nor home.

He faced the consequences of his lonely isolation
Of the choices that he made and the road that he had taken;
He died the way he lived, a rebel in your song –
How many today can claim this, from their murky billabong?

Banjo, don't you see? your rhymes no longer rhyme,
Your iambic pentameter has lost a beat with time,
You spoke of an Australia, young and proud and free,
Where men and women worked by day, and spent nights peacefully,

Where a gun wasn't necessary to see your kids to school,
Where if you stole another man's swag you were a bloody fool;
But these are not the values of the swagman of today –
He has no truth or honour, and knows that someone else will pay.

It gladdens me that you don't know how your land did fare,
And I'm glad to know that your billabong did not your swagman spare,
But most of all I'm glad to know, that one hundred years ago
Our Country wasn't politically correct, and nor were you Banjo.

*Tony Anetts*

## *Sacrifice*

Why can't the world remember,
The lessons of the years;
The horrors of each conflict
Bringing many bitter tears
To wives and daughters left behind,
Who pray for peace to reign,
So they may see their husbands
And their fathers once again.

A chap I know from Moree,
With a bonny child and wife,
He considered them worth fighting for
And so he risked his life
To resist the German madman,
Who wants to rule the world;
He's the type of Aussie soldier,
Who keeps our flag unfurled.

A daughter nick-named 'Whiskers'
By a fond and loving Dad,
Her little heart is breaking
And her eyes are ever sad.
She is old enough to reason,
Just why he went away
And nightly with her mother
For his safe return they pray.

I know he'll never weaken
When the battle's at its height;
It's his family he's protecting,
That's why he's in the fight.
Someday the war will finish
And he'll put away the sword,
That family's reunion
Will be his just reward.

*Raymond John Colenso*
*(AWM PR 00689)*

## Home Front, 1943

It is quite plain
Our people are fine democrats.
They loudly disdain
The Nazis and the 'little yellow rats',
And laud the soldiers of this 'free and mighty nation' –
Our way of life is better, they maintain.
(especially when you can dine on a pretty fair ration.)

Brave Boys, they fight
The battle for Australia's freedom
For us, our wives, for liberty, for RIGHT;
So in peace we shall therefore lead them
To the finest fruits of Victory: In them shall they invest
Secure their lives, provide for futures bright.
(From deferred pay they will naturally find the normal business interest.)

Meanwhile beware
Lest they should sweat in vain;
Let any but dare
To curb our ancient liberties: his then the pain
Of financial mights combined to drive him from the market.
For them and theirs, to Free Enterprise we swear.
(And even though the profit margin's down right now, turnover is up and hearty.).

*P. F.*
*Chaplain D. Trathen (?)*
*(AWM PR 00218)*

## *Advance Australia*

Forget about our fighting men
And join me in a cheer,
Who gives a damn for the Navy
If the painters get their beer?

Don't worry about our sailor boys
Who man the corvettes sleek,
Here's to the Home Front
At twenty quid a week.

This is the news to cheer the lads
Whose hours aren't nine to five,
And who don't know in the morning
If, by night, they'll be alive.

If you don't believe me, ask them,
And I wonder what they'll say
As they fight on in the islands
For six-and-six a day.

So when the pubs are open
Down tools and drink your fill:
The news'll make them happy
In the swamps on Bougainville.

*T. L. Haselden*
*(AWM MSS 1204)*

## *Horrors of the Home Front*

So you're weary of taxes, my masters?
You're bowed 'neath the burden of debt?
   And your delicate palate is pining
   For dainties your purse cannot get.

Why, we'll welcome you here in the jungle,
The only taxation we pay
   Is our blood and our strength and our manhood –
   Come join us my friends and be gay.

We'er not bothered be seeking the solace
Of oysters, fresh eggs and champagne;
   See our fattened and fond exultation
   When bully beef greets us again

Why suffer the ill-mannered jostling
At Randwick when races are there?
   Be with us in our Coral-girt Eden –
   We've endless supplies of fresh air.

Why fritter your time and your temper
As black market liquor you seek?
   Come and share our Bacchanalian revels –
   Two bottles of beer every week.

Why bewail that girlfriend's unfaithful,
That Yankees have shouldered you out?
   Take a trip to our tropical island
   Where the damsels are never about.

Why complain of the shocking milk shortage,
Let cows and their milkman go hang!
   Try a sip of our sterilised water –
   You'll love its medicinal tang.

Why disgorge thumping fees to your Doctors
For luxury livers and gout?
   Why, it costs us not even a shilling
   For treating malaria bouts.

So be free from their strikes and their lockouts,
Be sure like we are of our pay,
   With us you'll be certain of working
   For twenty-four hours every day.

So to hell with harsh civilisation,
Be damned to your tyrants so vile!
   Grab a rifle and share our good fortune
   On this our Utopian Isle.

*'Black Bob'*
*Lt A. L. O'Neill (?)*
*Bougainville*
*(AWM MSS 1328)*

## Ballad of the Base Wallahs

Now the common frontline soldier, he will go where he is told,
But the cute Cut-lunch Commando such harsh treatment can't be sold.
For the common frontline soldier runs the risk of getting shot.
Which the shrewd Cut-lunch Commando knows is foolish tommyrot.
And the common frontline soldier at most things is quite unskilled.
He fights horrid Japs and Nazis, and he ends up getting killed.
But the brave Cut-lunch Commando, if he feels he *must* get shot,
Boldly breasts the bar in Pitt Street, where he sinks pot after pot.

Now the common frontline soldier, when on duty overseas,
If a little sleep he scrounges he must share it with the fleas;
But the tired Cut-lunch Commando always knows his 'P's and 'Q's
Has a feathered bed and playmate to improve his hard-earned snooze.
And the common frontline soldier when he sails to do and dare
Has no financial worries, for the Army pays his fare.
But the poor Cut-lunch Commando as he fights the Barracks War
Has to pay his way (then claims it on his good old 'TS4').

Now the common frontline soldier in his jungle-green array
Is scarce a tailor's model (though he scares the Japs away);
But the sleek Cut-lunch Commando is Beau Brummel to the life,
With more stripes than any zebra and his pants creased like a knife.
And the common frontline soldier wades through mud and never whines
But although himself he's filthy, sees his rifle barrel shines,
While the great Cut-lunch Commando wades through supper at each dance.
And his desk-chair up at the barracks shines the backsides of his pants.

Yes the common frontline soldier has his little hour of fame,
But his certain end's a white cross with his number and his name;
But the bold Cut-lunch Commando knows that when at last he's dead
It will be without his boots on, and by God. 'twill be in bed!

So, my common frontline soldiers, of the story here's the nub:
Join the Royal Cut-lunch Commandos... fight the war from pub to pub

*'Black Bob'*
*Lt. A. L. O'Neill (?)*
*Sydney, July 1944*
*(AWM MSS 1328)*

## Bougainville 1945

We've nineteen dead on the Buin Road,
    Ten more on the jungle track,
And all day long there's a broken tide
    Of our wounded streaming back.
We've fought all night by the Hongorai
    With never a bite or sup,
And tomorrow's back-page news will quote –
    Our soldiers are 'MOPPING UP'.

As dawn awakes with a jaded eye,
    Discarding its misty pall,
White crosses mourn on the Numa Trail
    For fellows who gave their all;
In Tsimbas ridges, Boraken's groves,
    They drained to the dregs hell's cup;
The blood they gave was a passing thing:
    They merely were 'MOPPING UP.'

The screaming silence of ambushed swamp,
    The horror of obscene bog,
The vicious foe in a filthy league
    With blanketing rain and fog
Are trifling things, which the critics know
    Should never hold heroes up.
Good Lord, why this isn't war at all:
    We are simply 'MOPPING UP'.

We make no claim to heroic mould
    But this little boon we ask –
Those armchair critics please send up here
    To share in our 'simple task';
When they're on intimate terms with Death
    And have tallied the blood-cost up,
Maybe they'll coin a more adequate phrase:
    Than casual 'MOPPING UP'.

                'Black Bob'
            Lt. A. L. O'Neill (?)
           (AWM MSS 1328)

## *From Us You'll See No More*

I've been looking down on earth again,
Since Nippon toed the line,
And though I know your thoughts are gay,
I'd like to tell you mine.

I'm just as thrilled as are you all
To think the stoush is o'er,
And I'm sure to date there's no regret –
From us you'll see no more.

The thing I'd like to ask you though,
For all of us passed on,
Is that you'll honour promises
To those who know we've gone.

We don't want mourning for your loss –
There are plenty of our kind –
But see there is a decent go
For those we've left behind.

It didn't matter when I went,
I left no one to weep,
But plenty [of] chaps who took the count
Had wife and kids to keep.

And it's for them I think tonight;
They gave their all – your dad;
It's up to you to see they get
The deal they might have had.

Young Tim who bought it in Tobruk,
And Blue at Alamein,
And Snow was knocked in Syria;
I see them now again.

Then Smithy over Shaggy Ridge,
And Slim in the Wewak show;
Their thoughts were for their dear ones home
As their strength was ebbing low.

T'was Tony on the jungle trail,
My God! he fought for life;
"It's not that I'm afraid to die,"
He said, "But my kids and wife."

I crudely stroked his burning brow,
Said, "Take it easy sport,"
As long as I am still on deck
I'll see they want for nought."

But I met my match in Borneo,
And the job is still to do,
Are we to break that promise to him,
Or can I look to you?

And this is only one of scores
Of cases of the sort;
Can we depend you'll see to them
That now the battle's fought?

You promised each and all of us,
On joining in the fray;
You'd care for us and ours if need
Be, when we went away.

We hoped you wouldn't have to though,
But there, 'What is to be.'
And now with all the war guns stilled
My friends we look to thee.

The wars are fought for principles
And when the battle's won,
The job of putting things aright
Has only just begun.

The world has failed in bygone years
To win the fight for peace;
But if you right that fault this time
We'll rest in perfect peace,

*G. A. G.*

## *What Have We Done to Deserve This?*

I wonder whom we've got to blame
For what goes on today,
Why manpower men are going home
And five-year chappies stay.

I could ask Mr Dedman why,
But that's no use I guess –
I know he wouldn't say that he
Had caused this awful mess.

I went to see an Air Force chap
To book a passage home,
He said you'll have to wait a while,
There's manpower men to come.

I wandered down towards the docks
To find myself a ship;
They told me only manpower men
Were going home this trip.

I slowly wandered back to camp,
Alone in grim despair,
Arriving just in time to see
Some more men leaving there.

I didn't have to ask them why,
I know without a doubt;
They'd told me several days before
Some boss would get them out.

A chap with two years' service up
Pulled out the other day,
He used to drive a taxi cab,
But soon the bricks he'll lay.

Yet one chap here, a QX man,
Is waiting with the rest
For six long years he's soldiered on
And surely needs a rest.

There's one great fear in all our minds:
The demob crowd back home
May be discharged ere we can find
Some way across the foam.

With no one left to hand us out
Our ticket marked with 'D',
We'll have to soldier on through life
And never will be free.

*Anon*

## *To the Guy Who Pinched My Dame*

It's while I'm sweating and fighting in this place they call Tobruk
That I got her message saying, "Getting married, wish me luck".
No I didn't do my onion, war rages just the same,
But I'd love to pen this message, to the guy who pinched my dame.

Don't think I'm blessing you for sitting on the fence,
For not slapping on the old khaki, for you may have shown some sense;
But I'm out off in the desert, bought myself a heap of grief,
And I'm getting gaunt, gut rotted, while waiting for relief.

But I am here and you are there still that ain't my moan,
But you might have pulled a white man's act, and left my dame alone.
She was the apple of my eye, talisman, lone star and guiding light,
But the little head I loved so well, now shares your pillow at night.

You tell me that you're not to blame, she'd heard the mating call,
But she is easy meat, a lonely girl, and you know how women fall.
I don't know, maybe you're smart to dodge slaughter, dirt and strife,
You laugh at all the mugs out here, who fight to keep you safe.

I wasn't there to watch my dame, I thought her worth fighting for.
Oh! what's the use, you get the cream, while I am at the war!
Wish her luck! She'll need it, when she counts the whys and buts,
She will find her idol lacking, not in charm – but guts.

*Anon*

## *Growin' Old*

They say you're growin' old when your memory starts to slip,
And your knees go kinda wonky when up the hill you trip,
You like to reminisce on things that used to be around,
Long before the dollar took over from the pound.

If you mention 'knobs of blue', scrubbin' boards and clothes props up the yard,
And tell of all the virtues of Jolson, Valentino and things written by the Bard,
They shake their heads and wonder about the affect of all your years;
'Tis hard to make young folk comprehend when memories turn to tears.

You dined on rabbit stew 'n vegies when the hunters drifted in,
And you boiled the tea leaves o'er and o'er and re-rolled bumpers
before they hit the bin,
You remember bread and dripping, darning needles and patches in your pants,
And how you swelled with pride when allowed to dress up for the local dance.

You mended shoes with cardboard and dined on speckled fruit,
The mattress was filled with horsehair and bedding was of calico
topped by the finest jute,
You went to the 'flicks' on Saturday arvo' to see the features, a cartoon and the rest,
The price, for kids, was a zack (sixpence) and the heroes – they were the very best.

I guess growin' old compares with the modern motor car,
It travels miles and miles and then begins to show that it's not up to par,
Bits wear out and the upholstery starts to sag, so you apply a little polish,
But it, like you, is growin' old, yet the journeys that you shared are ones that
you now cherish.

If growin' old means memories, then I've got quite a few,
Of epsom salts, castor oil and camphor to ward off bouts of flu,
And home-made toys, gramophones and the local township band,
An' waiting on the milko, and his horse, with billy can in hand.

We drove our horse and sulky to church 'n Sunday school for which we dressed up fine,
For Sundays were often picnic days and for them we did pine,
Our games were often rough with skinned knees and elbows quite normal,
An' those days were days of wonder, a sheer delight for most were quite informal.

The media say we're elderly when we reach fifty-five,
But that's a lot of nonsense, I'm long past that and very much alive.
And yet I guess we begin to age the moment we are born –
It's not the years that make us old 'tis becoming all forlorn.

So if you, like me, have accumulated quite some years,
Cling tight to the memories of 'the good old days' e'en tho' it may mean tears,
And if growin' old brings aches and pains that make you want to grumble,
Give thanks for the grace of God who gave you time – 'tis then you'll feel
quite humble.

*Bill Phillips*
*1998*

## The Flag

As the century turned our colonial states drew up a constitution,
And we became a federation of States, a Nation, a veritable institution,
We held a competition, to design ourselves a Flag for all to rally to,
The glorious Southern Cross was there and a star to represent the States,
plus the old Red, White and Blue.

This flag that we adopted, Union Jack and all, made us feel united,
It gave us national identity and in it we delighted,
It revealed that we were 'The Great South Land', as 'The Cross' so proudly showed,
And 'The Jack' told where we came from, its heritage on us bestowed.

We owe much to mother England for it gave to us our birth,
The early Pommy settlers, they opened up the land 'n' made us realise our worth;
Some were convicts, criminals of note, but their contribution gave us a mighty start;
The soldiers and free settlers also gave us something toward our great big heart.

There were many early troubles, with cruelty directed to natives and the convicted,
It was quite normal, 'twas the way of life, but our growth was not restricted,
Further colonies were developed and they just grew and grew, yet we were not one nation,
So founding fathers gathered to give to us a future and international station.

The British flag of Union revealed that we belonged to an ever growing Empire,
So that great badge of honour featured high upon our flag, what more could we aspire?
Our Mother Country was defender of the freedoms that captive nations seek,
And called upon its fledglings to stand and fight 'ere they could hardly speak'.

Tested in China, and against the Boers, the New Australians showed courage never seen before,
And when the Kaiser threatened, to the Union Flag they rallied, with patriotism galore.
At Gallipoli they truly showed their mettle as, united under 'Jack' and 'Cross',
They gave our Nation pride, plus an ever conquering spirit, and showed them who was boss.

When on to France the Anzacs marched, the First World War soon was over,
And not a man who served dishonoured the Federation Flag, if history you discover;
They were proud to be Australian and to be acknowledged as the best,
They saw no shame in a 'Union Jack' and treated their Aussie Flag as a cut above the rest.

Between the Wars, when poverty was rampant, Australians rallied around the Flag
That men had gladly died for and called upon almighty God to help remove this snag,
And when our Politicians sought to overcome and motivate our spirit,
It was with Flag, and the Anzac courage, they urged our Nation not to limit.

Then tyranny, it struck again when Hitler's men and Tojo, sought to use their might,
And Anzacs were called again to assist our embattled Motherland even tho' it meant a fight;
So we fought again with the flag of Federation flying high atop the mast,
And under this oft' bloodied ensign we won a victory that we pray will last.

One hundred years have almost gone, and we can proudly stand alone,
Now they respect our voice upon the International stage, for we are not a clone,
Some say we ought to untie the apron strings and shed the Union Flag,
I doubt that Mother England would deny our freedom, nor our desire to brag.

If we decide to fly a different flag representing our maturity and Oz's new direction,
Don't ask that we should feel ashamed and cause an insurrection,
I'm bloody proud of my Australia mate, as I'm sure you'll be of yours,
And as time goes by you'll learn to honour the 'old' Flag, despite its many flaws.

And if you've come from other lands and want to be an Aussie,
Learn first to speak our language, then our history of honour and Anzac spirit, and then you'll find a possie,
'Tis so easy to set aside the efforts of our fathers and say 'their tales are just a drag';
If we are *all* to be Australian, let's salute our mighty Flag!

*Bill Phillips*
*1997*

## *Aboriginals Were the First to Settle*

Aboriginals were the first to settle
   On this great Aussie land,
With spears they showed their mettle
   When they tried to make a stand.

As the English had a modern gun
   When they landed on the shore,
The Aboriginals had to run
   Not knowing what was in store.

Their culture and their way of life
   Was far behind the times
Of the modern English man and wife
   Who annexed the country for home and mines.

*Herbert M. Boys*

## *Our Australia*

Australia has a rugged beauty, its people diversified and proud,
They call our country 'lucky' and say we're arrogant and loud;
We're known to boast and brag and pull a leg or two,
We've got a sense of humour that irritates a few.

Our History is of dark men who walked the land 'til colonists arrived,
We're told of exploration, outlaws and the dark men now deprived,
Of new towns and opening up the land, of rushes to fields of gold;
There were settlers with high hopes and governors who were bold.

We've learned to cope with famine, drought and sometimes fire and flood,
There have been times we've had to shed our blood;
These things have built our character and taught us how to win,
It has taken sheer determination and a lot of Aussie guts but we did it with a grin.

Our land is vast and there's opportunity for those who come,
They have to leave a place somewhere and never beat a drum,
We welcome all, regardless of colour, race or creed, who come to be an Aussie,
Prejudice is catching, so leave it all behind if you want to find a possie.

When times are tough and others might despair
An Aussie shows his courage and ensures a 'go' that's fair;
We're Euro, Asian, Abo, Pom, Scot and Irish so we're the perfect brew,
But it's the mix of all we stand for that helps a mate pull through.

New Aussies come to settle and master soon our tongue,
They learn of pride and sacrifice, the things I learned when young,
Of Anzacs and later generations who emulate their style,
And they'll be as proud as I am when they've been here a while.

Some curse our politicians, 'coppers', 'abos', 'wogs', and 'slopes',
That's simply our tagging game but it makes us sound like dopes;
We're classless they will tell you, so you're all just one of us,
It's hard for visitors to comprehend and some wonder why the fuss.

If we are to be Australian, we are to be as one,
Not divided by the things that our forebears might have done;
There are heroes in our graveyards and I'm sure they'd find it strange,
That we've not passed our history on as generations change.

There's oft debate about who owns this rugged plain,
We've overlooked the fact that *Terra Australis* is God's domain;
Indigenes rage and claim to tracts we've come to love:
It's not the land that's 'lucky' it is those who acknowledge the Master up above.

The things that do the damage to the image we portray,
– When there are moments I feel ashamed to even say 'g'day' –
Are kids on drugs and alcohol-related crime, past bitterness and hate,
I don't care who you are, or where you're from, but if you learn to overcome,
I'll consider you a mate.

The year 2000 will see the world arrive at our front door,
They'll come to see the beauty of our rugged distant shore,
We'll show again our courage, our manners and our flag,
Our athletes will strive as others have before and if the cheers inspire them,
they've got it in the bag.

If you call yourself 'Australian' then you're the proudest on this earth,
It's not a title that comes easy – you have to show your worth;
It means a fight, occasionally a tear, and you'll have to show your strength,
The old have paid their due and the young will too, at length.

Let us stand together, mixed races yet one band,
The nations of the world are coming to see our land,
They'll want to know why we rarely experience failure,
It is because we are part of this land we call Australia.

*Bill Phillips*
*1997*

## *"Gee, I Love this Country!"*

As I sat in the mall on a bright and sunny day amunching my 'Big Mac',
This little bloke came and sat on the bench beside me confiding that he'd
been to see the 'Quack',
"Didn't cost me a cracker! Now where in the world could you beat that?" he asked.
I guessed that he was unemployed and agreed that he lived in a battlers' paradise
as we sat and basked.

We talked about the white and sandy beaches and the warm and rolling surf,
And he confessed that he'd never seen the sea until he'd left his patch of turf,
He'd been a drover, a farmer 'til the drought it drove him east
In search of something better than the harshness of the bush 'n' thought
"I might become a Priest!"

Not to be outdone I told of my story in reverse: a city bloke come to see the bush,
I'd felt the pain of joblessness and told of a battle with a different kind of push,
He said he'd thought all city blokes were toffs 'n' out of depth in a coastal plain,
But I seemed to him a decent type 'n' not a snob at all 'n' he'd felt a little pain.

We chatted on and talked of travel 'n' places that we'd seen,
To see if there was some common ground and experiences of places that we'd been,
Our conversation rolled thru' Alice, Darwin, the Isa and over to Albany,
There were bits of Longreach, Prosperpine, Hobart Town, Moree and it was kinda uncanny.

He'd been to 'most all the places that I had visited and we found a common bond.
We were one it seemed, two Aussies asitting on a bench,
linked by a devotion to the land of which we were fond;
We talked of our employment, homes and family and the price of this and that.
'N' raised a collective eyebrow of the inquisitive passers by who stared as we had our little chat.

We had travelled far and travelled wide and I'm sure our paths had crossed.
As we traversed this brown yet glorious land oft' stark and betimes storm tossed.
'Twas agreed that the 'stay-at-homes' cannot love that which they have not seen,
For we have grown to love the diversity of climate, people and the stories that we glean.

I 'spose that I should mention, he was black, myself a shade of white.
But we sat with arms around the others shoulder and laughed 'til it was almost night,
For we had the commonality of oneness with this most wonderful of lands.
And as we parted my friend exclaimed "Gee, I love this country!" and on this we shook hands.

My friend was a bush and townie man 'n' I hailed from the bustling city,
Yet we set aside the prejudices that are common – more's the pity –
And we'd shared a day that neither will forget and we found no need for reconciliation,
For such things are for the separated so we hauled down the barriers caused by years of separation

I guess, as years roll on, I'll remember that day upon a bench –
Tho' I forgot to ask why he'd been to see the 'Quack', for parting had been a wrench;
But I'll remember always the common bond that had been developed,
And our common exclamation of "Gee I love this country!" It was more than I had hoped.

If I can but urge you, reader, whether of residency old or new,
In this land that God has given us, to get on out and see if our love is true.
And you'll increase your knowledge and your pride as our predecessors have done,
'Til you feel as one with earth and man and 'til all your bias is gone.

Yes indeed – this is a splendid land and truly, I love this land!

*Bill Phillips*
*1999*

## My Friends who Stayed at Home

I'm pulling off my colours and slinging my web away
I'm going back to Cairo to draw my bloody pay,
I'm fed up with being a soldier, so help me Christ I am
Chewing mouldy biscuits & bloody bread & jam.

I'm fed up with fighting Germans out on my bloody own
When I think of good old Aussie & my mates who stayed at home
I'll bet he's walking up the street with his chest puffed out with Pride
And skiting to his cobbers how he saved his bloody hide.

And when I said to Mother "I've volunteered to fight"
She said "God bless you son & bring you back alright".
They called me a chocolate soldier a five-bob tourist too
They said "You'll never see the front or even get a view".

They said "You'll have a picnic across the ocean foam"
And they weren't game to face it my mates who stayed at home.
They're not bad shots either when on the rabbit track
But there ain't no bloody danger – the rabbits can't shoot back.

And here's me in the trenches where I've got to hide my head
For fear some German bastard will fill it up with lead,
They shine before the barmaids full of brag and skiting
And at the old street corner is where they do their fighting.

A billiard cue is their rifle, a bar their firing zone
For there ain't no bullets for my friends – the ones who stayed at home.
So I'll pick up me old Lee Enfield & buckle me web about
For I'm only a bloody private but I'm going to see it out

And, if I stop a bullet, I'll die without a groan
And my cobbers will put the kybosh
On the bastards who stay at home.

*Ronald William Flew*
*8 December 1941*
*(AWM PR 00526)*

## *The Freedom of the Press*

There 'ave been some funny stories
    Said my cobber 'Bob the Bot'
(By those chaps they call reporters,
    I could shoot the bloody lot)
Of soldiers they met in Malaya
    And places they have been,
Tales of parties and big dinners
    That no soldier's ever seen.

"They can write some pretty tall ones,"
    He continued with a grin,
"Fourteen courses for a dinner
    With liqueurs, beer and gin.
There's no doubt they are liars
    And 'ave reached the 'ighest grade
They should drop their jobs reportin'
    For born lawyers they was made."

Now we come from o'er the water
    From the land we calls our 'ome
And their writin's made me angry
    So I scribbled out this poem;
If by chance I ever meet one
    'E'll stop shootin' off his gob:
I could teach him such a lesson
    If he'd take my flamin' job.

Take me place on roll call,
    Also try our bully beef,
With those concrete mixer biscuits
    'E would find his rarest treat;
Marchin' full rigged all the mornin'
    E' would miss the old car seat,
Whilst the wearing of my bluchers
    Gave him blisters on his feet.

Give him just a quart of water
    To do him all the day
For washin', shavin', drinkin',
    And five & six for pay;
With guard duties of a night-time
    And when day breaks, old son,
Take 'im on maneouver
    And give him the biggest gun.

Take 'im out into the jungle
    Make 'im keep up in the line
Where 'e'll likely get his nose skinned
    Just from tripping over vines,
With perhaps a touch of 'eat rash
    Or a good attack of 'ives
It would make that smug reporter
    Realise that 'e's alive.

And when he's learned that lesson
    'E may write the wrong 'e's done
Explain that training in Malaya
    Leaves little time for fun;
When he's back, a correspondent,
    Though he doesn't need a gag,
You should read a different story
    In that old Australian rag.

Yes there's been some funny stories
    Thus concluded 'Bob the Bot',
They've often made me head ache
    And I've wished that I was shot,
For I'd rather have a skin full
    Of that good old Aussie grog
Than reading of mug reporters
    Shootin' off their bloody gob.

*Anon*

## *The Folly of War*

The cannons roar, the bullets whine,
The soldiers' dreaded fate,
The reason why, not clear to see
Thoughts of logic, far too late.

Where hide the ones who make the war,
Who fashion all the rules,
Not for them the battlefield
This honour – left to fools.

Yet fools we are, we men of arms,
Who hold our honour high,
While those who make this world of war
Care not that soldiers die.

Vested power to politicians
Who, for greed, would sell their soul,
But never they in gunshot sound
For them, no bells do toll.

Never yet in history's time
Were problems solved by force,
Still Man must pay the devil's price
The biblical rider, on a pale horse.

Where men of science boldly tread
No man has been before,
Yet humanity prospers not a whit
When it comes to the folly of war.

*James D. Young*

## Soldier's Farewell

I've saddled up and dropped me hooch,
    I'm going to take the gap,
    my Tour of Duty's over mates,
    and I won't be coming back.

I'm done with diggin' shell scrapes
    and laying out barbed wire,
    I'm sick of setting Claymore Mines
    and coming under fire.

So, no more Fire Support Base
    and no more foot patrols,
    and no more eating ration packs
    and sleepin' in muddy holes.

I've fired my last machine gun
    and ambushed my last track,
    I'm sick of all the Army Brass
    and I sure ain't coming back.

I'll hand my bayonet to the clerk
    – he ain't seen one before –
    and clean my rifle one more time
    and return it to the store.

So, no more spit and polish
    and make sure I get paid
    and sign me from the Regiment –
    today's my last parade.

*Mike Subritzky*

## *Midnight Movie*

*To Jimmy B from Huntly - I hope you find Peace, mate.*

A quiet night in the barracks,
    around midnight he starts it again,
    he's yelling about some damned ambush,
    and calling some Viet woman's name.

He always yells out he's sorry,
    so sorry for all of the pain,
    but every night around midnight –
    he kills her all over again.

His life's in a kind of a freeze frame,
    he can't move on from the war,
    and every night just after twelve
    he's back in the Nam once more.

Back with the old 'Victor' Company,
    back in that same Free-Fire-Zone,
    and no bastard told those young Kiwi Grunts
    they patrolled near a wood cutters home.

When the Lead Scout signals it's Charlie,
    the Platoon melts quietly away,
    the 'Immediate Ambush' sign's given,
    and the Safety Catch slips onto 'play'.

There's five in the group in pyjamas,
    as black as a midnight in May,
    and the Killing Ground moves into picture
    then the Gun Group opens the way.

Black figures are falling around him,
    now he's up on his feet running through,
    and they're sweeping the ground where they dropped them
    as he 'double taps' a screaming torso.

At the Re-Org his fingers are trembling,
    the Platoon Sergeant gives him a smoke,
      then it's back to the bodies to check them –
    and his round hit a woman in the throat.

There are blood trails leading behind them
    and entrails are spilled on the track,
      but the woman who screamed once is silent,
    two rounds exit right through her back.

The jungle seems silent and empty
    as they dig down and bury the mess,
      then it's check ammunition and weapons
    and don't dwell on the past, just forget.

Another night in the barracks
    and Jimmy is yelling again,
      it's that same old Vietnam movie
    that's spinning around in his brain.

He always yells out he's sorry,
    so sorry for all of the pain,
      but every night around midnight –
    he kills her all over again.

*Mike Subritzky*
*Cassino Barracks 1974*

## Digger's Rest

I worked at the local hospital.

The old Diggers were different to other patients.
There was one old bloke lost both legs to nicotine.
He learned to smoke in the war.
He would raise the flag every morning and
sit in his wheelchair all day in the sun.

Always a smile and a story.

Feel the cannon blasts, and hear the bugles call!
Rally to the flag, charge the salient wall!

No, none of that stuff,
just stories of old mates in far off times,
only yesterday to his cataract eyes
staring into the distance as he told of
stealing vegemite from the store at Changi;
The Japs thought it was boot polish.

He laughed.

Even though you expect them to die,
it's always a shock when they go.
I went to his funeral.
They played the Last Post over his soldier's grave.
It was very sad for me.

It brought back memories of old Diggers.
Uncles who survived Changi and The Rail –
if anyone can say they truly survived,
there in the Repat.
And the old aunts who continued to visit their men
for the rest of their lives.

*Peter Tremain*

## *Just a Simple Soldier*

He was getting old and paunchy and his hair was falling fast,
And he sat around the Legion, telling stories of the past,
Of a war that he had fought in and the deeds that he had done:
In his exploits with his buddies, they were heroes, every one.

And 'tho sometimes, to his neighbours, his tales became a joke,
All his buddies listened, for they knew whereof he spoke.
But we'll hear his tales no longer, for old Bob has passed away,
And the world's a little poorer, for a Soldier died today.

No, he won't be mourned by many, just his children and his wife,
For he lived an ordinary, very quiet sort of life.
He held a job and raised a family, quietly going on his way;
And the world won't note his passing; 'tho a Soldier died today.

When politicians leave this earth, their bodies lie in state,
While thousands note their passing and proclaim that they were great,
Papers tell of their life stories, from the time that they were young;
But the passing of a soldier goes unnoticed and unsung.

Is the greatest contribution to the welfare of our land
Some jerk who breaks his promise and cons his fellow man?
Or the ordinary fellow, who in times of war and strife,
Goes off to serve his Country and offers up his life?

The politician's stipend and the style in which he lives
Are sometimes disproportionate to the service he gives,
While the ordinary soldier, who offered up his all
Is paid off with a medal and perhaps a pension, small.

It's so easy to forget them, for it is so long ago,
That our Bobs and Jims and Johnnys, went to battle; but we know
It was not the politicians, with their compromise and ploys,
Who won for us the freedom that our Country now enjoys.

Should you find yourself in danger, with your enemies at hand,
Would you really want some cop-out, with his ever-waffling stand?
Or would you want a Soldier, who has sworn to defend
His home, his kin, and Country, and would fight until the end?

He was just a common Soldier and his ranks are growing thin,
But his presence should remind us, we may need his like again,
For when countries are in conflict, then we find the Soldier's part
Is to clean up all the troubles that the politicians start.

If we cannot do him honor while he's here to hear the praise,
Then at least let's give him homage at the ending of his days;
Perhaps just a simple headline, in the paper that might say:
OUR COUNTRY IS IN MOURNING, FOR A SOLDIER DIED TODAY.

*Anon*

## *Lest We Forget*

*Written on the sad occasion of the death of Fred Kelly who, at the age of 101, was not only the remaining Anzac survivor in NSW, but also an inspiration for everything that is good in today's society. My wish would be that those of us who live in safety and comfort today will do everything in our power to ensure that this freedom is not lost!*

REST IN PEACE

A hero left this earth today, so gallant, brave and true
He fought to save our country, he fought for me and you.

He represented selflessness, on that Gallipoli Campaign
'Lest we forget', we hope and pray those efforts weren't in vain.

This is the time to stop and think, to calculate the price
That all folk pay in conflicts, of human sacrifice.

On reflection, those who died, gave all that they could give
But were survivors fortunate, with a tortured life to live?

It seems they serve a sentence too, memories Oh so grim!
Of suffering, squalor, blood and guts, losses of life and limb.

And then there are the stories of bravery and courage and mates,
Sharing in times of adversity their fears, their loves, their hates.

So don't let these soldiers of valour, fight the good fight for nought;
Let's play our part, each one of us, to gain the results that they sought.

To stand shoulder to shoulder, together, each one of us aware
That we're all in the battle together to 'ADVANCE AUSTRALIA FAIR!'

*Val Wallace*
*30 December 1998*

## *The Inspiration of Anzac*

There's a day in April that's sacred
    To the memory of HEROES who died,
That we might forever have Anzac,
    As a symbol of national pride.

They lay in the hills of Gallipoli,
    They sleep by the Aegean Sea,
But their souls march on to the glory
    Of an immortality.

No tombs of chiselled masonry
    Distinguish them from Foe,
But just a simple wooden cross
    With AIF below.

They displayed the highest courage
    For which they paid the highest price
And a grateful country speaks with pride
    Of their deeds and sacrifice.

They were the flower of our nation
    And chosen by standards so high
That only the physically perfect
    Were good enough, even to die.

They sauntered down the city streets
    With independence and pride,
Because they were volunteer soldiers
    And it made them feel different, inside.

They spurned all routine orders,
    Were undisciplined and raw,
With a flair for sport and games of chance
    And few ideas of war.

They scorned the heat and glare
    Of Egypt's burning sands,
While they cursed the blinding sandstorms
    And the filth of Pharoah's lands.

Through the dust and grime of desert camps
    A comradeship was born
That levelled all distinctions
    Where the 'rising suns' were worn.

They were cobbers, united thru' thick and thin
    And proud of the manhood that blossomed,
A breed of men perfect and destined to be
    The bravest things God always meant them to be.

And they proved it with reckless abandon,
    As the story of Anzac will tell,
With the men of New Zealand beside them
    And a British division as well.

And you've not forgotten Lone Pine Ridge,
    Or Quinns, or Sari Bair,
And you'll never cease to wonder
    How they got a footing there.

With their ranks all shot to pieces
    And their lines but thinly held,
Those Anzacs went down fighting
    With a courage unexcelled.

And those who were left gazed around them
    With eyes strangely softened and wet,
Searching for cobbers still missing,
    To find them with eyes fixed and set.

Oh, God of Battles! sound that trumpet
    That summonses men from the fray,
And outlaw this senseless destruction
    That crushes out life in this way!

They went there in their thousands
    But they didn't all come back,
For some went on a different road
    On a one-way beaten track.

With a smile upon their faces
    They've gone beyond the clay,
Bequeathing the glorious heritage
    Of ANZAC DAY.

*Jack C. Black*
*(AWM PR 83 130)*

## *The Old Soldier*

It's Tuesday the Third of March Nineteen Hundred and Ninety Eight,
    An old soldier died this morning, fifty-three years too late;
    And the nurses in the nursing home hated to be near him
    'Cause he'd spit and curse and fume, and cause a mighty din
And the doctors were glad to see him go, he was dangerous in their eyes
    He'd knocked one out with a single blow, and he was twice his size,
    And when he'd snarled at visitors, and spooked the other old folks
    They took away his privileges, his magazines and his smokes.
And they lectured him on manners, and called him a disgrace
    When at night he woke from screaming, lathered in sweat, pale faced.

An old soldier died this morning, fifty-three years too late
    But the nursing home's not mourning for the latest turn of fate,
    And the doctor chatting to the pretty nurse, has something else in mind,
    'Cause soon he'll be on the golf course with others of his kind,
And from cross the road the wind will bring the sound of children's laughter;
    And in the trees the birds will sing and will for ever after;
    The day goes on and before very long the passing might never have been,
    No lasting sorrow nor mournful song, for nasty old men, it seems,
So go and put him in the ground – and mind you bury him deep –
    That way we won't hear the sound, of him screaming in his sleep.

An old soldier died this morning, fifty-three years too late,
    With no regrets in going, nor pity in his fate.
    But what cruel trick life gave him and who designed the law;
    That would slip his mind back in time, and make him relive the war;
Back to the tropical jungles, with sweat and mud and rain,
    Back to the yellow terror he visits again and again,
    Where the very land around him is trying to kill him as well
    With the crocs and snakes and malaria, he lives in living hell.
It's no wonder he was cranky in his final golden years,
    When he heard the screams of the dying in his nightly sleeping ears.

An old soldier died this morning, fifty three years too late.
    His mind went back to war in ninety-seven and ninety-eight,
    And the sight of the gardener, pruning in bushes on bended knee,
    Was to him the enemy sneaking, as plain as plain could be;
And when the Docs came to get him, he caused such trouble and strife
    But little did they realise, he was fighting for his life.
    And so he suffered daily at the hands of a hidden foe
    Hunted and haunted nightly, by fears we'll never know.
Why now so many years later should he fight all over again
    When surely he has already fought, more than most other men?

An old soldier died this morning, fifty-three years too late
    He spent three years in Changi, Weary Dunlop was his mate,
    And the Burma Rail was built with blood of men that he called mates;
    And all of those men and most of his sight was lost behind Changi's gates
And, though he lived over fifty years past the end of that terrible place,
    That a part of him had died there was written on his face;
    And fifty years of silence had its own nasty price
    Because in one single lifetime he had to live it twice.
Rest in Peace now, old soldier, you have deserved it yet,
    And may the rest of us remember Lest We Forget.

*Ron Wilson*

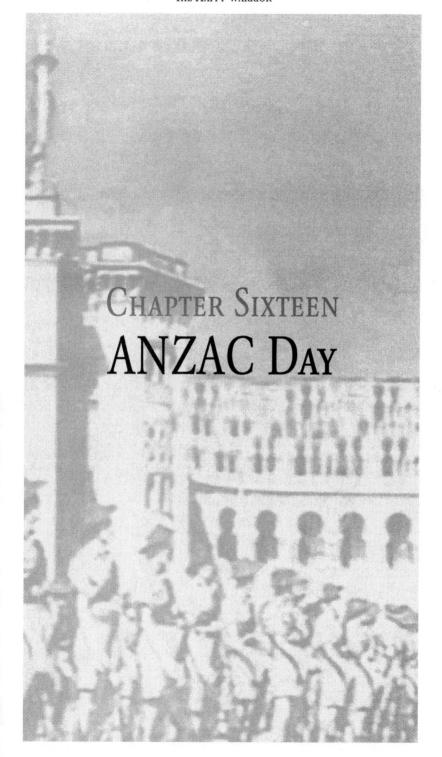

# Chapter Sixteen
# ANZAC Day

## *Anzac Day*

I saw a kid marchin' with medals on his chest.
He marched alongside Diggers, marchin' six abreast;
He knew it was ANZAC day, he walked along with pride,
He did his best to keep in step with the Diggers by his side.

And when the march was over the kid was rather tired.
A digger said "Whose medals son?" to which the kid replied:
"They belong to my daddy but he did not come back
He died up in New Guinea on a lonely jungle track."

The kid looked rather sad then a tear came to his eye.
The Digger said "Don't cry my son, and I will tell you why,
Your daddy marched with us today – all the bloomin way.
We Diggers know that he was there – it's like that on Anzac Day."

The kid looked rather puzzled and didn't understand,
But the Digger went on talking and started to wave his hand.
"For this great land we live in, there's a price we have to pay,
And for this thing called freedom, the Diggers had to pay.

"For we all love fun and merriment in this country where we live,
The price was that some soldier, his precious life must give.
For you to go to school, my lad, and worship God at will,
Someone had to pay the price so the Diggers paid the bill.

"Your daddy died for us my son – for all things good and true,
I wonder if you can understand the things I've said to you?"
The kid looked up at the Digger, just for a little while
And with a changed expression, said, with a lovely smile:

"I know my daddy marched here today, this, our Anzac day,
I know he did, I know he did – all the blooming way!"

*Anon*

## *The Unknown Soldier*

*James Young's son, a Major in the RAE, commanded the detachment that had the honour of returning the remains of the 'Unknown Soldier' home.*

The long quest on foreign soil for an Unknown Soldier ends,
His country wants him home at last, back here among his friends.

With fanfare, pomp and glory the honour guard will stand
As they raise this Unknown Soldier from out this foreign land.

Then proudly will they bear him through the green French countryside,
Long gone the muddy trenches, where he and many died.

He is coming home a hero born aloft on golden wings
To rest in the Nation's Capital, take his place with lords and kings.

To lie in state, on Aussie soil his holy place of rest,
A symbolic choice from thousands of our youth, our very best.

The honour we bestow on him, this unforgotten man,
Belongs to all his cobbers who fell in a foreign land.

Tho' many years have passed away since this young soldier died,
His tomb will stand for all to see, a font of national pride.

At last our soldier rests in peace, in simple dignity,
He harkens not to words of praise nor honour does he see.

Lying there so proudly, the country's flag his pall,
As ghostly footsteps echo across the great King's Hall.

The Nation's grateful people show a mark of their respect
To bear their head in silent prayer, sleep well, lest we forget.

Flanked by youthful comrades standing guard until that day,
When he makes the final journey to the tomb wherein he'll lay.

As a day of national mourning it moves the young as well as old,
Old soldiers sit and ponder absent comrades, brave and bold.

A hushed silence greets his casket as down the avenue it comes,
Borne by the Nation's leaders, marching slow, to muffled drums.

The bugler blows the Last Post as our Soldier goes to rest,
Where future generations can salute Australia's best.

*James D. Young*

## *The Last Parade*

The blazing sun was high above
    The steamy jungle shade,
Soldiers standing side by side
    The battalion's last parade.

Not here the sound of cheering
    Though duty has been done,
Suffice it is to hear no more
    The rattle of the gun.

Along those dark, damp jungle trails
    Where snipers wait and hide,
Where friend and foe look just as one,
    Here innocence quickly died.

Not easy is the battle fought,
    No beginning, who knows the end?
Ours not to reason why
    Just advance, withdraw, defend.

Now others face the hidden foe,
    Bring forth the bold and brave!
No more to feel the sting of death
    See the victory of the grave.

By definition be they veterans,
    Those who muster here today,
To hand on a proud tradition
    Then just quietly fade away.

To journey home with head held high,
    In each heart a promise made,
To honour those who paid the price
    And missed the last parade.

*James D. Young*

## *Of the Regiment*

You'll see me march on Anzac Day,
With grey and thinning hair,
And you'll say "The poor old bugger
I wonder why he's there?"

I am there because – once I served
Near China on snow-clad barren hills,
And sweltered in the summer heat –
Encountered different ills.

I have lived on crowded troop-ships
Crossed the China Sea by plane.
I have slept in steamy jungles
And been drenched in tropic rain.

I have walked across the pipeline,
Heard the sound of ambush gun.
Listened to the monkeys' chatter,
Paced a trishaw just for fun.

I have lived in hootchies awful
On the soil of foreign land.
And I've sat at night for dinner
With my feet in river sand.

And I watched a young friend die
And kept marching through the day
And I wonder why I did it,
But seldom had a say.

So you see me march on Anzac Day
I'm old, a little bent,
I'm a soldier – proud to be,
A member of the Regiment.

*Margaret Gibbons*

## *The 25th of April*

The twenty-fifth of April is always a special day
No matter what some people think, or what some people say.
It's a day for remembrance, a day for 'rejoices',
'Specially when we hear the old familiar voices.

So we get together each Anzac eve
In a place called Caulfield Central,
And for most of us, as it's our annual 'run':
Attendance is essential.

We answered a signal that came by mail
It's message loud like thunder,
Which simply read "It's time again chaps
To meet your mates from *Warramunga*."

We were met at the door by Lefty and Bill,
While just inside were Smouge Smith and Ray Gill;
And Lloyd Wicks with Georgeson, our Eight Mess talker,
Were being ear-bashed by 'Vicrail', Doug Walker.

We had a great night, which was intended,
As usual, were sad when it all just ended.
And when the beer went off there was great sorrow:
"Don't forget Chaps, we march tomorrow!"

Next morning we rose early, which was no mean feat;
As usual, Jimmy Georgeson produced a real treat.
But somehow breakfast wasn't the same this year
As 'Skipper' (Jimmy's little dog) was no longer here.

We mustered about ten in Swanston street
And listened to the bands and marching feet
Of the Army, as they'd gone first this year;
As for us, it was wait and give forth a loud cheer.

Came eleven o'clock it was our turn to go,
And the order was given to "Lash up and stow";
Of course it was shouted by the one with the chest,
Gunner T. Mal McDonald, who stands out from the rest.

Then off we moved in perfect file,
As this has always been our style,
To march to the music and keep the beat:
'Tis funny how some have two left feet.

Don Walker at our head was again to be seen
Decked out in 'number ones' as he always has been.
The sun was bright – how our medals did shine
As *Warramunga* 'steamed' up the steps of the Shrine.

We mustered well into the twenties this year –
A number that's not bad to boast –
And after the march, to the base for a beer,
For the Airforce have long been our host.

With money in the centre to buy lots of 'jugs'
It gave time to look at old familiar 'mugs'.
Yes, the Stokers were there and of course, quite loud,
We found 'Joe' Jelleff and old 'Bluey' Stroud.

With a glass in his hand and, as usual, so merry,
Is the one and only by name of 'Chris' Cherry;
Find with him, devouring a sandwich of steak,
Of course, you have guessed it, was Geoffrey Quinnfrake.

So, after we'd eaten and drunk all in sight
And were starting to look a bit of a fright,
'Twas home we decided we'd all best appear.
Then, we departed: "See ya next year?"

*Tim Lawrance*
*18 September 1981*
*(Ex Stoker, HMAS* Warramunga *1943–46)*

## Soldiers on Anzac Day

Old Soldiers marching in a line, ranks one behind another,
Remembering dead comrades, each one they still call Brother,
And women march the footsteps as their Sisters fought and died,
Some children marching hand in hand ask why their Grandpa cried.

Young Soldiers follow in their path continuing tradition,
Respect for those who went before and would follow to perdition.
Maintaining all the customs and the stories left behind
For future generations of Soldiers then to find.

Battlefields and deeds of war, all thoughts of yesteryear,
Gallipoli to Vietnam at last have led them here
With all the conflicts in between where Soldiers died in service,
So honour's left and soul's respect for Veteran and for Novice.

Dead Soldiers returned to Australia in their Comrades thoughts, so sad,
Remembering their sacrifice and friendships' pride they had,
And those who only gave their limbs, their blood or sanity,
They gave without regretting and they gave it willingly.

But as they look from heaven on the fields they battled for,
They see a thankless people, polis rotten to the core:
Deceitful greedy businessmen and criminals are rife,
Is this what they all fought for? Is this worth human life?

They answered conscience call that their country shouted loud,
They gave their best, they gave their all and did Australia proud.
The cost was never counted – not the wounds and not the pain
But the question of Dead Soldiers: "Did we really die in vain?"

*WO2 Paul Barrett*

## *My Pilgrimage*

Seven thousand Aussie lads lie dead on a distant shore,
They died to give us nationhood but nobody seems to care anymore,
I've wept for them at the place they bled, on a hill by Anzac Cove,
Where the Anzac legend of courage and nerve left nothing else to prove.

I draped our flag upon the grave of a cheeky boy of sixteen years,
Who, with his mates, was landed at Gallipoli to fight for peace, not cheers?
And as I gazed across the rows of many a common soldier's grave,
I reflected and displayed my pride in these who paid the price of being brave.

With map in hand, and Turkish guide, I walked the Anzac battlefields and wondered 'How the Hell?'
And read the plaques on monuments that their foes have placed where they fell,
For our Anzacs had earned respect for both fighting prowess and compassion,
They would not yield, and bloody battles fought, yet with foe would share their ration.

I served with mates a generation later and sought to emulate their style,
The nationhood and Anzac courage bequeathed to us was undergoing trial,
We fought as hard and paid the price that all soldiers do regret,
And thousands more young Aussie blokes now lie in places we must not forget.

They were heroes then, at Gallipoli and along the Kokoda Trail,
And all the places where they fought are forgotten as our memories fail,
I made my pilgrimage to their graves for they gave us value not found in banks,
They gave the greatest gift to folk like me and you, so we owe them a prayer of thanks.

I've prayed that our sons will not be called again, to resist a tyrant's greed,
For the price we pay is a price too much to bear, despite a soldier's valiant deed
And many a wife and mother has to endure the loss of a loved one who was called,
A soldier knows what must be done, yet knowing leaves him not enthralled.

As I stood among the rows of graves in Bomana, near 'The Track',
Then later at Simpson's Plot by the Dardanelles, I thought I heard a crack,
I heard again the sound of shot and shell and knew how they had felt,
I had come to pay respect to these whom I do honour, so in silent prayer I knelt.

Australia owes so much to these men who died to give us life,
We must learn about their deeds, thanking God that we did not face their strife.
My pilgrimage was personal, for I lost a mate or two, and I feel the sacredness of their rest,
They pointed me to Christ, who also gave His life that we too could share the best.

If you by chance do visit Turkish shores, go pay your tribute to those who gave Australia pride,
Or do the same in New Guinea or Bougainville; it's not too tough, you'll take it in your stride,
Why not a moments silence on Flanders Fields or Tobruk, as you pass through,
Give meaning to your holiday; let the spirit of old Anzacs brighten up the crew.

And if you think that wars are a waste of lives and you are dead against them,
So were they my friend, but it was our way of life they valued so the tide they had to stem,
I had to go and visit, my pilgrimage to make, as I did some years ago to a hill called Calvary;
They have not shared the peace we have, yet what they gave
the world I wish to tell, 'twas their lives to set us free.

*Bill Phillips*
*1997*

## *Their Service – Our Heritage*

From Colonial Heritage they came, enduring hardship and adversity,
Which bred in them disdain of authority so they resorted to humour and mockery,
Life too short to tolerate pomposity, they rather thought common purpose the greater need;
This rugged band showed initiative, tenacity and a fierce determination to succeed.

A unifying spirit grew that dismissed the burdens of their station,
Drawing them together to become a vibrant, virile nation;
These federation youngsters did not hesitate when called to go and stem the flow,
When Kaiser Bill and Ilk sought to conquer Europe and deliver a fatal blow.

From city, town and country shed they came to meet the challenge of the fray,
It might cost an arm, a leg, a life, but what true blue Aussie lad would let this stand in his way?
The spirit of their heritage was quite unique and had a special quality,
'Twas an energy powerful enough to inspire them to overcome this emergency.

They soon were trained and shipped to fields of battle and many a mother cried,
For upon Gallipoli and other foreign shores they fought and bled 'n' died,
Their selflessness and mateship, courage and determination, meeting every challenge and never giving in
Ensured captive nations' freedom, for they had not gone to fight, they had gone to win.

These federation youngsters bravely fought to bring our Nation recognition and pride;
Their heartbreaking sacrifice changed the course of history for they had stemmed the tide,
Now friend and foe salute them, ponder their compassion and fine qualities,
Which we now proudly share for their spirit has lifted Australia to the skies.

A generation later were called to emulate their deeds,
And won a mighty victory with the indomitable spirit that every Aussie heeds;
So we see in times of bush fire, flood and tragic moments their spirit live again,
And when Olympic challenges face us we'll remember 'Their Service – Our Heritage' and victory attain.

*Bill Phillips*
*1999*

## *The Sacred Dead*

I stand with head both bowed and bare
To honour the sacred dead,
Gone, yet never to return,
Matters not what words are said.

The path of honour and virtue,
Once trod by the brave and the bold,
Young men who followed the colours,
Young men who will never grow old.

Let bugles blow and flags half mast
In exultation of their glory,
Those valiant souls we left behind
Let history tell their story.

Behind closed eyes a picture grows
As troops march home from war,
Spoilt by the countless empty places
Which were filled by men before.

May their sacrifice be not forgotten
Let their aureoled presence shine bright,
Each individual, a national hero
Who lost their last great right.

*James D. Young*

## *Anzacs*

What mean these great white ships at sea, ploughing their eastward tack,
Bearing their precious human freight, bringing the spent men back?
They mean that Australia has been there, they mean she has played the game,
And her wonderful sons have won their share of everlasting fame.

Battered, and worn, and war-scarred, those who had left their land,
Strong in their glowing manhood, by England to take their stand;
Those who had sailed, when the war cloud burst, out on a distant foam
To the tune of "Australia will be there!" Thus are they coming home!

What mean these absent numbers, the gaps in the stricken line?
You will find the graves which tell you, on the trail by Lonesome Pine,
On the slopes of Aki Baba, on Koja, Chemen's brow:
They died the death of heroes, as Australia's sons know how.

Eager for battle they leapt ashore at the cove where their name was won,
They stormed the cliffs of Sari Bair, where the death trap gullies run;
In the lead-rent scrub by Krithia, on the banks of the Kereves Dere,
High on the shell-swept ridges – Australia has been there!

There is silence on the beaches now, the battle-din has fled
From the gullies, cliffs, and ridges where they charged up, fought and bled.
There's a little cove that's sacred – north of Gaba Tepe Hill –
To the glory of the men who died, and a name that never will!

And now on the fields of Flanders, 'tis eternised once more:
At Pozieres, Armentieres, Messines, Bapaume, and Bullecourt,
At Polygon Wood, and Broodseinde, by the frozen Somme and Aisne
In the snow-clad front-line trenches – Australia is there again.

There are great white vessels sailing, and they bear the joy and pain,
And the glory of Australia's sons who have not bled in vain;
Tho' crippled, helpless, maimed for life, tho' more than death their loss,
There is more than life in the glory of the burden of their cross.

Greater than jewel-decked Emperor, greater than ermined King,
Clad in their faded suits of blue, the men that the white ships bring:
What tho' their crown a bandage, stretcher or cot their throne,
Splints or a crutch their sceptre, the Anzac name is their own!

*EMC.*
*Durban, 1917*
*(AWM PR 00743)*

## *Why Wear a Poppy?*

"Please wear a poppy," the lady said
And held one forth, but I shook my head.
Then I stopped and watched as she offered them there
And her face was old and lined with care,
But beneath the scars the years had made
There remained a smile that refused to fade.

A boy came whistling down the street,
Bouncing along on carefree feet;
His smile was full of joy and fun
"Lady," said he,"May I have one?"
When she pinned it on he turned to say,
"Why do we wear a poppy today?"

The lady smiled in her wistful way
And answered, "This is Remembrance Day.
And the poppy there, is the symbol for
The gallant men who died in war,
And because they did, you and I are free
That's why we wear a poppy you see."

"I had a boy about your age
With golden hair and big blue eyes,
He loved to play and jump and shout
Free as a bird he would race about,
As the years went by he learned and grew
And became a man – as you will, too.

"He was fine and strong with a boyish smile
But he seemed with us such a little while
When war broke out, and he went away –
I still remember his face that day.
When he smiled at me and said goodbye,
I'll be back soon, Mum, so please don't cry!"

"But the war went on and he had to stay,
And all I could do was wait and pray.
His letters told of the awful fight –
I can still see it, in my dreams a night,
With the tanks and guns and cruel barbed wire
And the mines and the bullets, the bombs and fire.

"Till at last, at last, the war was won –
And that's why we wear a poppy son."
The small boy turned as if to go
Then said, "Thanks lady, I'm glad to know,
That sure did sound like an awful fight,
But your son – did he come home all right?"

A tear rolled down each faded cheek,
She shook her head, but she didn't speak
I slunk away in a sort of shame
And if you were me, you'd do the same.
For our thanks, in giving, is oft delayed
Though our freedom was bought, and thousands paid,

So when we see a poppy worn,
Let us reflect on the burden borne
By those who give their very all
When asked to answer their country's call
That we at home in peace might live,
Then wear a poppy. REMEMBER – and give.

*Anon*

# CHAPTER SEVENTEEN
## PRAYERS

## A Soldier — His Prayer

*A scrap of paper fluttered into the hands of an Eighth Army soldier sheltering in a slit trench during the battle of Agheila in the Western Desert. On the paper were written some verses. The author has never been traced. Perhaps, in his own words, he fell 'Triumphed in the Dust' of the Western Desert. The verses have been preserved in 'Poems from the Desert' by Members of the Eighth Army (Harrap).*

Stay with me, God. The night is dark,
The night is cold: My little spark
Of courage dies. The night is long;
Be with me, God, and make me strong.

I love a game; I love a fight,
I hate the dark; I love the light,
I love my child; I love my wife,
I am no coward. I love life.

Life with its change of mood and shade.
I want to live. I'm not afraid,
But me and mine are hard to part;
Oh, unknown God, lift up my heart.

You stilled the waters at Dunkirk,
You saved your servants.
All your work is wonderful, dear God.
You strode before us down that dreadful road.

We were alone, and hope had fled;
We loved our country and our dead,
And could not shame them; so we stayed
The course, and were not much afraid.

Dear God, that nightmare road!
And then that sea! We got there... We were men.
My eyes were blind, my feet were torn,
My soul sang like a bird at dawn!

I know that death is but a door,
I knew what we were fighting for;
Peace for the kids, our brothers freed,
A kinder world, a cleaner breed.

I'm but a son my mother bore,
A simple man, and nothing more,
But, God of strength and gentleness,
Be pleased to make me nothing less.

Help me, O God, when death is near,
To mock the haggard face of fear,
That when I fall – if fall I must –
My soul may triumph in the dust.

*Anon*
*(AWM PR 00392)*

## Bomber's Prayer

Under the shadow of thy wings
Protect us Lord,
Thou Master of all living things
Extend thy might
And guard us as we fly
The long bleak stretches of the night,
Protagonists of law
And immemorial right.

And from the hunter's snare
Deliver us
The high flung nets of light
The shrapnel's ugly spite
The lurking kite
And peril instant everywhere.

If errand done,
With pinions maimed and crew spent
There rests
No hope to reach the kindly nests
Where blithely sings
The guardian sea about our island home,
O gather us yet closer, Lord
Content
Beneath the shadow of thy saving wings.

*Chaplain D. Trathen*
*(AWM PR 00218)*

## A Soldier's Prayer

Our Father, which art in Heaven, hear my prayer;
Death strikes all around me everywhere.
Give me the strength temptation's power to baulk,
That I may honoured be where'er I walk.
If upon me the grim hand should be laid,
Give me the strength to take it undismayed.
Bless thou my country's cause, defend the king,
And to my dear ones peace and solace bring;
Grant us each day a place among the brave,
And, if I fall, new life beyond the grave.
Amen

*Anon*

## *"Casting All Your Care Upon Him, for He Careth for You".*

*1 Peter 5–7*

Have you ever felt disheartened with the turmoil and the strife,
  That surrounds you as you journey on your way?
Have you ever thought the load you carry, more than you can bear
  As you tread along the weary road called life?

Have you ever felt the burden of your troubles and your cares
  To get greater as each weary day goes by?
Or does the road get rougher with each faltering step you take,
  As you in your weariness, despondent sigh?

Have you ever felt the need of one in whom you could confide,
  Who would help you, share your burdens and your woe?
Who would guide you o'er the roughest road,
  And give you cheer and comfort as you go.

Have you ever looked to Jesus, who will all your burdens take?
  Who said, "Come and cast upon Me all your care"?
For through life He will sustain you, for He careth much for you
  And He'll never ever leave you nor forsake.

He will give you strength and comfort, He will give you joy and peace,
  He will be a present help in time of need,
And when this life is over, and you leave this vale of tears,
  He will still be with you in Eternity.

*W. J. Baker*
*Canungra*
*6 July 1944*

## A Mother's Prayer for Her Son

As Thou didst walk the lanes of Galilee,
So loving Saviour, walk with him for me,
For since the years have passed and he is grown,
I cannot follow – he must walk alone.

Be Thou my feet that I have had to stay,
For Thou canst comrade him on every way;
Be Thou my voice when sinful things allure,
Pleading with him to choose those that endure.

Be Thou my hand that would keep his in mine,
And all things else that mothers must resign;
When he was little, I would walk and guide,
But now I pray that Thou be at his side,

And as the Blessed Mother folded Thee,
So kind and loving Saviour,
fold my dear son for me.

*Anon*

## *A Soldier's Prayer*

Oh, Lord, our Father, up on high
Harken to this soldier's cry!
As on bended knee I pray
For loved ones far away.

    Bless my mother sweet and fair,
    My love for her none can compare,
    Guide and guard her every way,
    Keep her safe from day to day.

To my father give solace,
May his name I ne'er disgrace,
In years gone by he did his part,
May I but have his fighting heart.

    To sisters all, and brothers too.
    Give thy guidance strong and true;
    In this hour of toil and strife
    Teach them tolerance, love of life.

To each true and loyal friend
Thine understanding, love, please lend,
And each comrade at my side
Through this turmoil safely guide.

    Oh, Lord, our father up on high
    Harken to my feeble cry!
    To this struggle bring surcease
    Grant us everlasting peace.

Lord, our Father, in your keeping
I leave them all, at work or sleeping;
Grant to me, Oh Lord, I ask,
The strength to do my chosen task!

                  *Cpl R Lawrence (?)*
                  *(AWM PR 00392)*

## *The Airman's Prayer*

Almighty and all-present power
Short is the prayer I make thee,
I do not ask in battle hour
For shield to cover me.

    The vast unalterable way
    From which the stars do not depart
    May not be turned aside today
    The bullet flying to my heart.

I ask no help to strike my foe,
I seek no petty victory here;
The enemy I hate, I know
To thee is also dear.

    But this I pray: Be at my side
    When death is drawing through the sky,
    Almighty God who also died
    Teach the way that I should die.

*Anon*
*Milne Bay*

## The Captives' Hymn

Father, in captivity
We would lift our prayer to Thee,
Keep us ever in Thy love,
Grant that daily we may prove
Those who place their trust in Thee
More than conquerors may be.

May the day of freedom dawn,
Peace and Justice be reborn.
Grant that nations, loving Thee,
O'er the world may brothers be,
Cleansed by suffering, know rebirth,
See Thy kingdom come on earth.

*Anon*

# Ranks & Glossary

## MILITARY RANKS

| | |
|---|---|
| Bdr | Bombardier |
| Capt. | Captain |
| CO | Commanding Officer |
| Cpl | Corporal |
| CQ | (Short for CQMS - Company Quarter Master Sergeant) |
| Dvr | Driver |
| Ft/Lt | Flight Lieutenant |
| FO | Flying Officer |
| Gnr | Gunner |
| L/Cpl | Lance Corporal |
| Lieut Col | Lieutenant Colonel |
| Lt | Lieutenant |
| L/Sig | Lance Signaler |
| Maj | Major |
| Pte | Private |
| RSM | Regimental Sergeant Major |
| Sgt | Sergeant |
| Tpr | Trooper |
| WO | Warrant Officer |

## GLOSSARY

Note: the compilers of 'The Happy Warrior' would welcome further information regarding the terms listed below, or in relation to other terms mentioned in the book. Such information would be included in future editions.

| | |
|---|---|
| AASC | Australian Army Service Corps |
| ack-ack | Anti-Aircraft guns (slang) |
| AEME | Australian Electrical and Mechanical Engineers |
| AIF | Australian Infantry Forces |
| AOs | Admin Officers or Admin Orders or Area of Operations depending on context. |
| AWM | Australian War Memorial |
| Aust. Gen. Trans. Coy | Australian General Transport Company |
| Batt. | Battalion |
| Bangalores | An explosive device used to clear obstacles |
| Beast | Cannot find specific reference indicating anything other than savage animal |
| bint | A girl or any female (slang) |
| blighty | England – "to cop a blighty" – to be injured seriously enough to warrant being returned to England for hospitalisation or rehabilitation |
| boobies | Booby traps |
| Brens | A type of machine gun (British) |
| Brownings | A type of machine gun (British) |

| | |
|---|---|
| bumble | (v) to stumble around ineptly, (n) an inept person |
| CAP | A type of toxic gas |
| Caribou | A type of military aircraft |
| chocos | Reservists |
| Claymores | a type of mine |
| CTO | believed to be a form of leave or time-off |
| DME | thought to be Department of Maintenance Engineering |
| Foux | thought to be slang for Focke (?) or Fokker aircraft |
| HE | High Explosive |
| hicks | Locals |
| HQ | Headquarters |
| Hun | Germans |
| Itie | Italians |
| Jap | Japanese |
| Jerry | Germans |
| Kitties | Kitty Hawk aircraft |
| LO | Liaison Officer |
| Mungaree | generic term for food - from middle-eastern (possibly arabic) expression |
| NEI | Netherlands East Indies |
| Number Nine | Form of medication - may have been a laxative or placebo. |
| OC | Officer Commanding |
| OPSO | Operations Officer |
| Pippers | Young or junior, Officers |
| P40 | A type of aircraft |
| P51 | A fighter aircraft (Mustang, United States) |
| QX man | A Queenslander — soldiers who joined up in Queensland had QX as a prefix to their regimental numbers |
| RAF | Royal Air Force (Britain) |
| RSL | Returned and Servicemen's League |
| Stuka | German Bomber Aircraft |
| Tommies | British Soldiers (slang) |
| UXB | Unexploded Bomb |
| Ulu | In the bush; in the middle of no-where; beyond the black stump. |
| UNIIMOG | United Nations Iran-Iraq Military Observer Group |
| Verey candles | Flares |
| Vickers | A type of machine gun or a type of aircraft depending on context |
| Wog | person of Mediterranean or Middle Eastern extraction or appearance (slang) |
| wop | Italian, or person of Italian appearance (slang) |
| Zero | A Japanese fighter plane |

## *We Shall Keep the Faith*

Oh! You who sleep in Flanders' fields,
Sleep sweet - to rise anew,
We caught the torch you threw,
And holding high we kept
The faith with those who died,

We cherish, too, the Poppy red
That grows on fields where valour led.
It seems to signal to the skies
That blood of heroes never dies,
But lends a lustre to the red
Of the flower that blooms above the dead
In Flanders' fields.

And now the torch and poppy red
Wear in honour of our dead
Fear not that ye have died for naught
We've learned the lesson that ye taught
In Flanders' fields.

*An American, Miss Moira Michael, read "In Flanders' Fields" and wrote "We Shall Keep The Faith" in reply.*